TEACH ME: AN ETHNOGRAPHY OF ADOLESCENT LEARNING

Cultural Shopping and Student Lore in Urban America

Ellen FitzSimmons

International Scholars Publications
Lanham • New York • Oxford

Copyright © 1999 by
Ellen FitzSimmons

International Scholars Publications
4720 Boston Way
Lanham, Maryland 20706

12 Hid's Copse Rd.
Cumnor Hill, Oxford OX2 9JJ

All rights reserved
Printed in the United States of America
British Library Cataloging in Publication Information Available

ISBN 1-57309-400-5 (cloth: alk. ppr.)

∞™ The paper used in this publication meets the minimum
requirements of American National Standard for Information
Sciences—Permanence of Paper for Printed Library Materials,
ANSI Z39.48—1984

To all my kin, "fictive" and otherwise.

Contents

Introduction..1

Chapter 1: Gangs..11

Chapter 2: Family..35

Chapter 3: Mentors..57

Chapter 4: Play..85

Chapter 5: Social Structure.......................................117

Chapter 6: Science Explorations...............................149

Chapter 7: Standardized Tests..................................177

Chapter 8: Fair Testing?..213

Chapter 9: Teach Me...233

Chapter 10: Afterword...247

Bibliography...255

Index...265

Foreword

*William H. Schubert, Ph.D.
The University of Illinois at Chicago*

My enthusiasm for this book by Ellen FitzSimmons grows out of my work as an educator for more than thirty years. I will begin by referring briefly to certain key themes or dimensions of that work and comment on how Dr. FitzSimmons expands on it and creates her own original contributions.

One of my deepest educational concerns has been what young people learn from their experience both in and out of school. During my elementary school teaching days, it was clear to me that students brought a vast array of knowledge, skill, values, and dispositions to the school setting. Then and now, as a teacher educator and professor of curriculum studies, my concern runs deep when I seldom see teachers build on the values, dispositions, skills, and areas of knowledge that students already have emerging within them. At all levels of teaching, I have made it a habit to try to build on the expertise that students bring to the educational encounter. I have been impressed with instances in which I have seen other teachers do this, infrequent as they have been, and I have learned much from them. Long ago, I concluded that building on student strengths leads to a far more productive form of teaching and learning than the all-too-predominant practice of identifying and dwelling on perceived deficits. The latter diminishes self-confidence and devastates the learning process.

This book vividly shows how a conscientious teacher (in this case, Dr. FitzSimmons as ethnographer and classroom volunteer) came to know a number of students, identified their interests and concerns, and built on their strengths to open new doors of learning and growth for and with them. Her work helps to validate the commitment that this process of building on students' capacities, experiences, and insights can increase understanding of what I consider to be the most basic curriculum question: What is worth knowing, experiencing, needing, doing, being, becoming, and sharing?

I have searched the literature for insight to help me better pursue this commitment to address the basic curriculum question *with* students. Early in my career, I turned to the progressive tradition of John Dewey and others whose work reflects and extends its spirit. The work of John Goodlad, J. Harlan Shores, Carl Rogers, John Holt, A. S. Neill, and Herb Kohl helped me build on the perspectives of Dewey for elementary school students. Over the years, I have added Boyd Bode, L. Thomas Hopkins, Carter G. Woodson, Ralph Tyler, James B. Macdonald, Dwayne Huebner, Maxine Greene, Paulo Freire, Joseph Schwab, Elliot Eisner, William Pinar, Madeleine Grumet, Michael Apple, Henry Giroux, William Ayers, Janet Miller, George Willis, Jean Anyon, Max van Manen, especially Ann Lopez, many of my current and former doctoral students, and more (including my own children) to the list that helps me along this pathway. Understandings they provide enable my resonance with Dewey's progressive organization of subject matter—that is, the assumption that the most sound education begins with the genuine concerns and interests of learners (what Dewey labeled *the psychological*) and connects these with what Dewey called *the logical* (i.e., funds of knowledge from the disciplines and from more experienced others).

It brings me great delight when the efforts of colleagues and students expand and extend my understanding of how to connect Dewey's *psychological* and *logical*. Ellen FitzSimmons has done just that. In this book, she has shown that a deep concern of students derives from what might be termed their *call to learn*, captured in FitzSimmons's powerful phrase, "Teach me." By becoming close to the students of the inner-city school she studied, FitzSimmons has learned about the diverse curricula of their lives; and she teaches us that curriculum, teaching, and evaluation are embedded in family life, gang activity, play, and a panoply of other experiences in the lives of these pre-high school adolescents. Her ethnographic skills (as an anthropologist) are coupled with her insights about teaching and learning (as an educational researcher) to provide challenging interpretations of the interplay between school and nonschool experiences. For instance, in dialogue with students about standardized tests, she illuminates the perceptive ways they thought about questions that test-makers hardly could have anticipated. In this encounter that FitzSimmons provides, the need to ask students about their own education is thrown into bold relief.

It is especially noteworthy, too, that Dr. FitzSimmons takes her work to another level, as well. She is not a detached researcher, nor does she strive for that status as an ideal; however, she does try to provide fair and unbiased renditions of what she studied. Ethically, she could not merely stand by to watch the lives of the adolescents unfold. She wanted to participate and to contribute. When she heard the call *"Teach me!"* emerge from them, she could not resist. Knowing that their teachers and parents had time and energy to do only so much, and without diminishing the good that they often did accomplish with the children, FitzSimmons depicts how she used resources at her disposal to help the students invigorate their aspirations to pursue the perennial curriculum question for their own lives, a question that asks and re-asks: "What is worth knowing, experiencing, doing, needing, being, becoming, and sharing in my life and in the lives I influence?" She provided inspiration, enthusiasm, resources, journeys, visits to laboratories, access to computers and books, and ongoing mentorship that responded to the students' interests and concerns and enabled them to fashion their own personal curriculum.

What we have in this book is the lore of a teacher who is simultaneously a researcher and who is foremost an advocate for children. As a researcher, Dr. FitzSimmons provides a kind of student lore, as well, wherein she illuminates the complex and variegated life-worlds of students who are too often the object of stereotype and unidimensional characterization. By her actions to respond to the implicit cry, "Teach me!," she portrays a unique coupling of advocacy, research, and action that enriched the students' lives. This illustrates a fundamental issue for researchers to address about the pull to remain detached and the push to help and inspire. In helping the students she portrays, Dr. FitzSimmons has enabled them to help themselves as they move into the next phase of composing their lives. I commend her efforts and accomplishments and look forward to her next steps.

William H. Schubert is author or editor of Curriculum Books: The First Eighty Years *(with Ann Lopez, 1980);* Curriculum: Perspective, Paradigm, and Possibility *(1986);* Reflections from the Heart of Educational Inquiry *(edited with George Willis, 1991);* Teacher Lore: Learning from Our Own Experiences *(with William Ayers, 1992);* The American Curriculum: A Documentary History *(edited with George Willis, Robert Bullough, Jr., Craig Kridel, and John Holton, 1994); and* Turning Points in Curriculum *(with J. Dan Marshall and James T. Sears, 1999).*

Schubert has also served as past president of the John Dewey Society and the Society for the Study of Curriculum History. He is the current vice-president of the American Educational Research Association.

INTRODUCTION

According to the 1990 census report, the school where I spent two years gathering data lies at the heart of an area where 55 percent of the people live below the federal poverty level. Although 79 percent of the residents are employed, the yearly average per capita income is only $8,306. The neighborhood crime rate used to be twice that of any other part of the city, but it decreased 11 percent during 1996–97, and was down 18 percent in 1998. Gang affiliation is estimated at around 75 percent but is also decreasing.

The school was built to serve the children from a public housing project constructed during the late 1950s. In 1997, 494 pupils from prekindergarten age through eighth grade were enrolled there. One hundred percent of the student body is African-American. Almost all of the children (99.8 percent) qualify for federally subsidized food programs.

The Chicago Board of Education placed this school on academic probation because 15 percent of its students did not perform at or above national norms in both reading and math as measured by the Iowa Test of Basic Skills (ITBS or "Iowas" as they are popularly called). In 1997, 11.7 percent of the students in grades three through eight met that criterion in reading and 17.1 percent met the standard in mathematics. According to the preliminary results of the 1997 ITBS, 54.8 percent of the school's first grade students tested at or above national norms in mathematics, but only 27.9 percent tested at those levels in reading; the number of fourth grade students who tested at or above national norms was 34 percent in mathematics and 15.4 percent in reading, and the number of seventh grade students who tested at or above national norms in mathematics and reading was 10.7 percent. The Illinois Board of Education placed this school on its Watch List because the students' Illinois Goal Assessment Program (IGAP) scores were consistently low, showing no improvement throughout the years. If judged solely by these boards' criteria, the students' scores appear to support John Dewey's (1896/1972, 273) assertion made over one hundred years ago: "The weakest point in our school system has been the grades from the fourth to the eighth, whether tested by methods used or results reached."

A friend who worked at the school eased my entry there. She described the student body as "bounded," saying that they were limited by their isolation (poverty), lack of resources (poverty), and social situations (poverty), and by their parents' and their own lack of experience (poverty). She hastened to add, "They're good children, and they try hard." So, in April 1996, I made an appointment with the school's principal, who offered me a group for my dissertation research. She said, "I think the now sixth graders, if they don't go into a seventh grade slump, would be the best group to work with. They've been trained to work as a team."

I swallowed hard. Seventh graders can be difficult, as many parents and teachers alike will attest. They are "neophyte teenagers." One day they can be sweet and helpful; the next, they can be sarcastic and sulky. Sometimes, as Monti (1994, 1) says, "they can work hard at making themselves unlikable and succeed handsomely at it." Seventh graders are in a state of flux: their bodies are going through incredible changes, and their moods swing erratically. They are newcomers to what I call the Hormonal H--- (heaven and hell) years. One day they seem so grown up, and the next they act like babies again. Yet, even as adolescence is a period of "storm and stress" (Schonert-Reich and Offer 1992, 57), it is also when teenagers make real discoveries about themselves and the world outside their families. During this time, they take great strides toward the development of abstract thinking and reasoning capabilities (Dewey 1910/1985, 231–32). It is a critical time during which children develop habits they carry throughout their lives. I was excited that I would have the opportunity to interact with a group of teenagers and document some of their changes and development as they occurred!

Twenty-four students sat at their desks, in rows four across and six deep, with skinny aisles in between. All wore the school uniform of black pants or skirts and plain white tops. Their classroom teacher introduced me and indicated I was to talk. They looked quietly expectant. I told the children who I was, explaining some of my study objectives and my interest in studying the students. I said I would spend two or three days each week traveling from room to room with them.

To break the ice, I proposed that we could get to know each other better by taking weekend field trips to places that interested them. Hands were raised, very politely. "Could we go to a haunted house?" "What about Workout World?" "How about the natural history museum?" "Or the aquarium?" The suggestions soon came faster than I could scribble them on the board; hand raising quickly dropped out as a prelude to speaking. The noise level became tremendous. Finally, I had to call a halt. I had run out of board space, and I had three months' worth of suggestions. I asked the students to rank their choices on a piece of paper so I could put together a group for each trip. I told them we could add more places later and that I would make myself available on weekends to do whatever they wanted when it fit all of our schedules. I ended up spending every weekend—Saturdays and often Sundays, even during the summer—for over two years working and interacting with the children.

We were together in school, at museums, on field trips, and in each other's homes and neighborhoods. I do not think they asked to go places they thought would please or impress me. If they did, they would have had to suffer through those excursions. We planned and strategized our time together. We read and discussed books, worked on science projects and school assignments, spoke at student forums, and took school-sponsored field trips to Washington, D.C., and

Springfield, Illinois. On more informal field trips, we explored a zoo and fifteen museums. We attended two basketball games and one funeral. We learned to use chopsticks and sampled "weird foods" at any number of city and suburban restaurants. We jumped double Dutch, played hand-clapping games, hunted rabbits along the railroad tracks, and lurched after frogs along streambeds. We shared personal and academic triumphs and a number of disappointments. We learned together, shifting the role of teacher among us.

I have structured my data as an ethnography. The data sets include transcribed and annotated field notes, verbatim notes of conversations, child-produced documents, school records, various reports, photographs, and video and audio tape recordings. The audiotapes are few in number; as soon as the children saw me pull out my tape recorder, they grabbed it to record rap songs (most often the lyrics of Notorious B.I.G.). Videotapes were made wherever we went. Sometimes I filmed; at other times, the children filmed. The child-produced films permitted me to see what interested the filmer and served as another type of data. I taught the children how to use my 35-millimeter camera. As a result, I have many carefully composed photographs of our group, as well as numerous unintentionally snapped pictures of sidewalks and feet.

Since my primary informants were minors, I asked parents or legal guardians to sign a release permitting me to quote the children in this work or in any subsequent publications arising out of this research. Releases were also secured for all adults' quotations. In one instance, an administrator revised an earlier statement in order to clarify it. In another, a teacher expanded on her original comments. I asked the students to choose their own pseudonyms. I selected pseudonyms for the adults when, for sake of clarity, the text required me to use names.

What emerged from my study is a record about and, in many instances, by teenagers—data that show how they perceive their realities, structure their experiences, and learn about themselves and their world. The information I gathered was *triangulated*; in other words, when the children made comments or claims, I

Introduction

attempted to verify them through additional sources such as other children, teachers, or parents. I used public documents—newspapers and school records, for instance—to document certain other things.

I also checked my analyses and those of the children by repeatedly reviewing the videotapes and my field notes. All videotapes were transcribed by hand and checked for accuracy before I asked the children to review their quotations to see if I had transcribed them correctly. All contributors had the opportunity to elaborate or modify their statements at that time or to request that specific quotations not be used. I checked my analyses and conclusions with the children to see if they agreed I "had it right." Unverifiable statements were extremely rare, specific to certain individuals only and occurring most often during my first few weeks with the children. Wherever possible, I also consulted other researchers' works to see whether my data agreed or differed from what they had found. Points of disagreement were rechecked; the differences and possible reasons for them are discussed in the text.

The data I collected did not add up to a picture of adolescent culture as an integrated whole. Moreover, here lies one of the major differences between my data and the data in traditional anthropological ethnographies. At first this bothered me. The model for culture that I was trying to apply suggested I should have found more integration, a greater sense of direction, than my data presented. Then I realized that traditional anthropological ethnographies, by and large, focus on adults. They chronicle daily life with the goal of describing how adults make sense of their world, how a culture functions as an organic whole. They provide adult perspectives of culture and the strategies adults use to shape cultural pieces into a whole.

The seventh graders I studied were simply not adults. They did not have an adult perception about their culture that might have included a sense of an ideal whole, about how to create a wholeness, or even that a wholeness was something they should strive to create at this particular point in their lives. They were learners in the process of learning about themselves, their culture, and their world. They were individually learning about life *while* they lived it, as well as structuring and guiding their actions by their experiences. Although their actions were frequently directed by their desires to link varied experiences, they oftentimes affected linkages without having either a template for the end product or an awareness of how those linkages might affect the final shape.

These children's perspectives were self-referenced, context and time dependent. My data clearly showed that many different experiences were used to shape how the children operated. As Dewey (1896/1981) suggested, it became nearly impossible, even with the children belonging to the age-graded cohort classified as adolescents, to reduce their individual experiences to a singular "experience." Their perspectives were personally based, grounded in what they could remember from their even-earlier childhood lessons and in what they were learning at the moment, with vague and very general ideas why some of those experiences might be useful to them in the future.

Another significant difference between my data and the data of other ethnographers who work in societies that recognize adolescence as a distinct life stage, either differentially experienced or not, is theoretical. Whereas other ethnographers show the process by which adolescents are prepared for and integrated into adult society, they typically cast the children of those societies into one of two modes. They classify them as *culture acceptors* conforming to the (traditional) program (Mead 1928; Turner 1967; White 1993) or as *culture rejecters* at odds with social norms. (See Thrasher 1927; Carpenter et al. 1988; Monti 1994).

After studying these particular seventh graders, I concluded that they fit neither classification completely. Total acceptance or rejection of enculturation (education) lessons was never universal across the group or even typical of certain individuals. Rather, the children individually chose to accept or reject specific lessons, and their choices were time, space, and context dependent. Sometimes the children would pick and choose in ways that suggested they had no idea how the pieces might ultimately fit together or even that some of the pieces should fit together. In other words, these children were *culture shoppers*.

Cultural shopping differs from the *patterned* model Pitman et al. (1989, 3) proposed for adolescents acquiring culture. That model implies children look to acquire things that will fit a predetermined conception of what the end product should resemble. The manner in which the children I studied set about learning their culture and other things they wanted to know was nowhere near as structured or simplistic.

The way these children actually acquired information and experience was analogous to visiting a mall with many different kinds of shops under a single roof. It is possible to buy a variety of things at a mall because the different shops carry many kinds of goods. Shopping can be a solitary or group activity, or it can be an occasion on which an adult drags an unwilling, disinterested child along. Some shopping trips are planned, while others are spontaneous; likewise, some purchases are carefully strategized and some items are impulse purchases. Sometimes only a single item is bought. At other times, the shopper might buy several items. Still other times, nothing is bought. Some purchases are made with a goal toward complementing or replacing something the shopper already possesses. Some are bought simply because they are new or novel. Some items are classified as bargains too good to be passed up, and others are rejected as being too costly or not worth the price. Sometimes the individual purchases can be combined into an ensemble. Other times, they are simply unrelated items. Some purchases can be real mistakes. Others can start a trend.

Cultural shopping is simply what I found that these particular children did (and, I suspect, what all children do) in the process of living their lives and of learning about things and people. My data most clearly describe the children's attempts to accumulate information, knowledge, and skills in order to make sense of, learn from, and function in the different, sometimes separate, worlds with which they frequently came in contact: home and family, school, church, and the streets.

In this introduction, I present the broad phenomenon of interest that underpinned my research (what adolescent school children want to know, why they want to know it, and how they go about learning what they want to know), raise theoretical questions about culture and its acquisition, and propose the cultural shopping model to illuminate and explain the data. In the chapters that follow, I detail and discuss what the children do, the people with whom they interact, and some of their in-school and out-of-school experiences.

Chapter 1 concerns the children's community and its problems with gangs. In this chapter, the children talk about the effect that gangs have had on their lives and discuss their own, their school's, and their community's efforts to short-circuit gang influence. The data lead to questions about peer culture, culture change, and revitalization movements. Chapter 2 deals with certain types of familial relationships. Blood ties and fictive kin are discussed, and questions are raised about the role that kinship plays in daily life and educational, institutional settings. Chapter 3 focuses on the numerous adults with whom the students have chosen to interact in informal mentor-mentee relationships. It describes a number of the children's efforts to enlist adults to help them. The data detail the roles into which the students cast the adults who have agreed to help them financially, socially, emotionally, and academically. It also documents changes in the scope and breadth of those relationships through time.

Chapter 4 concerns some of the various games and child-initiated, -organized, and -directed play activities in which the children engage. Questions are raised concerning the educative value of play in terms of modeling adult behaviors and trying out "what if" scenarios, as well as about the social organizational structures expressed in gender-separate and mixed-gender activities. Chapter 5 explores what the children want to know, what they feel they should know, and why. It raises questions about the possibility of using the leadership roles that were documented in single-gender and mixed-gender informal field trips to effect better learning in the classroom. Chapter 6 concerns science lessons and experiments. The broad topic of science permits the students to discuss how science is taught in their school. In this chapter, I use information from the children's discussions about science to raise questions about the use of technology to supplement classroom lessons, student motivation, transferred interest, and gender.

Chapters 7 and 8 concern standardized tests and ten students' discussions about why they answered practice test questions in the manner they did. The data raise questions about the use and application of such tests to gauge learning and achievement and the effects that the tests have on the student's learning. Chapters 9 and 10 are where I draw together the various strands that run throughout the children's ethnography, setting it against the backdrop of some current sociopolitical events in the city where they live. I detail changes in specific children's lives and circumstances that occurred since the start of my study.

I have included lengthy quotations from many of the children because, after all, they and their thoughts were the focus of my research. The quotations enable the reader to work toward an understanding of who these particular children were, what they felt, and what they wanted to know and why, better than anything I could write alone.

These data fall under the classificatory heading of student lore, a subset of curricular scholarship called educational lore (Schubert 1986 and 1993; Schubert and Lopez-Schubert 1981; Schubert and Lopez 1994). Within the subsets of this category, teacher lore, administrator lore, and parent lore can also be found. All of these encompass accounts and stories about curricular journeys.

Curriculum has traditionally has been thought of mainly in terms of tangible products such as policy statements, lesson plans, pedagogical guides, and textbooks. Although it still includes academic content, "more recently it has also been considered as activities and/or learning experiences" (Schubert 1986, 11).

The Latin root of curriculum is *currere*, literally "to run a course." The implication is that life itself is a course, that life itself is "curriculum." Under this interpretation of curriculum, educational lore finds its validity as a scholarly endeavor. Educational lore reports are important for a number of reasons, not just because they provide interesting and useful data about what people are doing and thinking. If teachers and administrators are serious about educating children in the best possible manner, they must try to understand the social and personal factors that have shaped and affected their charges' lives. They need to use that knowledge to design and structure a curriculum that helps students learn more because it takes advantage of the children's prior knowledge: information they bring with them from the streets, from home, from their churches, and from previous formal educational experiences. Teacher, parent, and administrator lore accounts provide adults in those capacities a voice through which they can explore their experiences and perspectives, while student lore data sets provide a voice to students detailing their explorations of what they believe is worth knowing and experiencing. As Schubert (1993, 42) succinctly put it, "Educational lore has long been a basis for decision and action in the realm of educational practice."

Much of the information contained in this book was distilled from my doctoral dissertation in curriculum design (University of Illinois at Chicago, 1998). My hope is that the data and analysis will be valuable to parents and educators alike, both as documentation of "their [the children's] ways of looking at it" (Schubert 1993) and as a basis for some of the decisions and actions that affect them.

CHAPTER 1
GANGS

A particular north-south street in the children's community forms the dividing line between gang territories. The children said different gangs control the various buildings in the public housing project where they live, too. At any time a building, or even an individual floor, can become a contested site where gangbangers try to "hold on to a position of leadership in their own building" (Lemann 1992, 259).

The school lies to the west of the housing development, across the dividing-line street. When the children emerge from their apartments in the projects, they must cross in front of other buildings that may be controlled by a gang hostile to the one controlling the building in which they live. Then, the children must cross from that gang's territory to another's in order to reach their school.

The children claimed that when the projects were first built in the late 1950s, they were beautiful. Jasmine spoke as if she remembered those days:

> When the projects was built, it was perfect—no troubles, an' the flowers an' playgrounds was decent. Long time ago, it was pretty. Long time ago, it had grass an' flowers.

Biggie advised:

> Well, now [the housing authority] fixin' it up again. There was a time when they start not to give a care, an' that when the kids start killin'

theyselves, an' jumpin' out the windows an' stuff, an' then they decided to put bars up on the windows. Then that was when they started havin' gates up like, on that roof that the little kids start jumpin' on, an' the kids leapin' out the second floor an' stuff, an' gang-bangers up there started shootin'.

The children reported that, in the past, shoot-outs regularly erupted without warning in the "field" between project buildings. Jasmine maintained there has been a change there, too: "Now when you go outside, you walk wherever you want. But it used to be that you couldn't cross the open field. It used to be like that." She explained further, "When the gang-bangers got really bad, that's when the [housing authority] put a cap on it. For a while, it [the project] call the 'graveyard' 'cause a lotta people die in the projects with the gangs, drive-bys, walk-ups..."

Biggie interjected, "But now the gangs—the *gangs* tryin' to turn the *gangs* around, an' they got [housing authority] security an' more policemens [around the project]. People just got tired of the gangs."

Now gang members often warn both bystanders and the school when there will be daytime shooting. One school administrator said, "They [someone in a gang] will call the school and warn us to send the children home early, sometimes." Biggie agreed, "They sometimes let you know ahead. They sometimes do that." Jasmine thought that if you stayed outside "after you been warned, it you' own fault if you get shot."

Nighttime in the neighborhood, however, can be hazardous and noisy. According to the children, after dark when the gangs are at war, no warnings are given before gunfire erupts. As young as these children are, they have learned to "hit the deck" when they hear gunfire and to identify the sounds of different weapons—the high-pitched *pshew* of rifles, the mid-range *braaap-braaap* of semi-automatic weapons, and the *pop-pop-pop* of handguns. They reported that during wars, recruitment periods, and especially during holidays, the gunfire racket throughout the projects made it hard to sleep.

Yet, when Biggie and Moochie talked about their route to school, they stressed how safe it was at the time, as compared to previous years. Our conversation about gangs and safety followed reading selections from *There Are No Children Here* by Kotlowitz (1991). The boys claimed to be personally acquainted with the book's main characters, Pharoah and Lafeyette, because they lived in the same neighborhood. As Biggie commented, everyone knew them because "they's famous." However, until they read the book, the children had thought the fame stemmed from those boys being the subjects of a video starring Oprah Winfrey. The children were quick to point out similarities and differences between what they read and what they knew from their personal experiences.

According to Biggie, "You don't have to hide in no garbage cans or nothin', an' every day we go to school, don't nobody start shootin' or nothin'."

Moochie added, "We can cross the street now. Anybody say we cain't cross the street, that ain't true."

They reported that most of the daylight shoot-outs have been moved over to the local park. One time, before I was made aware of the danger, I proposed to Biggie and Moochie that we go to the park. They laughed, poking each other in the arm. Moochie, feigning incredulity over such a stupid suggestion, struck his forehead with an open palm. "Cain't go there."

"Why not?" I asked.

"*Pop! Pop! Pop!*" Biggie replied, holding his right-hand thumb up and forefinger extended, punctuating his words with the downward wrist movement that explained it all.

Terrell confided:

> Well, I used to go to [the park] but I don't go there now [because of] . . . the gangs. Lots of different gangs there. They just accuse you of bein' in a different gang 'cause of where you live. Well, like, the park has different gangs in it, an' each [project] building, it got a gang, an' dependin' on which building you live in, they think you in that gang.

Recently, some of the larger project buildings have been torn down. The demolition followed a study that showed it would be more expensive to renovate the buildings than to wreck them and build new housing. As the result of a 1987 Act of Congress and a landmark court decision rendered in response to a lawsuit initiated by this housing project's residents, replacement units were mandated. Consequently, new townhouses are going up all over the neighborhood, on vacant land as well as on lots that were specifically cleared for construction. The smaller project buildings are also being cleaned up and remodeled. Frequently, however, considerable time elapses between the vacating and razing of buildings.

Homeless people, drug dealers, and gang-bangers have been known to squat in the vacant apartments, boot-legging electricity and using the spaces for their own activities. With so many apartments vacant and so many boarded-up buildings awaiting demolition in every housing project throughout the city, there is no practical way to keep all the squatters out.

Some project residents with no criminal backgrounds and a solid history of paying their bills are being offered the chance to move into the new townhomes. Others are being offered apartments in different public housing developments. Still others have qualified for Section 8 rent vouchers that enable them to move into privately owned apartments in other areas of the city and suburbs while still paying only a portion of their income for housing. The children's neighborhood seethes with activity; people are on the move.

The children reported that some of the gang members who once lived in the demolished buildings have relocated to the suburbs or elsewhere in the city. Lemar asserted, "I know this 'cause that's where they tried to move us [to the suburbs], an' that's where they [the housing authority] movin' all the gang-bangers to already." The children also said that some of the gang members who once lived in now-demolished apartments in other housing projects have moved into their neighborhood and their housing project. The children were afraid there would be new trouble, maybe even another gang war, as those gang members tried to establish themselves by carving out or expanding territories and boundaries in their new community. In 1997, one particular war between gangs whose territories abut each other was very short, lasting only a week or two. It ended on Halloween night. Two youths were killed.

"Until it [a gang war] over, it's not safe around. Too many people get shot [in a gang war]. There gotta be a peace treaty, or the police gonna step in an' start steppin' on all of 'em," Biggie commented.

"They won't have no kids if they keep shootin'," said Moochie.

The school is supposed to be off-limits to gang activities and recruitment. The school has adopted a strictly enforced uniform policy of a plain, white top and black skirt or pants. The reasons for this action included reinforcing the school's neutrality, reducing competition over clothing, and eliminating the wearing of gang colors. (See Lowe 1997 for additional justifications for the adoption of a school uniform code).

A school administrator explained:

> We had discretionary funds to buy solid white tee-shirts with no imprinting on them that could be used as loaners, and [we] keep them in the Parent's Room. Sometimes the children would come [to school] with dirty sayings or drug emblems on their shirts, and we'd make them turn them inside out, but the problem was when they started wearing embroidered designs, and when you turned them inside out, you could still see them. So, we'd send them for loaners [school tee-shirts] if they were available. They were sent around [to the assistant principal's office] for some act of misconduct and they would commit acts of misconduct deliberately to get out of school. And they were gang drug dealers who hadn't made their quotas that month, so when we sent them home, they had a legitimate reason to be out of school. So, we noticed who was gone—and when—and we decided to buy tee-shirts and keep them in the Parent's Room. So, now they have to stay in school.

Biggie complained that the uniform colors themselves inadvertently created a problem. "Every color here is a gang color. Our school uniform is a gang color, too. You know, we ought to have a police officer to come in at my school an' give us an update on the uniform colors of the gangs, 'cause I think students should know what to wear an' what not to wear."

One teacher maintained that as many as 75 percent of the school children had "gang ties." Official statistics about gangs in the neighborhood seem to support her contention. During a short walk down the school corridor, this teacher pointed out one student whose father was a gang leader, another whose uncle led a rival gang, and a girl whose mother was living with a gang-affiliated drug dealer. She told me that "gang signs" included carrying amounts of money to school that "they have no business having," hanging around with older or younger children, wearing coats or shoes with certain color combinations, switching one shoe with someone else, rolling up one pant leg or the other, having either the right or left ear pierced, and wearing a baseball hat backwards with the bill on one side or the other. (See Lemann 1992, 227 for an explanation of the two large national gang divisions and symbols associated with them).

Biggie stressed that misinterpretation of these kinds of signs can be dangerous. "If you have you' hat on the wrong way, you got one comin'. They thinking you a gang-banger."

Terrell attributed some of the uproar and nonfocused activities that occur in the school to gang members: "Kids just get distracted more 'cause [of] the gangs. Like in [teacher's name] class, the kids can't behave, an' they in gangs."

I asked, "Which gang?"

He replied, "Lots of different gangs, an' those kids just out of control—[our teacher] says the best thing to do is just walk away. One minute they be talkin' they language, an' the next they be fightin'."

In the spring and in the fall, there was a palpable undercurrent of tension that seeped into the classrooms. The gangs were recruiting. Biggie explained there were code words "like 'What you ride?' 'How you ride?' 'What you down with?'" He added, "Long as you know the right answer, that's the point."

I asked the children about the factors that drove someone to join a gang. My questions emerged after a chance encounter with a boy in the assistant principal's office. The boy had been sent there for some behavioral infraction in his classroom. He was a small boy who appeared to be approximately ten years old, but was actually fourteen. He slouched in a chair, waiting for the assistant principal to arrive to determine the appropriate punishment for his misbehavior.

I had not seen him before, but this was because he said he had "just transferred in" from an alternative school for "problem" children where he had spent the previous six weeks. After a short discussion about why he preferred that former school to this one, the rest of our interchange went:

"I hate this place. I can't wait to get to ninth grade, and then drop out."

"What do you plan to do then?"

"Sell rocks [rock cocaine]."

"In a gang?"

"Yeh."

"Is that really a good idea?"

"You get to drive a big car [made a driving motion] an' make money."

"Yes, but gang people don't always live long, do they?"

"You get a gun, an' blow-off folk."

"Do you know any gang members?"

"Yeh, my uncle who lives over there [gestured toward the housing project]—my uncle is a gang-banger an' he got the whole building. Yeh, an' he's a [housing authority] guard, too."

"Well, it seems to me selling rocks can't be very profitable if your uncle has to have another job."

The boy put his head down on the round table where he sat and said nothing more. I left the room, chilled. He was transferred out of the school shortly afterward.

At the time of this conversation, I was unaware that "many people involved in the underground economy also work at legally declared jobs" (Bourgois 1995, 6)—both adults and, according to Monti (1994, 14–125), teenagers. I wish that I had thought before I reacted to the boy's words. As an ethnographer, I know better than to make an evaluative comment. Had I not effectively put an end to the conversation by making a comment that implied a judgment, I most likely would have secured additional information. I will never know if that boy was being truthful or not, or simply embellishing the facts to appear tough or to bolster his self-esteem.

Lemar said he believes that people join gangs because they need money or food. He added he did not understand why people in need do not approach their families first for help. "Gangs will give you food or money, but they always ask you to run the D's [sell or deliver drugs] or they make you do corners [watch for police or sell and deliver drugs on a specified street corner]."

Terrell said, "Some kids join to make a name—a bad name—an' to get girls."

"They think because they tough, they get the girls," Biggie added.

Moochie interjected, "Kids join 'cause they think they got protection. They tryin' to be bad. They get protection from other gangs, an' they think they got someone to love them. The gangs, they pump they [the members they are trying to recruit] head up."

Jasmine scoffed: "They actually call theyself 'family.' Girls join 'cause other girls encourage 'em. They say, 'It's good. It's more fun. You be out every night an' have fun.'"

I asked, "Why would girls want to go with a gang member?"

Terrell replied, "Some girls like tough guys, an' they gots money they flashes. But the people who gots jobs have the real money, but they don't flash it."

I had heard that gangs were recruiting younger and younger members. "Yes," the boys agreed, "they called 'shorties'." They added that they thought the reasons that gangs wanted young members was because, "in case somethin' go down bad," a child would most likely receive either a "station adjustment," at best, or be sent to "juvie," at worst. From what I gathered, a station adjustment is a "talking to" or scolding that occurs down at the police station, and being sent to *juvie*, or juvenile hall, can result in a police record that will be sealed if the child stays out of trouble until he or she becomes an adult. I asked Terrell, "Say, do you know how young some gang members are? I mean the youngest?" He replied, "I saw some like seven—five, around school."

Folb (1980, xxi) has suggested that ghetto teenagers have a "preoccupation ... with survival," so I asked the children how they negotiated walking around the neighborhood and avoided being harassed by gangs.

Jasmine responded, "I don't talk to 'em. I just keep goin'."

Biggie commented, "If you don't want nobody to whup you or nothin', then stop tryin' to be tough. That's my opinion."

Moochie offered, "Jus' act crazy, like, you walkin' down the street talkin' to you'self or singin'."

"Or drool," Ed added.

Biggie elaborated, "You answer 'neutron' [no affiliation], or act retarded, an' start slobbin'. It help you a whole lot."

These tips, the "art and artifice" of which Folb (1980, xxi) and Anderson (1990, 177) spoke, were similar to the one Biggie gave me about street survival (i.e., "You gotta walk like you mad, like you on a mission, an' then won't nobody bother you").

The children claimed their strategies have saved them from experiencing what another urban boy went through with the gangs most of the time.

> By the time he was in eighth grade ... [he] was already being harassed by the gangs. 'They pick on me a lot,' he says. 'They come into my face, say I'm a coward, taunting me, pushing me, any time I come

around. . . . If it's a whole group of them, I might get a little fear in my heart, but most of the time I'm not afraid of them'" (Lemann 1992, 300).

Moochie, who has taken karate and self-defense lessons through the after-school sports program, bragged: "One time they [gang members] jump me. But, they don't really know how to fight. They give 'soft taps' an' that's why it take so many of them to jump you."

Terrell related how he avoided being pressured to join a gang.

> The gangs don't put no pressure on me. They don't put no pressure on me 'cause I don't hang 'round that crowd [gang-bangers]. I go to the library an' come to the house, so if I don't look like I got nothin' to do, they don't pressure none. But if it look like you got family pressures, they really go after you. Like, if they know your mama use the drugs or somethin'.

"Although the data are not always consistent, research suggests that the proportion of youths who become delinquent increases from about age 12 through 15" (Ksander and Berg 1988, 209). Despite the fact that these children are precisely within that age bracket, I doubt that they are actually *in* gangs themselves, and I never had any hint during the times I was with them that they were engaged in delinquent behaviors.

Moochie explained his reasons for not joining a gang.

> It's stupid. If I join [a gang], that'll make everyone livin' in my house a member, automatically. Like, if they want you an' you ain't home, they drive-by an' get one of you' family. I don't wanna get popped [shot]. An' another reason, I don't wanna go to jail. You can get hurt, 'cause they on you. But, *you* catch the bullet an' make *they* money. That's *all* you get. You be a human shield an' a moneymaker—another foot soldier. Ain't no way I'll join!

Jasmine promised:

> I won't never join. It's stupid, an' you can come an' beat me you'self if you ever hear I join. You get beat in or you have to do some boy [have sexual relations] or kill somebody. Well, maybe not kill 'em—just hurt 'em so bad they ends up in the hospital.

Jasmine's information was corroborated. Being *beaten in* to a gang is an initiation rite in which the wanna-be gang member submits to being hit, beaten, punched, and more by a number of his or her same-sex gang members for a certain length of time. The beatings can take different forms: the wanna-be runs between two lines of gang members who try to attack him or her, or the wanna-be must submit to a one-on-one or group fight. Evidently, according to my informants, willingness to go through being beaten in proves the sincerity of the wanna-be's desire to join the gang and also proves toughness. Being *beaten out* is essentially the same kind of rite, although it is intended to signal disengagement from the gang. "Doing," or having sexual relations, in order to become a gang member is sometimes an alternative girls can take to being beaten in or out. It involves what my informants called gang sex. One of the children told me a cousin had elected this option when she joined a gang at age thirteen and, as a direct consequence of her initiation, bore a child at age fourteen.

Another very real problem the children mentioned concerning gangs was strictly social. Once a person joins a gang, everybody knows about it. That person wears the gang insignia, hangs around with other gang members, and usually drops his or her former friends and associates unless they belong to the same gang.

Gang culture dictates that fellow gang members are classified as friends or "family" but requires that rival gang members be considered enemies, even if they had been friends before their affiliation with different gangs. Gang members supposedly look out for one another and protect each other. Problems might arise, however, when and if someone quits a gang at a later date. There is no fail-safe method to alert everyone that an individual is no longer affiliated. The rival gang's members might still "go after" that person, thinking that he or she is still a member of the other gang. In addition, the children advised, the former gang member's friends become enemies after that person leaves the gang. The students thought that the only solution to this type of problem was to move out of the area altogether.

The children complained that people frequently assumed they were gangbangers or involved in illegal activities because of where they lived and their age. Moochie was particularly sensitive about such stereotypes. He recounted that once, when he was selling candy at the local sports arena to raise money for his class trip, "this cop kicked my butt hard 'cause he thought I be sellin' drugs or stole the candy or somethin'." The children never hinted they have considered that other variables such as their sex or ethnicity might play as large a role, or even larger, in other people's assumptions about them and their activities.

Biggie said, "The problem is everybody in the project don't live this [gang] kinda lifestyle."

Moochie agreed, "Nope, it ain't true."

Biggie continued, "It's 'cause some kids do things wrong an' they—we're actually good kids. I'm a good kid. I grew up an' lived in the projects. I never did drugs or joined no gang. I got in trouble with my mama, but not the law. Every kid in the projects is not a bad kid."

"Truth."

"Folks focus on the bad," said Biggie.

"They bend the truth," Moochie said. "We may do some stupid stuff, but no gangs."

However, some of the children did mention relatives who belonged to gangs or were in jail because of gang activities. They recounted gang-related shootings and deaths they had witnessed or that had involved people they knew. Almost every child had some sort of gang story to tell.

One child related that a cousin had been shot, "paralyzed from the neck down, [when] crossin' the field [in between project buildings] durin' some shootin'. He ran. He panicked." Another told, in sketchy terms, about a seven-year-old girl who had been accidentally run over during a "cruising drive-by."

A drive-by can happen when gang members go out "cruising" in a car or van, checking out their territory to "see what goin' down" and who is around. If they note rival gang members hanging around, they might shout insults from the safety of their car, spray the crowd with gunfire, or drive over the curb and down the sidewalk in an attempt to intimidate or disperse them. Drive-bys, according to the children, are deliberate actions aimed at other gang members. Apparently, what happens during a drive-by depends on the mood of the moment and how high current tensions are running among the different gangs.

The children made clear distinctions among the various kinds of gang-related activities that often resulted in injury or death. They cautioned that drive-by shootings should not be considered the same as random or walk-up shootings. Random shootings were aimed at no one person in particular, while walk-up shootings were deliberate, brazen, and very personal one-on-one assaults.

I thought the child who reported the drive-by had simply heard about the incident. However, he assured me that he had been standing next to the girl when she had been struck and that he had "jumped out the way."

In July 1997, Twan's older brother, Emmitt, was fatally stabbed in an altercation with a gang-banger. Apparently, Emmitt saw a man beating up a woman on the street. He stepped in to help her. The man left but almost immediately returned with a knife. He stabbed Emmitt to death. It was never made clear to me whether all of the involved parties were gang members.

The children told me about the event, and when I asked if the police had been called during the altercation, they scoffed, "Not hardly." Terrell claimed, "Don't never be no police here." The incident never appeared in the newspapers, as far as I know, although the street talk was that Twan's brother survived the stabbing long enough to identify his attacker for the police who questioned him in the hospital.

Biggie's anguish over Emmitt's death was palpable. "Twan's brother is *dead*—his big brother! That's how [Twan] got his shoes, his clothes, everything!

His brother is *dead*! Stabbed—he twenty-somethin'—yah, the [names of two gangs] in it." Tatiana related that ever since the killing, Twan had been afraid to sleep alone, a statement that produced sympathetic sighs and nods from the rest of the children who had been discussing Emmitt's death. Kay summed up the affair with "It was a tragedy," adding she did not think Twan had received any counseling.

In early December 1997, a shooting occurred on a Saturday night. A former student at the children's school was killed. More than likely, he had been a gang member. However, no gang wars were in progress at the time he was killed. Apparently, he was neither an intentional target nor the victim of a walk-up, so his death may well have been the result of a random shooting. The children were abuzz with gossip about the incident.

They talked about how the funeral had been attended by "alla his twenty-six kids an' his girlfriends" and how the number of cars had stretched far down the block from the church where services were being conducted. They speculated whether his children would qualify for Social Security benefits, and they wondered how the mothers of those children would take care of the babies since "they daddy dead, an' the welfare changin'."

Jasmine related that she had heard the shooting happened near a store "on the end [toward the limits of the housing project's sixty-acre site], an' it was probably gang related. Kay called me an' told me; Kiki called me an' told me; an' my grandma, she live over there, she called me an' told me. Tatiana say she was standin' right there, but I disbelieve her, 'cause if that true, she be havin' flashbacks an' everything."

The assistant principal also told me about the shooting. I searched the local newspapers for a report of the incident without success. Moochie explained the lack of coverage. "They [the media] don't come over here." His comment and Terrell's reinforced the belief that the housing project is "a world unto itself, completely cut off from the institutions and mores of the wider society" (Lemann

1992, 266) and the streets are "a kind of domain that allows a young person a range of activity and movement not directly subject to adult or establishment authority or control" (Folb 1980, 76).

Some of the children I asked about gangs volunteered that they do not, and would not, hesitate to call on "family" gang connections if and when the need arises. In fact, one boy who claimed to have family-based gang ties admitted that he had used those connections when he felt a teacher was picking on him unfairly ("He always pull on my ear for no reason!"). He said that he had called his Uncle Ray-Ray, a local gang leader, into the school to put "some mental pressure" on the teacher and to threaten unspoken things if the situation did not improve. Another boy boasted with some pride that no one, including his teachers, "had better mess with" him because if they did, he would tell his grandmother who belonged to a gang. He reported that his grandmother was well known for "goin' off, an' when she do, she call on [her son, also a gang member] to help her."

The only time I was personally involved with anything that even remotely concerned gangs was almost a non-experience. Most of the students entered school through one of the side doors facing the housing project across the street. Before school began on Class Officers' Election Day in 1996, I positioned myself in front of those doors at a table, hoping this strategy would maximize my chances of snaring the seventh graders and getting them to vote. My table was ringed by a number of children, none of whom were seventh graders. I thought this odd but, because they were there, felt I should be sociable. I asked them their names. They all turned out to be related to Lemar in some fashion—brothers, sisters, or cousins. They kept glancing at the door each time it opened.

I asked, "Are you waiting for Lemar?"

"No."

"Don't you have to eat breakfast?"

"No."

"So what are you waiting for?"

"Lemar, he say stick by [you], today."

"Did he say why?"

There were negatives and shrugs all around. The bell rang and the children dispersed to their classrooms. Later that same day, I took some of the seventh graders to the library, a distance of approximately two blocks. They ran the entire route, past the "rat alley," and quickly across the main thoroughfare. I wondered, as I hurried to catch up with them, why they were not ambling along like usual, chewing gum, kicking stones, and fooling around. The trip back to school was a repeat of the dash to the library. That afternoon, the seventh grade teacher came to me. "You know," she said, "I apologize for sending you to the library today. We just found out it was the 'sweeps' and it was dangerous."

Sweeps used to occur with great regularity in the housing projects. These efforts, organized and conducted by the city police department, were intended to clear out illegal tenants, drug dealers, and gang-bangers, along with their guns and drugs. Although the dates and schedules for such actions were supposed to be secret, word generally got out ahead of time somehow. In the past, some sweeps had turned violent; at other times, because of leaks, they netted very little in terms of illegal tenants, firearms, or drugs. Sweeps had become less frequent once the project renovations had begun and after the housing authority had hired its own police force.

I found it astonishing that the children had apparently known about the pending sweep since early morning (they guarded me at the door before school began; they ran to and from the library) but that the teachers were unaware of the action planned jointly by city police and housing authority police until the afternoon! If gang members call the school to warn of upcoming confrontations, should law enforcement officials do less?

As part of the school's efforts to deter students from thinking about crime and drugs as glamorous, the seventh graders were shown a film called *Picket Fence*. Biggie summarized, "Well, to get to the whole story, the moral was: If you sell drugs, you gonna get caught up any ol' way." Moreover, as part of their health program, they viewed a video on gangs that included interviews with former gang members. They also discussed gangs during class with a professional moderator and listened to testimony about gangs from a parent who was a former gang member. She admitted she had joined the gang (name unspecified) when she was a teenager in order to "belong." She told them she quit after she had been shot a second time. The first time she was shot, she was hit in the neck; the second time, the bullet lodged near her spine. She said she had to be beaten out of the gang, but it was worth it because she had her life.

Jasmine believed the veracity of this testimony and added, "I know this for a fact 'cause I have a cousin, she used to be in a gang an' she quit. She moved an' they let her go. Usually, it the same for girls as boys, you get beat in an' they beat you out."

Two field trips were taken to reinforce the classroom lessons about the social consequences of drug use, drug dealing, crime in general, and gangs. One trip was to a local halfway house where, as Biggie reported:

> A man talked us through the whole drug an' substance test. He was showin' us how the tests should get done an' the different methods, like through the hair, through the urine, through blood things, through a blood test, an' many others. He said you have to be careful with this urine 'cause if you get it mixed up, you get the wrong person sent to jail.

Regarding the other field trip to the county jail, Ceana related, "The man at the jail ask if anybody know anyone who ever been in jail, an' everybody's hand went up."

Tatiana recounted the experience in more detail.

> We had a lecture from about thirty-eight inmates—six women—about what it was like bein' in jail. They mention that the kids gettin' somethin' they own families didn't—they gettin' to see the inmates face-to-face instead through a three-inch glass. They say the kids could pick what they want to eat an' they could not. An' [girls' names] was

sittin' in the first row an' they was single out for a lecture on good behavior. We had a good day.

In March 1997, a group of Caucasian youths accosted and severely beat an African-American boy from a different neighborhood in the city. The media emphasized the racial aspect of the beating. On April 10, the seventh graders composed letters to that boy. What they wrote is very telling about how they perceived the incident and interpreted it in terms of themselves and their own experiences. The notes they mailed to the boy are reproduced below exactly as the children wrote them.

Art expressed the sentiment shared by his classmates.

> Everybody hopes you fully recover from your tragic experience. I guess you could say God was watching over you when you came out of your coma on Good Friday.

Corelle sent this letter:

> Sorry about what happened to you. Hopefully, you're not in a gang of some sort and that was the reason or they did it out of jealousy or they just pregadoris [prejudiced]. I hope you're OK!

Wynona's letter said:

> I am so sorry for what happen to you, that's why all of our people need to come together as a family and stop the crime. I just want to say that the world cares for you, *leas I think they do* [italicized words crossed out]. Well, I care for you and I hope you feel well I mean better. And God bless you and your family and this world. We need to help broken hearts. A broken heart hurts.

DeDe wrote:

> I heard on the radio the news what happened to you and I am very sorry that it happened to you. It could have been me and anyone else. I think that is not right for people to just do something like that for no reason and everytime I wake up I think about whats going to happen to me, if I am going to live this day or what because it seem that every day kids and adults are getting kill and I hate when that happens because I live in a big place now in the projects and so I think about it all the time. I just want to say God Bless you and I will pray for you.

One of the major differences between my data and those of Thrasher (1927), Folb (1980), Monti (1994), and the numerous other researchers who have investigated gangs most likely lies in the fact that their informants were gang members, whereas the children with whom I spoke disavowed gang affiliation both currently and in their past. These other researchers were able to investigate real phenomena, whereas the data on gangs I was able to collect from my informants were generalizations about the gangs, accounts of activities gangs carry on in public, and the children's feelings about gang activities. It may be that the children knew more about gangs than they were telling, or perhaps their contacts with gangs and gang members were really limited to periodic encounters in the streets and their school.

Some of the data these particular children provided about gangs appeared to be contradictory. On the one hand, they described the gang situation in their neighborhood as improved, saying they could cross the street, traverse the open field in their housing project, play outside their buildings now, and walk around their neighborhood without fear of being shot. On the other hand, they claimed that gangs were still active, still shooting and still doing drive-bys, and they worried that another gang war was imminent. I attribute much of the contradiction to the fact that the children were not personally involved in gangs but simply reacting day-to-day to ever-changing, local situations and circumstances in which gangs might or might not figure.

The children's personal feelings about gangs and gang membership were ambivalent. They maintained that they rejected gang involvement for themselves; yet, two of them said they would not hesitate to call on gang connections they have should the need arise. The reasons they refused to become personally involved with gangs were (1) they believed that they had a choice, (2) the cost of gang involvement was perceived to be high, and (3) they had support for their decision not to join from their families, churches, community, and school.

The children's emphasis on personal choice appears to be at odds with social models that assign adolescents a much more passive role in relation to gangs and delinquent behaviors. Nichols (1991, 244) analyzed gangs and delinquent behaviors in terms of this latter approach:

> It is much more 'costly' for a young, inner-city, black boy to take school seriously and avoid the lure of street crimes than it is for a suburban, middle class boy of any race. The costs to the urban black include ridicule by his peers and those who wield money, power, respect, and influence in his community, as well as the physical danger of rejecting the criminal path dictated as 'normal' by ever-growing gangs. Peer pressure is strongest at exactly the time when a boy's manhood is emerging. Detest them though we might, gangs serve a vital social function for the young people who belong to them. The relative absence of positive adult male role models at this time of life makes gangs more attractive as mechanisms for earning respect and a sense of belonging.

Although the children's comments that youths join gangs to "belong," to get "love," and to achieve a sense of "family" agreed with Nichols's last statement, on the whole, these reasons were obviously not enough to persuade them to join a gang. Biggie said he believes "you gotta make up you' own mind." These children counted the costs of joining a gang as too high for consideration. Was this because they have seen the true cost of gang involvement firsthand?

Moochie reiterated that the price was very high. "They just be shootin'. They steal, kill, beat up everybody. They think they bad. They end up dead."

Biggie indicated that he believes gang-bangers are deluded. "They think they takin' from us when they takin' from theyselves. They think like, they gonna live longer, but they really shorten they lifetime."

The children's attitude toward gangs may well have developed in part, too, because their school, unlike some of the ones Monti (1994) studied, acknowledged that gangs exist both in the community and within their walls and has taken steps to make certain the children learned about the price society exacts for criminal behavior. In this instance, the school might actually be doing the job Dewey

(1916/1985, 25–26) believed it should—that is, acting as a positive formative influence, as a steady, integrating force to balance the gangs' negative influences. But could part of the difference between these children and those Monti (1994) studied be due to their attending a school with an Afro-centric curriculum that stresses pride, self-determination, and personal responsibility, also?

The critical role that schools play with regard to gangs cannot be overemphasized. At least two researchers, Bourgois (1995) and Monti (1994), have suggested that attending school might actually introduce children to gang members and facilitate gang involvement. Bourgois (1995) has identified school as one of the institutions that fosters feelings of alienation, the precondition upon which peer pressure to join a gang and to become involved in illegal activities can operate.

He wrote:

> School is obviously a powerful socializing force, but it is by no means the only institution pushing marginal children into street culture and the underground economy.... When asked how they ended up on the streets most of the dealers blamed their peer group.... They learned a great deal during their school day—but almost none of it was academic. Most important, they spent their time cultivating street identities both inside and outside the physical confines of school (Bourgois 1995, 194).

And, Monti (1994, 44) found that:

> schools [bring] most of the community's children together for seven hours each day during the better part of the year. Children [are] curious about gangs.... Each school day provide[s] them with an opportunity to explore what it mean[s] to be a gang member along with the school's regular curriculum.... It was clear that there were times when youngsters were more interested in gangs than they were in their academic pursuits.

Further, Monti (1994, 162) asserted that gangs are an "exaggerated, better organized, and meaner version of the 'peer culture' that operates in all schools in varying degrees" and that many children found gangs and gang membership highly attractive.

There is no doubt that the children with whom I interacted were also watching and learning about gangs in school, from their peers, and perhaps even from some of their own family members. From their reports, most of their peers were not involved in gangs. Here, at least, at the children's school, opportunities to study gang members at close range worked as a deterrent for joining gangs, as some of their comments revealed.

I saw no evidence that any of the children who chose not to become involved in gangs had been pressured not to join by their classmates, had made a joint decision not to join, or had promised to support one another in those decisions. I saw no evidence of the existence of even a peer group of gang rejecters. Instead, I will argue that only on the basis of the similarity of their individual choices can the term *group* be applied to these particular children at all.

One of the most critical elements of culture—the requirement that cultural practices be generationally passed—is one that Monti (1994) failed to consider when he developed his definitions of *peer culture* and *gangs*. The children indicated that the gangs about which they knew were not just composed of adolescents and pre-adolescents but included adults of both sexes, too. I suggest that it is the adult component that gives these gangs their real subcultural elements: adaptive, learned behaviors, specific to a set of activities that are passed generationally from individual to individual. Therefore, my definition of peer culture is at odds with Monti's (1994) analysis of the nature of gangs. Yet, because there is that generational component to gangs, even though Monti (1994) failed to recognize it, I believe he correctly labeled gangs as a subculture. He noted, on page 161, that gangs create a "particular worldview for their members and put it into practice. The creation of a worldview by any collection of human beings is vital work, and the fitting of that worldview into the ways in which persons conduct their daily lives is their culture."

At the same time they individually rejected gang affiliation, two of the children with whom I spoke indicated they had or would have no qualms about using gang connections to effect changes and shifts in power relations. I wonder whether their willingness to use their family gang connections in order to countermand what they perceived as unfair treatment by those in power in the school was a reaction to one of the "multiple and contradictory relations of power" (Apple 1995, xi) that they found in school? Or did their expressed willingness to use gang ties to achieve their own personal ends support their literal internalization of their school's motto, "By any means necessary" (the famous phrase Malcolm X repeatedly used, documented in a 1964 interview quoted in Myers 1993, 181)?

Twenty years ago, it might well have been that the children's parents had to make accommodations and negotiations with gangs in order to survive in those same project buildings where they now raise their children. Perhaps these same parents are determined to keep their children from having to make the same kinds of choices. I know from discussions with four of the children's parents that, as far as they are concerned, gang membership is not an option for their children.

According to Biggie, Jasmine, and Moochie, the community's effort to change the reality of daily life in the projects, to rid their neighborhood of gangs, has been to form tenant associations and men's organizations charged with making certain that, as far as possible, the buildings are "clean" both of garbage and gangs. These grass-roots kinds of citizens' efforts to solve local problems have been bolstered and legitimized by those of local church organizations, law enforcement officials, and the housing authority. They seem to have been somewhat effective in changing the degree to which gangs control life in this neighborhood today. It is also apparent that the school has responded to the larger community's increased concerns about gangs by providing formal curricula that enable the children to make informed choices about gang involvement.

Would a revitalist model explain the community's apparent shift away from tolerating gang presence and activities, and gang involvement, and the seeming contradictions that emerge in the children's discussions about gangs? The term *revitalism* has traditionally been applied to phenomena as disparate as Cargo

Cults, the Ghost Dance, Millennium Cults, The Great Awakening, and Nativistic Movements. In general, both secular and religious revitalist movements emphasize change. Depending on the movement's goal(s), changes can reintroduce or reinterpret older customs that were discarded, lost, or forgotten; or changes can create a hybrid set of beliefs and activities. These kinds of movements are quite different from simple nostalgia for the past. Movements such as these are dynamic and vital.

Revitalization usually happens when a number of people become convinced that certain aspects of their present "lifeways" no longer satisfy their needs (Wallace, 1956). Revitalist movements typically are a cultural response to perceived deprivation and/or oppression. As such, these movements often emphasize the elimination of alien elements, whether customs, goods, values, or people.

According to Wallace (1956), individuals under extreme stress from external or internal pressures develop and join revitalist movements. Usually, one or more persons are responsible for instituting and leading revitalist movements. They are joined by others who share their beliefs that present circumstances must be changed.

Their collective efforts to change the circumstances under which they find themselves produce rapid changes from different directions. Changes are tackled enthusiastically and energetically. Clashes of views that split communities along political lines are common in secular revitalization movements. These splits lay the foundation for future political action. The natural course of such movements leads to structural reorganization that eventually solidifies and becomes the basis for new, routine behaviors. In other words, revitalist movements are transformative efforts. In this neighborhood, the impetus toward revitalism was quite clearly related to the fact that "people just got tired of the gangs."

Chapter 2
Family

When I taught introductory anthropology classes, I always asked the students to move into small groups and brainstorm the question "What is a family?" Because the student body was so ethnically diverse, the question generated almost as many definitions as there were students. Interestingly, their models revolved around "family" as a social unit bound together by kinship or jural ties. Usually one brave person would begin the class discussion by saying, "A family is a married couple [male and female] and their child [or children]." Inevitably, someone would interject, "What about an unmarried couple and their children?" Then, the students would offer other definitions similar to the following:

"A family may be a married or unmarried couple and her children, his children, and their children."

"But what about a couple, his, her, or their children, and one or more sets of parents or other relatives?"

"Or what about a same-sex couple and his/her/their children?"

"What about people you call 'Aunt' or 'Uncle' but who really are just good family friends? Are they part of the 'family'?"

Typically, the discussion moved from blood and jural relationships to exploring whether residence and household activities could be used to define "family." What do families do? What are the responsibilities of family members to other family members? Do all families work to socialize their children? Does every family do things the same way? Does everybody get a hand in the socialization process, or is it a job one member gets? Aren't those activities based on residential proximity rather than social ties? Do they always live together? Do they all contribute to the running of the household, or do some family members get a free ride? Why do we have families anyhow?

The foregoing illustrates the problems inherent in defining and generalizing something as fundamental to social organization and socialization as *family* and *kinship*, sets the stage for a discussion about the meaning and importance of such social ties for community life, and leads to questions about the effects a larger scale kinship model might have on a school. The seventh graders with whom I worked used family and kinship models in their attempts to link and integrate the different social spheres within which they operated. They created networks of people whom they classified as kin and called upon those individuals to help them gain access to information, resources, support, and power.

These seventh graders have grown up in a predominantly African-American community. Most of them live in a public housing project. Some of their families have lived in the same project for over thirty years. According to the state-issued report card, their school is described as having a population that is 100 percent African-American. Although official statistics characterized the student body in those terms, Biggie and Ed disagreed. Once, during a conversation where I asked whether they thought they might like to attend a more ethnically diverse school, they said they already had diversity in their school because two members of the student body were white.

Biggie explained, "They mamas' white, so that make 'em white—Oh, we 'posed to say 'Caucasian.' So, that make 'em Caucasian."

Ed continued, "'African-American' is when both parents is African-American."

Because the answers the children gave were at odds with the usual macro-social definition of Caucasian and African-American, I double-checked with Jasmine and received the same response. I also asked her, "What if the father's Caucasian and the mother's African-American—does that make their kid Caucasian too?" She considered the question and replied, "I guess so, yes."

"So," I probed, "when one parent is Caucasian and the other is not, then the kid's 'Caucasian'?" "Yes." Yet, when I helped one of the students Biggie, Ed, and Jasmine had identified as white fill out her membership application for the local Boys and Girls Club, she checked African-American in the box that asked for her ethnicity.

These children's racial/ethnic classificatory criterion adds a new dimension to how one can think about the rule of "hypo-descent" (Harris 1964, 56). This rule states that the standard pattern in the United States is for those in the majority, typically Euro-Americans, to assign subordinate status to those in the minority—groups that include native Americans, Asians, Latinos/Latinas, and African-Americans. Was the children's ascription of what is usually considered "majority status" to two of their classmates at odds with this rule? Or was it a standard application of the rule? After all, in their community, Americans of African descent *are* the majority. In this instance, did the "traditional" majority classification (Caucasian) carry subordinate status implications? Or did the classification simply grow out of an awareness of difference?

In my experience, the children never judged any of the people with whom they came in contact primarily on ethnicity or any of the dynamics that categorical scheme implies. Instead, they most often described and related to others in terms of how those people behaved toward and related to them. Theirs was a very personal kind of classificatory scheme. Whether their attitude was an outgrowth of the school's Afro-centric philosophy or not, none of the children I asked could say. In this school, at least, ethnicity, in the full sense of the word, was neither denigrated nor extolled. It never was the criterion on which students based their sense of self-worth either. It simply was a non-issue.

Actually, ethnicity might now be becoming less of a self-esteem issue than it has been in the past, as revealed in a recent survey of 272,400 sixth- to twelfth-grade students published in the *Chicago Sun-Times* (May 1–3, 1998, 18). The data showed that, for 71 percent of the children, their own ethnicity or race made no difference in the way they felt about themselves.

However, because these children have grown up in this particular community and have attended a school with an Afro-centric focus, ethnicity, in the broad sense, might well be that "additional 'layer' of identity that [inner-city] youth . . . adopt as a matter of pride" (McLaughlin and Heath 1993, 222). Kay summed up the African Studies curriculum as she saw it: "We learn about our heritage ever since we was in Head Start. We study 'bout slavery an' stuff. We learn 'bout Kwanzaa. We learn about our ancestors."

As with many other things at their school, Afro-centrism was redefined to the point where it smacked more of postmodernism than what Black Nationalists and Pan-Africanists might have ever envisioned. (See Campbell 1996, 153-72, for a list of postmodern concerns, and Watkins 1993 and 1994 for a discussion of the historico-political roots of Pan-Africanism and Afro-centrism).

A school administrator, whose definition of Afro-centrism differed from that of Asante (1988), one of its most famous proponents, said:

> We are an Afro-centric school. But we keep in mind that in the real world you don't live in a total African world. You need to live with others. We emphasize pride, but we say 'move out and look and understand and accept other cultures.' I define Afro-centrism as African-American people dealing with one another in very positive ways, sharing, caring, working to build our place here in America. It's teaching African-American history but not disparaging others. It's talking about the differences but not in negative terms. There are differences, but they're not negative.

Chapter 2: Family

The principal maintained that this version of an Afro-centric model has made a huge difference in how the children act and feel about themselves. She believed that since they adopted this philosophy, the students, as a whole, were more self-assured and very "open and likely to give you a hug." The teachers and administrators reiterated time and again that they were trying to socialize their students, using the school's Afro-centric model to instill pride in themselves and their heritage and to develop personal responsibility.

What the teachers and administrators said they were trying to accomplish is close to what Dewey (1916/1985, 25–26) envisioned schools should do when he wrote:

> The school has the function also of coordinating within the disposition of each individual the diverse influences of the various social environments into which he enters. One code prevails in the family; another, on the street; a third, in the workshop or store; a fourth, in the religious association. As a person passes from one of the environments to another, he is subjected to antagonistic pulls, and is in danger of being split into a being having different standards of judgment and emotion for different occasions. This danger imposes upon the school a steadying and integrating office.

Many of the children in the seventh grade had younger and older siblings, half-brothers and -sisters, stepbrothers and -sisters, cousins, aunts, and uncles who also attended the school at the same time as they. A number of the seventh graders are "blood kin." Ed and Art are maternal first cousins. Kiki, Lemar, and Twitty are maternal first cousins. Twitty and Shanita are paternal first cousins, as are Moochie and Fred. Twan and Fred are related because Twan's mother and Fred's father are siblings. Biggie and Jasmine are maternal second cousins; Jasmine and DeDe are paternal first cousins, and both Jasmine and Biggie are cousins "somehow" to Keesie. However, Biggie is not particularly fond of Keesie because she once "jumped him" when they were in first grade. He has declined to publicly acknowledge their consanguinity, saying, "I won't claim her as no kin." Tatiana has an older stepsister (stepfather's child) and two full siblings (maternal connection) with whom she lives. She also has two younger half-siblings (paternal connection, different mothers) who attend the same school as she.

Some of the children lived in extended family situations where the composition of the domestic unit fluctuated. For example, one student and her mother lived in her grandmother's house, although in a separate apartment. That child's father is deceased. The child's oldest sister, her husband, and their children have stayed with them on occasion. At other times, the household has expanded to include either one or both of the other female siblings and their children, and the mother's husband. The child complained, "Holidays, there be thirty peoples—just too many peoples." (See Staples 1973 and 1985, along with Staples and Johnson 1993, for in-depth sociological descriptions of African-American families).

Tatiana, with her knack for summing up complex issues in a few, well-chosen words, described her school as the place where "we all family here." *Family* was both a real and symbolic notion that permeated, structured, and shaped many of the children's interpersonal relationships within and outside of the school. Many researchers, most notably Fordham (1985, 1986, and 1988), Stack (1974), and Aschenbrenner (1975), have written about the existence in the African-American community of the network of symbolic family members who have been grouped under the label *fictive kin*.

Fictive kin relationships appear to have grown out of a "helping tradition," also called "intra-Negro charity" by Powdermaker (1939, 136, quoted in Martin and Martin 1985, 61). Historically, the helping tradition was common in the African-American family and community. The extended family, churches, and other black care-giving institutions were the major providers of such help. Numerous researchers, such as Martin and Martin (1985, 63), Rawick (1972), and Herskovits (1941, 1966), have placed the roots of the helping tradition in Africa, maintaining that it was tenaciously retained during slavery, was predominant in rural Southern communities, and was transplanted to urban centers both North and South. Martin and Martin (1985, 65) believed that the helping tradition has "sunk nearly into insignificance today" primarily because African-Americans increasingly adopted "dominant urban values" that emphasized individualism, secularism, and competition. Yet, Fordham (1985, 1986, and 1988) implied that the collective spirit remains embedded in African-American cultural tradition. Since the tradition includes "helping" and reliance on others, she found it continues to be a powerful component in many African-Americans' social, economic, and political lives. She stressed that "kinship-like connection[s exist] between and among persons in a society, not related by blood or marriage, who have maintained essential reciprocal social or economic relations" (Fordham 1988, 150-51).

According to Aschenbrenner (1975, 12), the notion of family is not limited to a circle of real or assumed relatives; "play mothers and fathers" and "play sisters and brothers" are added

> onto an already full set of kin. . . . A woman without children or whose children have left home might 'take on' a play daughter. She will act like a mother to her or, at least in some ways, will play the part of mother. She will buy her play daughter gifts—usually at birthdays and at Christmas. The girl will play the part of 'daughter' by going to the store for her or doing some light housework, nothing too strenuous. Sometimes she may even stay overnight.

Fictive kin relationships are an immanently practical adaptive strategy. Stack (1974, 58) defined fictive kin as "those you count on" and stated that it is a device through which "people expand their personal networks." For example, Moochie's "grandmother," Ms. Jackson, is not his "blood kin" but has assumed the structural and systematic aspects of the grandparent role about which Smith (1970, 55–70) wrote. Moochie refers to Ms. Jackson as "my grandma" and treats her with the respect one would normally accord a real grandmother. The school authorities were unaware, until recently, that she was not a blood relative. Ms. Jackson works at the school and lives in an apartment in the same building as Moochie and his parents did until 1997 when they moved. Teachers frequently asked her to relate information about Moochie's work progress or attitude or behavior problems to his (employed) parents. She was called to be present whenever he was chastised for classroom misbehavior. Because she was in the school building, if Moochie forgot something at home, such as money for a field trip or a permission slip, he sought her out. He also informed her when his after-school plans changed. She knew what activities his parents might have had planned for the evening and sometimes gave permission for him to go to the library or to someone's house until dinnertime. She occasionally supervised Moochie until one of his parents returned home. She is interested in his social and academic development. Aschenbrenner (1975, 3–4) has documented that this is not all that unusual in an African-American community, since "the black child learns about the many facets of his society, and its values are transmitted from within his kin group, which is not limited to the conjugal family of parents and children."

Ms. Jackson also served as a pipeline from the school to home and back. She gathered information that pertained to Moochie and the school and conveyed it to both Moochie and his parents. She also communicated information from Moochie's parents back to the teacher. She operated *in loco parentis*.

She and I have had at least two long discussions about how to encourage Moochie to read more often and about different strategies that might help him stay out of trouble in the classroom. Plans and strategies were very necessary because Moochie professed to have great difficulty discerning and interpreting exactly what it was that his classroom teacher expected from him. As a result, he was often "in trouble."

Ogbu (1985, 58) called this kind of interchange the *folk theory* of child rearing. (See Allen 1985, page 282, for additional documentation of and a discussion about some of the "advice sources" African-Americans typically consult). He stated that inner-city blacks often asked other parents and adults for advice to guide "their relationships to children and to rationalize what happens between them and children." I would extend Ogbu's definition of folk theory to include asking for advice on how to guide children in relationships with teachers and to rationalize what happens in those relationships.

Chapter 2: Family

I know that pieces of what Ms. Jackson and I have discussed have been relayed to Moochie's parents because both he and his parents have made reference to some of those conversations when we talked. I do not know how much Moochie's parents relied on the information they received from Ms. Jackson, but it was obvious that they at least listened to what she had to say. I also do not know what Ms. Jackson "got out of" being Moochie's "grandma" because the opportunity to explore this dimension of their fictive kin relationship never arose. I suspect it is something similar to what Stack (1974, 58) discovered, that is, "A friend who is classified as a kinsman is simultaneously given respect and responsibility." Aschenbrenner (1975, 12) neatly summed up the benefits of a fictive kin relationship.

> When closest bonds are with family, what better way to show friendship than by extending family relationships? And what better way to bridge the generations? One can become agreeably involved, with the option of limiting the involvement.

The literature on fictive kin documents the development and shape of such relationships from adult to adult (Play Brother/Sister), from younger adult to older adult (Play Mama/Grandma), from adult to child (Play Mama/Daddy), and from child to child (Play Sister/Brother). However, I was unable to locate any information about the kinds of play relationships that I documented while I was at the school, specifically the formation of a Play Baby category and the adoption of adults by children as Play Mamas/Grandmas.

When we were discussing fictive kin relationships, Tatiana told me, "Here you can talk 'bout me an' Twan. He my Play Baby." I asked her what she meant. She said she considered him to be just like a baby brother and that they played together. On the bus ride to Washington, D.C., for example, she "dressed" Twan up in her sunglasses, then called attention to how silly he looked. Twan went along with the game, grinning but looking somewhat sheepish. Everyone recognized there was a special connection between Tatiana and Twan that was distinct from a boyfriend-girlfriend relationship.

Terrell talked about how Tatiana and Twan acted in public. "Tatiana, she say 'he my baby,' an' they be huggin' all the time." Waldo added, "Twan her 'Boo Baby.' She show favoritism to him, like when he talkin' [in class], she never put his name down." Because I looked puzzled, Lemar explained that a baby was often called a "Boo Baby" or a "Boo" because parents played peek-a-boo with their young babies and babies enjoyed playing it. Babies, up until the stage where they can walk and talk, are typically called "Boo Babies."

I consider Tatiana and Twan's relationship truly interesting as the sole instance I found of cross-gender "best friendship" among the seventh graders. It was more common for them, as for many older adolescents, to have a typical boyfriend-girlfriend relationship with a member of the opposite sex. Although younger boys and girls occasionally have best friends of the opposite sex, early adolescent children customarily pick same-sex best friends, as Thorne (1993), Lever (1976), and Goodwin (1990) have documented in their descriptions of gendered play.

Among the seventh graders, each set of best friends had one or more reasons for becoming best friends. For example, Keesie and Kiki were longtime best friends because they grew up together. Fred and Ed were more recent best friends because they shared an interest in basketball and a mentor. Moochie and Waldo were best friends since they liked to run after rabbits and catch snakes up near the railroad tracks together. A common interest in dogs and wildlife brought Terrell and Ken together as best friends. Princess and Susie were best friends because they discovered they both want to be writers. Kay and Sierra recently became best friends when they uncovered parallels in their family histories that included having mothers and older sisters the same age. Jasmine and DeDe are not only kin but also what the children called "talkin' buddies," meaning they discussed everything, all the time, every chance they had, together.

Best friends are distinct from *associates*. The boys typically classified other boys with whom they interacted on a casual social level, or on a temporary basis, as associates. For example, one boy might refer to another with whom he had worked on a school project as an associate. Interestingly, no seventh-grade boy ever used the word *associate* when talking about an adult or a younger boy. However, the boys did use the term when referring to slightly older boys, not yet adults. I never documented any instances in which they applied the word *associate* to a girl or girls. I also never heard any girl call anyone else her associate. The girls simply identified an individual by name, then added "my classmate," "another student," "somebody I know," or "a person I worked [on a specific project] with," if that were required.

Even more interesting about Tatiana and Twan's relationship, aside from the fact that it crossed gender lines, was Tatiana's conferring of fictive kin status on her best friend, much as an adult might confer such status on his or her best friend. Perhaps the only way that she could rationalize or legitimize spending so much time with Twan, who after all is a boy but not a boyfriend, was to pretend he was her baby. On the other hand, her designation of him as a Play Baby might have been because Twan stood only four-and-a-half feet tall "an' he so cute."

I was designated fictive kin to two girls and one boy with whom I worked particularly closely. My status in relation to these children was acknowledged and accepted by all the seventh graders. One of these three children actually called me "mama." When I first heard myself referred to in this manner, I was confused. When and how did this transformation from researcher to mama take place? What did this new status mean?

I first became aware of my fictive kin designation when Kay ran toward my car as I carefully negotiated it through wads of children spread all over the parking lot-playground behind the school. Over the rope-rhymes and general chaos, I heard her yell, "Mama!" I looked around for her mother, but she was not there. Kay raced over to my car and waited until I opened the door. By that time, Art had joined her, jostling for the position nearest the driver's side door. Kay snapped at him, "Get away from my mama!" Art backed away. I gave Kay a hug, asked her about her homework, and made a mental note to find out what being her mama meant.

During the day, I could not help mulling over what Kay had called me. I knew that the boys sometimes laughingly called me "Mother Hen," after I had exhorted them to "Come along, Chickens." They used the same appellation when they talked about their former teacher, a motherly woman named Henrietta, who had died. However, I could discern no reason that Kay should call me mama. To my recollection, I had treated her no differently than I had treated the other seventh graders, although Santa Claus had dropped a much-needed new jacket for her, in her favorite pink shade, at my house before Christmas.

An opportunity to explore what my new name meant came when I met Coco, Princess, DeDe, Tatiana, Keesie, Fred, Art, Biggie, and Lemar during our scheduled morning reading session. Normally, Kay would have attended, but she had gone to the school clinic to receive treatment for an asthma attack. I asked the group, "What's it mean when you call somebody 'mama' who's not your mama?" They did not have to think long before they answered. Their replies went far toward clarifying my newly acquired status and role.

Tatiana explained, "It mean you trust them, an' got feelin's for them, an' can always rely on them."

Added DeDe, "You do for them an' they give you somethin' special—presents or spend a lot of time with each other."

And Keesie's definition: "Someone that I care for, an' I trust. Someone that be there when you need them, an' they need you to be there. An' they loan you money if they want to."

Coco replied, "Someone to count on, trust, an' love, an' wish you they relation, [like] a sister or brother in real life."

"A real good friend," said Art.

For Fred, a mama is "a person you can trust, that be there when you need 'em."

Chapter 2: Family

For Lemar, it's "a person you can talk to."

Biggie added, "They you 'second mama.'"

Princess answered, "Someone you close to, by bein' with them all the time. These relationships last forever."

Then I asked, "What does that person have to do for you or your family? Like, do they have to give you things you need?"

Coco responded, "I don't ask [my Play Mama], but I tell her daughter to ask [her] if I need somethin'."

Tatiana said, "You get what you need."

"Do you have to give it back?" I asked.

"Yes," said Keesie, "you give it back when you finish with it."

Tatiana did not completely agree. "Sometimes. It depend on what it is. Money, yes, you need to give it back."

Finally, I asked the *big* question: "Well, Kay calls me 'mama'—so what am I supposed to do for her?"

"Whatever her own mama can't," answered Tatiana.

Coco said, "Put her on the straight an' narrow with a chat should she need it."

"Okay," I thought, "Now I've got it."

That the children relied on me to take play mama responsibilities seriously was borne out a few weeks later when one of the girls advised me, "Doncha know your daughter, Kay, messin' with that boy [name]?" There was no opportunity for questioning. She scurried off down the hall into her classroom. However, it was obvious that I was expected to *do* something. Finally, I decided to talk to Kay about "that boy." I had no idea if "messin' with" meant dating, teasing, or something else in this particular instance; but whatever it was, apparently at least one of her friends did not think it was good or appropriate. When I saw Kay, I made my statement as broadly applicable and as ambiguous as possible.

"Well, I heard you were messin' with [boy's name], and maybe you might want to think a little bit about what you're doing." Kay ducked her head, trained her eyes on the floor, nodded, and that was the end of that conversation. A week later, when I heard that Kay had stopped going out with "that boy," I wished I knew if it were my "mama" words that had caused the breakup or whether, like most thirteen-year-olds' relationships, this one had simply run its course.

One member of Kay's peer group had enlisted my assistance to put a stop to an association felt to be inappropriate or perhaps even dangerous. Obviously, she [they?] either did not feel able to talk about this with Kay directly or had tried to talk to her without success. Consequently, a hint was dropped to the adult believed to have influence with Kay—(i.e., her play mama).

Fictive kinship also allows kin certain freedoms regarding property and the rights to its use. It took me a long time to understand why the two girls and the boy who claimed me as fictive kin felt so free to poke around among my possessions and to ask if they could use or have some small thing, like a calculator, a few batteries, or a pen or borrow a video. Apparently, no doubt ever entered their minds that since I had those kinds of things lying around, I would share. The interchanges went something like this: "You using this?" or "You need this?" The questions were followed quickly by requests. "Can I use [or borrow or have] it?" It seemed, moreover, that the children observed limits to what they could reasonably expect to use or be given. Until I offered to let them work on my computer, it was never one of the things they asked to use. Once I began encouraging them to type papers and poems, play games, and "surf the Web," they have asked to come out to my house specifically because they needed to use the computer for some school-related project or download the lyrics to a song they wanted to memorize. Perhaps, the machine's cost, about which they were curious, deterred them from asking to use it until I indicated it was permissible.

Even more rarely, the children have asked for a loan to buy a gift for a parent or sibling. They were always quick to add that they would work to pay me back.

Chapter 2: Family

If they could not return the money, they volunteered one hour weeding my garden, cleaning the house, or doing chores I needed done for every five dollars I loaned them. They made it quite clear that they felt five dollars per hour was a reasonable valuation for their work.

This was not a "hustle" which Ogbu (1985, 55) claimed is one of the strategies some inner-city dwellers use to obtain goods, services, and money. I know the difference from experience. One of the student's mothers tried to hustle me for money with no mention of repayment. I did not give her anything, but someone else did. The mother was overheard in the school's parent room the next day boasting about how she had "hustled [name]" who apparently had "come across."

Stack (1974, 37–38) believed the exchange and redistribution of possessions, goods, and services among kin in African-American communities "bears a striking resemblance to patterns of exchange organized around reciprocal gift giving in non-Western societies." Such patterns of gift giving are embedded in well-defined kinship obligations, permeate the social-economic life of the participants, and redistribute goods that are in short supply.

Some of the seventh-grade girls gave me an informal lesson in how they believed redistributions should work. Whenever the girls came out to my house, they would play in my daughter's room. Because they came out so frequently, my daughter finally became resigned to having visitors in her room when she was home or away at school and whether she liked it or not. When she was home, they would run up to see her and talk. If she were at school when they came, they made her room their own. They pretended to make telephone calls, listened to her messages, turned on her television set, checked out her closet, and rummaged through her trinkets.

My daughter used to have a trundle bed for overnight guests. The girls would pull the trundle out and use the extra mattress for what can only be described as harem-like lounging. When my daughter got a new bed and Tatiana saw it, her first question was "What happen to the other bed?"

"I gave it away."

Coco asked, "Both parts?"

"Who to?" Kay inquired.

I replied, "Well, I gave it to [my stepson] because he moved out and needed a bed."

Tatiana sighed: "Well, then that's OK, 'cause if you just gave it away, you shoulda called me." "Or me!" Coco chimed in. "No, *me*!" Kay disagreed.

The girls' implications were clear. It was all right to buy something new, but it was not all right to simply give the old, still "good" thing away to a stranger. If someone in my immediate family could not use it, I should have offered it (redistributed it) next to someone in my fictive family.

Stack's (1974) discussion of redistribution referred to the ebb and flow of gifts and goods among adults in fictive kin relationships, not from adults to children. Gifts and goods, even freely given money, that flow from parent to child, and from play mamas and play daddies to their play children do not create obligations or debts. When a child needs something, and if the child's "own mama can't," the child's play mama might be able to provide it. If she can provide the goods, services, or money, she is expected to do so. If she cannot, she might loan the child the required object or money with the understanding that it be returned or repaid.

It also took me a long while to understand the relational implications of fictive kin status with regard to the real parents of my play children. I sometimes received telephone calls from those children's mothers that would begin with no introduction. I suppose they assumed I would know who it was. In one instance, Jasmine's mother, Reetha, asked me for the names of good furniture resale shops close to her new Section 8 apartment because the neighborhood was unfamiliar. She asked if, after she was paid, I might be free to go with her to look for "new furniture—not new—but new to me." I have also been asked to give her and her family rides home from school since I was "going in that direction." She and I have tossed around the pros and cons of different jobs Reetha was considering, and I have been asked to baby-sit my play daughter Jasmine and the twins when Reetha was working but the girls had a half-day at school. According to Ogbu (1985, 58–59), cooperating mutual-exchanges based on kinship or friendship include child-rearing duties. From my experience, they also include child-sitting duties.

Unlike Kay and Jasmine, my play son has never directly referred to me as "mama." He did, however, make frequent joking references to our "ties," such as the time he nudged my arm and laughingly reported, "They tryin' to kill my mama [at work], but that's OK 'cause I have another one just in case." Although Biggie and I have some sort of unspoken kinship, even Biggie's teacher recognized our relationship. She once advised, "You know that Biggie, he thinks he's your's and [your husband's] son, too." And the assistant principal called me one evening for Biggie's telephone number because she "knew [I] would have it."

My play son's mother has telephoned on various occasions to ask whether I could take him for a haircut when he came out (she sent the money with him), to bemoan how poorly he reads, to inquire whether I knew if the teachers assigned "creative writing" in class, to discuss strategies for starting a tutoring program for school children at her church (subsequently put into operation), and to recount "our boy's" triumph at the City Science Fair that I had been forced to miss. There have been times when we talked for hours. The calls, reports, and requests from both these mothers are perfectly natural if one is "family." Obviously Fordham (1988, 150) was correct when she asserted, "The term 'fictive kinship' ... is based on more than just skin color."

What I get out of the relationships my play children have created for me is simple and extraordinarily meaningful. I have received poems, touching notes, and presents that indicate a lot of thought and time was spent selecting or making them. The children have even included my biological children in their gift giving.

My "children" made a point of keeping me informed about what they were doing. They showed me their progress reports as soon as they received them so I could praise their grades or sympathize with them. They watched out for me when we traveled together. Since they think I "don' look rough an' [I] don' go smart," they gave me street survival tips, like: "You gotta walk like you mad, like you on a mission, an' then won't nobody bother you."

They remind me when I have, once again, forgotten to zip my purse, and repeatedly demonstrate how easy it would be to "G", or grab, my wallet. During the years I was conducting my research, they made sure no one vandalized my car in the parking lot either before or after school. Once, they even washed my car.

They have offered to weed my garden. They always cleaned up after themselves at my house without being asked. They have accompanied me to the grocery store, helped me comparison shop, and unloaded the bags. The girls frequently paid me compliments on my shoes and clothes and gave me fashion recommendations as well ("Now, you can't get that coat with all that curly, ugly hair all over it [a Tibetan lamb jacket]. People gonna be sayin', 'How you let her buy that ugly, curly-hair jacket?'").

When I have been sick, they have called to see if I am better, passing along folk remedies and advice. Moochie's "sure-fire" cough remedy was one I actually tried and found efficacious: "First you take a lemon an' cut it up in half or quarters, an' leave the rind on, an' then you boil it up, an' drink it like a tea. It nasty, but it work. Bring all the stuff up."

Some of the children have even picked up a few of my expressions, such as "There you have it," "Could have fooled me," "not a problem," "a ton of things," and, I am ashamed to admit, "Well, duh!" I had not realized that "a ton of things" peppered my conversations until Biggie wrote me a note asking me to pick him up for school because "I have a ton of things to bring." His teacher pointed out it was only natural for him to have picked up that phrase since I used it "all the time." I have also caught myself using one of the children's more colorful expressions on more than one occasion ("da'g," a multipurpose word that can be used as an exclamation, an adjective, or adjectival phrase). And, lastly, the children are all patient with my questioning; they give me thoughtful answers. I get respect.

My experience as play mama indicated that their families encouraged, or at least did not discourage, this kind of child-originated extension of family. Moreover, I discovered that "the play kin relationship is less intense and plays a somewhat different role [than real kin relationships].... It allows family members to 'play at' roles that are earnest in the family" (Stack 1974, 142).

The relational terms that structure intrafamilial relationships ("Auntie," "Mama") were not the terms these seventh graders customarily used when describing people or greeting people they saw in social situations ("Bro'," "Sister," "Cuz," and "Homey"). They used these more generic relational terms to acknowledge an acquaintance ("Yo, Bro', whassup?" or "Hi, Cuz!") or to establish a common understanding of ethnicity or neighborhood ("Doncha know, we homies?"). These kinds of appellations establish and reaffirm a more distant, almost undifferentiated relationship, even though they are loosely lumped into what is commonly thought of as the "kinship terminology" category.

Fictive kinship in the inner city may well be an adaptive mechanism serving multiple purposes. Kinshiplike connections have been called "lifelines" in the African-American community (Aschenbrenner 1975). In a society where capital, either real or cultural, is limited, fictive kin become a resource that permits access to scarce commodities. Fordham (1988) maintained that the African-American tradition of establishing fictive kinship "includes a political function as well."

Fictive kinship, which expands the external boundaries and internal divisions of consanguineous family, creates a unit where "the whole is greater than the sum of its parts" and provides a mechanism by which people pulling together for their common benefit can become powerful. Fictive kinship works to identify group members upon whom one can count for information, understanding, acceptance, and help. The relationship is reciprocal and based on a belief that, in a family, you give when you can to whomever's needs are greatest at the moment. The notion of fictive kin is based on an ideal family model where everyone personally associated with the unit cooperates for the benefit of all its members. As a result, when kinship extends beyond the bounds of the immediate family, it "provide[s] a model of cooperative behavior for others in the community" (Stack 1974, 128).

The anthropological literature is replete with both intra- and extra-Africa examples of fictive kin relationships. Its existence has been documented among non-African peoples as widely separated geographically as the Tubetube of Papua New Guinea (Macintyre 1993) and the Japanese (Kondo 1992). Euro-Americans sometimes even call their parents' best friends "aunt" or "uncle" (Schultz and Lavenda 1995, 556).

The common thread that runs through all the literature on fictive kin, including that of Stack (1974), Fordham (1988), and Aschenbrenner (1975), is that the election of an adult to kin status provides that person with a "recognized status," gives him or her a social role, justifies familiarity, enmeshes him or her in a web of relationships with rights and responsibilities, and eliminates the social disruption that dealing with an outsider on an intimate, prolonged basis might create. It is even more the norm than the exception for anthropologists to be taken in as fictive kin by some member of whatever group they are studying.

In light of the above, then, my election to kin status makes a great deal of sense. When I entered into the children's lives, I was an outsider, a researcher who asked many questions, an adult who was in their school and in their classroom but not a classroom teacher. I was an anomaly. How were they to classify me? How were they to treat me? How could they justify answering my sometimes incredibly personal questions, telling me all I wanted to know about them—their likes, dislikes, dreams, and lives?

I believe some of the children solved the problem by *adopting* me. Perhaps I placed the notion of adopting me in their heads by my behavior toward them, which they could have interpreted as similar to what they might expect from a kinsperson or what they had previously experienced from a play mama. In any event, the adoption put me in a more comprehensible context.

Because I was designated as kin to some of the children, the other children knew exactly how to relate to me. My kin status allowed me to do for my "children" what might be interpreted as "special" things without creating resentment among the other children. Frequently, the girls who were trying to cajole me to take them on a Saturday outing would ask, "OK, so who comin' 'sides Kay an' Jasmine?" and the boys discussed the numbers of bodies that could fit in my car around an assumption that Biggie would be coming, too.

My status as play mama permitted me certain rights and privileges with my play children that I did not have with the other seventh graders. At the same time, by virtue of our publicly acknowledged relationship, my play children could ask me more personal things and questions, joke around or call me to tell me about their needs and feelings more freely than the other seventh graders ever would or could presume. To their way of thinking, their kin status granted them rights of familiarity and access that the other students did not have.

In every instance I could find in the anthropological literature, an adult member of the studied group always made the outsider kin and found some culturally sanctioned rationale for doing so. I could find no documentation, in the traditional ethnographic literature or in the sociological descriptions of African-American families, of instances where the children actually elected an adult or other children to fictive kin status. Admittedly, this may be because adult anthropologists and researchers typically deal with the *culture bearers*, the adults, in any studied community rather than with children. Nevertheless, my impressions are that child-initiated adoption of adults as fictive kin may be a tradition, at least in the community I studied.

These suspicions are somewhat supported by the following quote from *The Journal of Ordinary Thought*:

> A little boy who lived in my building was so—I don't know how to put it in words—but he sort of adopted me.... He told his mother that they had to take care of me because now I had no one.... He said from now on his family would be mine.... I got to know this little boy, who is now a grown man, and his family. Still today I have a lot of love for Rodney and his family, who fondly call me grandma (Shepard 1997, 12).

I wonder how common the practice might actually turn out to be if more researchers looked for it.

I do not think it matters much whether the children used a traditional African-American method of creating fictive kin, whether their election of adults and other children to fictive kin status was a re-interpretation of a traditional method, or whether it was their own invention. Rather, what I found fascinating is that some of the seventh graders brought the symbolic kinship concept, with all its implications ("We all family here"), to school settings. It is actually a very logical strategy when one considers that children have "a somewhat narrow world of personal contacts" (Dewey 1900/1990, 183; see also Dewey 1901/1991, 233–35) and that when their worlds expand beyond the family, they must find and develop ways that help them cope with, succeed in, and make sense out of new social situations.

I wonder if these children were not forging that real, viable link between the so-often separated worlds of home and school, when they applied home-based social relation concepts (fictive kin and extended family) to the social relations they developed at the school. Did these seventh graders inadvertently hit upon a very practical way to introduce what Noddings (1992) called a "caring" approach to their in-school social relations and education? Could their approach work in other schools, on a schoolwide basis?

CHAPTER 3
MENTORS

There is some confusion about how, when and why mentoring actually began among the seventh graders. Although the administration had sponsored group advisory sessions for the older students in the past, no single, formally structured mentoring program under whose auspices "non-related adults paired up with adolescents in one-to-one relationships" (Schonert-Reich and Offer 1992, 8) had ever existed in their school. And, yet, during my first year (1996–97) of observation, a number of quasi-formal connections involving individual students and adults willing to be mentors suddenly developed.

One boy told me he had read about a child and his mentor in a book and thought the concept was a good idea. However, he took it no further than to talk about it with his friends. Another said he had seen an advertisement on television aimed at encouraging adults to volunteer as mentors. He reasoned that no adult would find him, so approached an adult he knew to be his mentor. A woman who had prior contact with the seventh-grade children volunteered to be a mentor. A school-based after-school sports program, sometime during its first year of operation in this school, provided student-participants with opportunities to link up with college students in mentor-mentee relationships. The seventh-grade teacher also might have planted one of the seeds for the mentoring idea in mid-September 1996 when discussing mentors in class. She told the students:

> Twitty Walters has been blessed with a mentor.... Mentors can help you get things you need. If you need a suit or a dress for graduation, ask your mentor. If you need help for college, ask your mentor. If you need any of those kinds of things, just ask your mentor, and your mentor will help you get them.

In 1997, she clarified her statement.

> My feelings about mentors are they are especially valuable to the students at [this school] in academics and maybe they can help in these other concerns. It depends upon the student/mentor relationship.

Her spin on a mentor's role might have developed because she frequently emphasized economic conditions with her students, having grown up "dirt poor in Arkansas." In any event, she actively encouraged the seventh graders to link up with adults willing to help them economically—socially if not financially. Her hopes were that every child who wanted a mentor would find one.

Many of the seventh graders followed their teacher's directive to find a mentor. Two of the girls sought, and found, "fairy godmother" mentors among the teachers at the school. These women were willing to help the girls amass, either through outright gifts, in return for "clerical" work and running errands, the $384 they each needed for their trip to Washington, D.C. More boys than girls found mentors. They claimed they did not look for mentors to help them financially. They said they wanted mentors for academic assistance and social guidance.

Biggie suggested a possible reason why some of the children did not link up with mentors.

> Some of the kids don't want mentors. I really don't know why, but [maybe] they have too much pride, or they feel they mom[s] can do it all. Too much pride—like, they don't need no help, they can do it all theyself.

The different kinds of informal mentoring that occurred in this school, among these seventh graders, had elements in common with formal mentoring programs described in the literature. Both formal mentoring programs and the mentoring concept as it evolved in this school provide opportunities for children to interact with adults. Nevertheless, fundamental differences exist between the two.

Formal mentor programs for adolescents are purposefully constructed with one or more goals in mind. Some formal programs are structured to simply expose adolescents to adults who act as role models; some have intervention, either academic or social, as their focus; and some create opportunities for success in education, work, and social life (Rhone 1992; Schonert-Reich and Offer 1992; Vanover and Utesch 1993; Sipe 1996; Koziol 1997).

However, at this school, no single, formalized program served to guide or shape all the mentor-mentee interactions. Further, the children's conversations about their mentor-mentee relationships indicated that the goals for each dyadic relationship were set and reset by the involved parties, primarily the children, through time.

All of the formal mentoring programs discussed in the above referenced works involved some kind of formal, specialized training of the mentors, themselves, before they were allowed contact with their mentees. In this school, no one associated with the school itself formally trained the adults who became mentors. The college students who acted as mentors under the auspices of the after-school sports program received some formal training in mentoring. However, the children with whom I spoke were unaware that this training had occurred. Whether a mentor received formal training before assuming, or being cast into, the role of mentor did not interest the children. For the most part, the mentors were simply people willing to spend time with the children, regularly interacting with them and also helping them in areas in which the children indicated they needed assistance.

From around September 1996 until April 1997, nonschool-based mentors were allowed to come to the school whenever they could to interact with their mentees, to tutor them or just to talk, apparently for however long they wished. In the case of teacher-mentors, they sometimes pulled their mentees from class to run an errand or help them pass out papers at a meeting. As the number of children with mentors increased, so did the number of children pulled out of class; and the number of hours the mentees spent out of class with their mentors escalated.

Finally, the classroom teacher objected. The seventh-grade teacher said that the erratic arrival of the mentors to collect their mentees was disruptive to the classroom routines and to the children's learning. She told me she would not mind it so much if, when the mentors took the children out of class, they worked with them on the material they would have covered had they been in class; but as far as she could tell, this did not happen. Her objections were more understandable in light of the following conversation about when and how often two of the boys met with their mentors during regular school hours in the 1996–97 school year.

Moochie said, "My mentor, we get together early Monday mornin' like, before we go to our 'specials,' an' maybe at lunchtime."

Regarding his own mentor, Art commented, "We'll meet Thursdays, like, eleven-thirty—right before we go to our 'specials.' If I get to my 'special,' he'll come pick me up an' we'll stay like, three, maybe four, in the afternoon."

The seventh-grade teacher met with some of the after-school sports program college students on April 29, 1997, and talked with them about her feelings. Yet, as far as I know, nothing was said to the teachers who continued to pull their mentees from classes to assist them.

When I checked again, in the fall of 1997, to see whether the boys were continuing to meet their mentors from the after-school sports program during regular school hours, they told me that their mentors had begun coming at a set time every week, and pulled them from class for one hour only to tutor them on their school assignments. Apparently, some compromise had been negotiated between these children's teacher and their college student mentors.

In December 1996, I asked the girls, "Tell me about mentoring. How did it start?"

Chapter 3: Mentors

Tatiana responded, "How did it start? It's 'cause Twitty Walters got a mentor, an' [our teacher] want everybody else to get a mentor so they could help them go to Washington, D.C., this year."

Said DeDe, "I made up my mind to ask one of my teachers will they be my mentor so I could go to Washington, D.C., so I ask [Ms. F.] an' she say, 'Yes,' an' now she's goin' help me go to Washington, D.C."

Coco added, "She [Ms. F.] gave her deposits an' everything."

Jasmine chimed in, "An' she got free candy." The girls all laughed at this comment.

Tatiana reported, "An' Fred's mentor [Ms. Sikes], she gave him twenty-five dollars toward his Washington, D.C., trip!"

"An' then she [Ms. Sikes] gave some to Ed!" Coco noted.

"That is *so* wonderful!" Tatiana said.

When I asked the boys the same question, they placed the origin of mentoring a little differently. Ed said:

> The way I got involved in it was, Twitty Walters got rid of her mentor [around November 1996] an' I see the good things she [Ms. Sikes] was doin' for Twitty, an' so when Twitty didn't want her, I say, 'I'll take her.' So I asked [my teacher] for the lady's phone number an' I called her up, an' then we got together an' we had a date, an' she came to school.

Biggie recalled:

> The way I got a mentor was through my church, an' this lady, she wanted to mentor me 'cause she saw I was doin' good, an' she wanted me to go forward in life, an' she didn't want to see me go the wrong way. So, I got into mentoring by she just came up, grab me up, an' she met my mom. She do lots of things for me. She talks to me, an' I get things like work. She gets me jobs. She just helps me a lot by showin' me what kids ought to do.

Moochie related:

> I was just at the after-school sports program one day [sometime during December 1995 or January 1996] an' Pete—he's my mentor now—an'

he start to come an' get me out my classroom, an' pull me out to the library, an' help me on different things, an' all that. An' then he took me to a meeting an' tried to start up a mentor program by showin' other people how me an' him get along, an' he just brought a whole lot of people to the program, an' that's how the other people got them mentors.

Art said:

> The way I got involved is a little bit of what Moochie just explained. Pete got a lot of people who wanted to mentor other children, an' I got my mentor this way—'cause I asked Pete if he knew anybody that knew a lot about math an' different expressions like algebra, percentages an' different things like that. An' that's how I got my mentor—through Pete. It's his friend. Pete brought him here 'cause I had asked for a mentor, an' then, soon [as] we met, we started meetin' up more an' we worked a lot of math.

Art's mother confirmed that he had been working on his mathematics with his mentor. "He's been working with his mentor—and his mentor said he'd teach him trigonometry. He's also been working with him a little on reading, and says he should be ready for the Iowas."

Since the students' approach to finding mentors seemed a bit free-form and very dependent on the children having close enough contacts with adults to feel free to ask them to be their mentors, I asked, "How do you go about getting a mentor?

Ed answered, "You gotta go out an' get you a mentor, not just sit around an' wait for somethin' to come to you."

Moochie agreed.

> It just like Old Country Buffet [a restaurant]. You don't sit around an' wait for somebody to come an' get you your food. You get up an' go get you' own food. You don't wait for you' mentor. You gotta do the right thing an' go an' get you a mentor.

When I rechecked with Moochie in the fall of 1997 about whether the after-school sports program originally included a mentoring component, he said he did not believe that it did. From Moochie's perspective, the mentoring component of this program developed only after the other college student-coaches in the after-school sports program saw how well he and Pete got along and decided that mentoring the regular participants in the program to strengthen their academic skills was a good idea. Moochie believed that the after-school sports program's mentoring component had not been planned but, rather, had evolved; and he was proud of what he perceived as his own pivotal role in its development.

The students first met Ms. Sikes, a local businesswoman, when she came to their summer school program to talk about her job [July 1996]. Afterward, she stayed to help in the class and reportedly offered to mentor a child [September 1996]. The teacher selected Twitty Walters, whom she felt could benefit from a mentor relationship. That child initially and, from all reports, reluctantly went along with this notion. She soon disengaged herself from the mentor relationship. The teacher, expressing incredulity, said, "Well, maybe she [Ms. Sikes] was too academic for her [Twitty]." Later, when the teacher finally determined that Twitty had severe difficulty reading, she modified her assessment about why Twitty abandoned her mentor. "She can't read, and maybe she didn't want Ms. Sikes to know." The girls place a slightly different spin on the "Twitty affair."

According to Jasmine, the teacher "chose her [Ms. Sikes] to be Twitty's mentor to get her to Washington, D.C."

Tatiana countered, "No, I heard Ms. Sikes want' Twitty Walters, but Twitty Walters didn't want Ms. Sikes, so now Ed got Ms. Sikes, an' he's working, an' he's blessed, an' he keep her for life."

Coco said, "I think Twitty spoiled, 'cause when Ms. Sikes was her mentor, she didn't wanna go where they used to go. She didn't wanna . . ."

"Ms. Sikes call her up on the phone, an' she didn't wanna talk. She shy," advised DeDe.

The boys spoke somewhat disparagingly about the girls' choices for mentors. Art began, "I think the girls pick mentors from school because—"

"To suck up," Ed interrupted to finish the sentence.

Biggie said, "It's basically like the girls, they don't want a mentor—"

"No, they just want money. They [the girls] don't work with them [their mentors]. They not 'real' mentors," observed Moochie.

The boys did not consider that the girls' seeking mentors who could help them financially might be because the girls' opportunities to earn money for the class trip were more restricted than their own. The girls often baby-sat but rarely for anyone who paid them. Twitty was the only girl in the class with a regular, paying baby-sitting job. The children were encouraged to sell candy to finance part of their trip. The girls said their mothers would not allow them to go over to the local sports arena to sell candy before or after sports events because it was not safe after dark. They reported that even some of the boys had been strong-armed and their candy money stolen. Neither of the girls who looked for a "fairy godmother" was a regular churchgoer and thus did not have a church congregation as an outlet for candy sales. The best they could do to raise funds for their trip was to sell candy door-to-door in their buildings and find mentors willing to donate money or permit them to earn money by doing simple chores for them. DeDe and Tatiana did not like going from door-to-door selling candy, labeling that activity "distasteful," so even this outlet was effectively closed to them by their reticence to knock on doors.

The boys, however, sold candy in their churches, door-to-door in the community, and at the sports arena. Moochie never felt that the arena was a safe place to try to raise money, refusing to return there because "this cop kicked my butt hard, 'cause he thought I be sellin' drugs or stole the candy or somethin'." The boys also did odd jobs such as sweeping out a local grocery store or working for Ms. Sikes.

I asked the boys if they expected their mentors to give them money.

"My mentor, she pay me when I do work, but I don't expect it," answered Ed.

Chapter 3: Mentors

Biggie explained, "I don't expect it 'cause the meaning of a mentor is 'someone who guide you on the right way.'"

Then Art replied, "No. Mentors, to me, is like the best thing you can have, that you get, in helping yourself, to help you or tutor you or to move on with stuff you need help with, but no money."

I asked the children how long they envisioned their relationships with their mentors lasting.

Tatiana and Coco replied (in chorus), "It is for life."

Tatiana elaborated, "When you have a mentor, it mandatory for life, 'cause how you gonna let them go?"

Biggie agreed, "I think I'll have my mentor for life. It gonna be a growin' relationship. We get along well. We love each other, look out for each other, help each other out. We like backbones."

The other boys were less certain about the longevity of their relationships with their mentors. Moochie said, "Well, it depend'. I mean, my mentor gonna graduate, an' maybe he movin' an' I lose contact, but for as long as he want, I'll be his mentee."

Art agreed. "It's like I can have him as long as he wants to be my mentor, 'cause when I ask him, he say he will be my mentor for sure next year."

Ed added, "I think I'll have my mentor for as long as I want, an' I can take advantage of the learnin' she can give. She like a second mother, an' she determined for us [Fred and me] to get what her two daughters got."

The literature on mentors never really delves into how long mentor-mentee relationships typically last. Perhaps this is because the literature only treats formal mentoring programs. The single set of statistics I discovered about the length of time a mentor-mentee relationship lasted concerned a particular Big Brother/Big Sister program (Sipe 1996, 15).

The researchers found that certain practices characterized effective mentor-mentee relationships: trust, involving the youth in decisions about how the pair would spend their time together, consistency and dependability of presence in the youth's life, adult responsibility for keeping the relationship alive, paying attention to the youth's need for fun, respect for the youth's viewpoint, and seeking and using the help and advice of program staff (Sipe 1996, 15). The characteristics of ineffective mentor-mentee relationships were attempts to reform or transform the youth by setting goals and tasks early in the relationship, taking an authoritative role, emphasizing behavior changes rather than developing trust, being inconsistent or undependable, insisting the youth play an equal role in initiating contact, attempting to impose values that might be inconsistent with the youth's, and ignoring advice of program staff (Sipe 1996, 15). Seventy percent of ineffective mentor-mentee relationships in the studied program disintegrated during the nine-month period between the researcher's first and second interviews, while 91 percent of the effective mentor-mentee relationships were still active at the time of the second interview (Sipe 1996, 15–16).

In a formal, structured program, do mentor-mentee relationships typically last only as long as the period of time that the program is in effect? Do the quality and effects of mentor-mentee relationships vary depending on whether the relationships were formed under the auspices of a structured mentoring program or not? Do some of the same things characterize effective mentor-mentee relationships in an informal program as in a formal program? If so, which ones are critical components of the relationship?

Almost one year later, I returned to the mentor topic by asking, "What exactly is a mentor's role?"

"Mentors—they help," said DeDe.

Tatiana answered, "A mentor give you special help—help with readin' an' math, too. When you go to college, you have your mentor, an' if you don't, how you gonna grow an' develop?"

Coco said, "It one-on-one."

And Princess explained, "It so you get more help than in class."

Chapter 3: Mentors

Lemar, a boy constantly and publicly accused of causing disruptions and of having a bad attitude, said, "My mentor [acquired in October 1997], he gonna give me help in the classroom an' work on my at-ti-tude." He added, "You know, [name of a teacher], she always on me for my at-ti-tude, so he be workin' on helpin' me improve it." Another child thought that it was good that Lemar had found a mentor but felt that he needed to do something else in addition to working on his attitude. "He should learn that rule: 'Keep the mouth shut.'"

Fred, who shared a mentor with Ed, his best friend, commented, "I got a mentor [Ms. Sikes] to help with readin' during the summer, an' I worked for money with my mentor for the trip [to Washington, D.C.]."

"My mentor do everything. When I had cut my hand like this," said Ed, holding up his bandaged hand, "she had called my mama, an' she came all the way to my grandmama's house just to get me an' take me to the hospital—like, she my second mama."

Fred said, "She get us like, what we need for projects."

According to Biggie, "It's important to have someone to help you to read, type, make corrections on things, have a second opinion with you. They [mentors] stick by your side, an' they can follow you through college—everything they can tell you. You don't know everything."

I pushed for more clarification. "How is a mentor different from a teacher?"

Coco responded, "You always got somebody on stand-by [when you have a mentor]."

Tatiana agreed. "You can always call your mentor up an' talk."

"—about problems an' personal things," Coco added.

"Well, I think the difference with like, the teacher in the after-school readin' [program] an' a mentor is you spend more time with your mentor, an' that's why it better," noted DeDe, adding, "An' when you do find a mentor, treat 'em right."

Biggie commented, "If I'm down, I can call her with a personal thing an' she'll cheer me up. She'll help me, keep me encouraged. She'll also help me try to find out what high school I want to go to."

The boys drew sharp contrasts between mentors and teachers. They said their mentors were more accessible than their teachers, more willing to spend time with them to make sure they had the concepts "straight." Ed explained:

> Well, like, a teacher in school, they get paid from 9:00 to 2:30, an' that's why I think you should have a mentor—for from 2:30 to whenever. You can call your mentor any time you want, an' your teacher say, 'Don't call me!'

Biggie, whose comments echoed those that Delpit (1993, 131–132) documented other African-American students used when describing "good teachers," said:

> My mentor with me, workin' with me. The teacher, she got the whole class to worry about. The difference between a mentor an' a teacher is a teacher give you your grades an' a mentor don't. The teachers, they more harder on you, an' they press you, they push you, an' that's good; but the mentor, she's not pushy.

Approximately one year after identifying mentors as people who could help them financially, the girls had recast their mentors as people to whom they could turn for help with academics and personal concerns. Tatiana explained:

> Well, like, if I need . . . help with a problem, like, on the Iowa test, an' I know estimation goin' be on it, an' if I have trouble with it—which I don't with estimation—I'd ask my mentor, 'Could you give me some tutoring for, say, seven hours?' So, when I get to the Iowa tests, I would be ready. When I get to the Iowa tests, I'd go straight to the ones I know, do the estimation, then do the ones I don't know. So, without a mentor—[shrugged].

DeDe contributed, "When we got finished with Washington, D.C., an' all that, I wanted [my mentor] to help me on my math an' my readin', so my score go up."

Chapter 3: Mentors

"We need more focusin' on our skills an' our readin' scores—" Tatiana noted.

"So we can get off probation," finished Coco.

Jasmine, who had not gone on the Washington, D.C., trip and had not found a mentor, spoke theoretically. "Mentors help. It is important to learn [in order] to get jobs because welfare—when I get older, I don't wanna be on welfare. I wanna have my own job so I can pay my own bills an' get my kids things."

DeDe continued, "An' find a house . . ."

"An' feed my kids without no welfare helpin' me, an' besides, welfare bein' cut off. I want my own job!" added Jasmine.

Coco said, "I want my own business! Computers—an' I need a mentor [to] help me get this."

I asked the girls whose mentors were all women, "Is there any reason why you picked women to be your mentors?"

DeDe chuckled. "You can go shoppin' with 'em. Tell 'em different things."

For Tatiana, though, gender was not a significant factor.

> No, there's no particular reason. There's really not. A man can do as much as a woman. A man can teach you how to add, subtract, divide, multiply. There's not a difference, though. A man can teach you everything a woman can. Like, Ed has a woman [mentor], so it's not a difference. As long as they got a brain an' intelligence, that all that matters.

Still trying to clarify how the children perceived the roles mentors played, I asked, "What's the difference between a mentor and, say, an aunt or uncle?"

Tatiana responded, "Well, my auntie be with me for life, an' my mentor be with me for life. I talk with her [my auntie] about personal things—*an'* with my mentor. But, my auntie would be there if I need her, like, say, if my mentor go out of town."

All the girls agreed with Tatiana's distinction. However, the boys said that they would ask their mentors for help with academic questions and problems before they would turn to their aunts or uncles for help.

I asked, "So what's the difference between a mentor and a godmother or godfather?"

"That's the same," Lemar replied.

Jasmine voiced agreement. "Nothin' really. They both help."

"—'Cept your parents pick your godmother, an' you pick your mentor," explained Coco.

Art reiterated this distinction. "It's—your parents pick your godmother an' godfather an' you—Me, I picked my own mentor, an' my mother picked my godmother, so I guess, it's a big difference."

"An' you ask your mentor mostly for help with your academics," added Tatiana.

Ed said, "Like, if you have a real godmother, you don't every time go to your godmother house. . . . She ain't like your mentor. Your mentor help' you study, but a real godmother, she don't help you study, she—"

Biggie interrupted, "Like, your godmother, she have kids of her own an' if your parents don't be there, she gonna 'mediately step in, an' your mentor can't do that 'cause they don't have it legally by law. All the mentor can do—Well, they can only go so far."

Moochie added, "Like he says, the mentor can only go so far; they can only do what they do—mentor."

"Who would you turn to first for help with your homework?" I asked. "Your immediate family, your mother, father, brother or sister, your godmother, your mentor, or your teacher?"

Coco answered, "My mama an' my father. I don't got no godmother."

DeDe said, "My mama, or I go to the library. So, if my mama don't understand, I'll try. I'll try to do it on my own, 'cause I ain't got no phone, an' all my

Chapter 3: Mentors 71

aunties live out south an' on the north, an' I don't have my mentor's telephone number, 'cause I don't have no phone."

"For me, an' I can't speak for the other boys," said Biggie, "but for me, it go—my family, then my mentor, then my godmama, then my teacher. You gotta find somebody in—like, a specialty area. You gotta pick 'em right, pick 'em good."

His ordering agreed with that given by Ed, Moochie, Lemar, and Fred. Lemar and Fred added that since they had no godmothers, they would go directly from asking their mentors to asking their teachers for help if the mentor were unavailable or unable to help.

I asked, "Is mentoring for homework help on a daily basis?"

Jasmine began, "A mentor is like a teacher, so—"

Tatiana pointed out a distinction between mentor and teacher.

> But you can't spend six hours an' thirty minutes with a teacher, an' you can spend that with a mentor, because the teacher just gonna give you the facts an' what to look up; but then you go to your mentor an' it's not all about gettin' the answers—it's all about helpin'. But, when you get the answers, you just go right on up to your head an' you can really process the information. Mentors come an' get you; you call, an' they help you.

"So, what do you think the mentor gets out of mentoring?" I asked.

"I think," Tatiana began, and then paused. "They might enjoy it. My mentor gets a smile 'cause she help me, an' a special thanks, an' she be proud."

DeDe answered, "She help me get my scores up. She'll be happy if I get my scores up an' work hard."

Coco said, "The person get looked up to."

"I think my mentor gets a good experience," said Ed, "'cause she had two girls, an' they grown, so she say she like hangin' 'round me 'cause she say I'm like a little kid an' all."

Biggie reinforced Ed's answer. "Well, my mentor call me her 'baby,' an' all her kids are grown an' all, an' she call me like her son or somethin'. She goin' 'round tellin' peoples that I'm a good student [and] I'm a good kid."

Moochie observed, "My mentor just enjoy me, an' I enjoy bein' with him. Mentors be doin' it out they own free love. It say 'Do unto others as you would have them do unto you,' an' if you do good deeds [and] you help other people, someone will help you."

Art said of his mentor, "He's a good big brother to me. I think he's had experience bein' a big brother an' he want more, 'cause his brother is in high school already an' he's about to graduate, so I'm like this little brother to him."

In 1996, the girls said that they picked mentors for help getting to Washington, D.C., the monetary aspect of the mentor-mentee relationship their teacher had stressed in class. In 1997, the girls' immediate need to amass money for that purpose had passed. Although they still included help with money as part of a mentor's role, the girls expanded what they asked of their mentors to include tutoring and advice on personal problems. The girls placed as much emphasis as the boys on the role model aspect of mentoring. In fact, Coco and DeDe joined Tatiana in wondering how it would be possible to grow and develop without mentors. The girls ranked the people in their lives to whom they would turn for help in descending order: (1) parents and older siblings, (2) godmother and/or mentor, and (3) teacher.

When I asked them why they would not approach their classroom teacher for academic help first, they said they believed that their classroom teacher was unable to give them the time and the individualized attention and help they felt they needed, even though they picked other teachers in their school as mentors. They stressed that they saw no real difference in the quality of the mentor-mentee relationship and that of a godmother-godchild. However, the girls expected their mentors to help them focus on academics while they did not necessarily expect

Chapter 3: Mentors

their godmothers to help with school subjects. They anticipated that both kinds of relationships would last "for life."

The boys' perspective on mentoring remained the same from 1996 through 1997. The mentor's role was consistently perceived to be to help them improve academically and socially, but not necessarily to provide them with money or jobs. The boys' ranked order for seeking academic help was (1) family or older siblings because those people were usually around when the boys worked on their homework; (2) mentor for help with a specific academic problem; (3) godmother, rarely, and only if they had one; and (4) teacher.

The boys all said that if their immediate family and mentor could not help with a specific homework problem, they would most likely wait to ask the classroom teacher the next day. The boys most often described their mentors in kinship terms, as a second mother or a big brother. They stressed that the quality of the relationships they had established with their mentors was closest to that of "real family" but, when pressed, stated that mentors were really not in the same category as *fictive kin* since "play" relations were not necessarily expected to help with academics. Further, they made no clear distinction between *mentor* and *role model*. The duration of the mentor-mentee relationship was seen as dependent upon both the mentor and external circumstances such as proximity. However, all the boys indicated they would like their relationships with their mentors to be ongoing.

What emerged from these children's discussions about mentors was that mentors were chosen because the children identified them as people who could, would, and did help the children obtain the cultural and financial capital they believed they wanted and needed to succeed. The girls' discussions about their "fairy godmother" mentors were evidence that they identified people who could, and did, help them amass financial capital. In addition, the desire to amass cultural capital was corroborated in a teacher-initiated survey of the 1996–97 seventh graders. This survey revealed that 17 percent of the boys and 42 percent of the girls believed that doing their "homework with help" would assist them to earn better grades and learn in school, and that 67 percent of the boys and 58 percent of the girls felt it was important to learn at school to "get a job."

Sipe's (1996, 19, emphasis in the original) study found that in formal mentoring programs *"in general,* it is not important to ensure same gender or same race matches in order to produce effective mentoring relationships." My data were somewhat to the contrary. A mentor's gender was not a factor that greatly influenced these seventh-grade boys' decisions about their mentors; three of them had female mentors. I believe that this might be because the boys had clear ideas from the start that they wanted mentors to help them focus on academics and social skills rather than to advise them on intimate, personal concerns. A mentor's gender was a concern for the girls, however, for a number of different reasons.

Jasmine, who had no mentor, alleged that, although she would like a mentor, she could never have a male mentor for safety reasons. "My mama told me, 'Don't get no man mentor,'—an' I ain't fin'a go to no man mentor's house! I cannot have no man mentor 'cause they play with kids!" She added: "I think you should have a woman mentor, 'cause the woman go through the same things that girls go through, an' you can talk to them 'bout the things that you goin' through."

At this point, Tatiana interjected, "Like the boys, the boys, they should have a man. They can talk 'bout how they developin' and the girls they can talk 'bout how they developin'." She then added that men could help girls as well as women could with academics.

These children, no matter what their gender, all considered their mentors people to whom they could turn for support and counseling, among other things. In terms of the boys, these data were at odds with what Lees (1993, 93) found. Her data showed that boys usually talked about "sport, or other activities, going places, and doing things" with each other and other males rather than about personal or academic issues.

On the other hand, Jasmine and Tatiana's casting of mentors as people with whom physiologic changes and development could be discussed is very much in keeping with what Lees (1993, 80) said typically characterized girls' relationships with other females. Unfortunately, Lees did not gather data on interactions and topics of conversations between boys and adult women.

My own experience talking with the boys was that, although they often discussed sports and other activities, they also talked to me about sexual development and behavior. On more than one occasion, they asked me questions that I would classify as highly personal as easily as they might inquire about the correct spelling of a word. The specificity of some of their inquiries caused me to wonder exactly how much and how technical I, as their nonparent, could legitimately become when I answered. Further, they frequently included me in conversations where they revealed very intimate details of their own and their friends' lives. My suspicion is that the boys never considered my gender to be an issue in those instances. Rather, I think they felt free to ask me about such things because they were hoping I might know the answers or direct them where to find the information. Or perhaps they meant to see if they could shock me.

I would add, moreover, that Tatiana's and Jasmine's idea that boys should have same-sex mentors like girls so they can talk about their physical development is typical human behavior. People often think the manner in which they do something is the best and believe others should follow suit; they frequently attribute the same motivations to other people that they have themselves.

The girls' waffling about the ideal gender for a mentor reflected the fact that they expected their mentors to play a variety of roles, depending on which need was paramount at the moment—money, academic help, or personal issues. I am somewhat hesitant to extend Jasmine's assertion that she and her mother link "safety" with the female gender to a general statement that all of the girls looked for women mentors because of similar concerns. I know that many of the girls have talked about safety, molestation, and rape in other contexts, and these apprehensions might well have generated some of their uncertainty about the ideal gender for a mentor.

None of the children ever mentioned ethnicity when describing their mentors or said it was one of the criteria they used when looking for mentors. Only three of the people the students chose as mentors are African-Americans, and this appears to have been more an accident of proximity than a purposeful selection based on shared ethnicity. The girls selected teachers in their school where the overwhelming majority are African-American, and Biggie found a mentor in his Missionary Baptist church.

Taylor (1989, 170) suggested that African-American children seek role models because they suffer from "lack of confidence and trust in themselves and in others in their social environments." On the one hand, this statement appears to be very true. The boys, in particular, appear to have chosen mentors who could serve as role models, although they stressed they looked for "specialist" mentors to help them with their mathematics and reading skills.

Perhaps an adult might interpret the boys' seeking mentors to help in those specific areas as their having shaky confidence in those skills, lack of trust in their own abilities and the abilities of others in their social environments. However, if an adult accepted this interpretation, he or she might miss a more fundamental reason for the boys to seek *role models* who also could help with their academic skills; that is, the boys were aware that there are things they do not know, need to know, and would like to know more about, both socially and academically. They were trying to both *learn* and *improve* academic skills, at a pace and in a manner that they believed guaranteed understanding. Unfortunately, in many instances, the boys did not feel they could accomplish this in class.

Biggie addressed this issue, one that Haberman (1991, 291) has already raised.

> The hard way to learn is gettin' the students the book an' not teachin' them, an' that what some of the teachers do, an' you begin to bore the students by just writin' the board work an' tellin' them to do it, then givin' you book work, tellin' you to do it in the classroom. That *ain't* teachin', an' it *no way* learnin'!

The girls, on the other hand, said they initially looked for mentors to provide financial help to go to Washington, D.C. While they were worried about paying for their trip, they never mentioned any other reasons for having mentors nor did they envision any other roles for their mentors to play. The girls sought mentors within the social network of teachers in their school, a milieu with which they were familiar and one which, by virtue of its familiarity and the gender of (most of) the teachers, might be considered safe.

Later, when the girls expressed a desire to improve their reading and mathematics skills, they turned to their already-in-place mentors for assistance. In 1997, Kay said the focal issue for the students was to "get our Iowa test scores up. Well, if we want to pass, we got to get our comprehension up." When improving their scores to the level required to graduate and to get the school off probation became the paramount concern at the beginning of the school year in 1997, all the children who had found mentors began intense work on academic subjects with their mentors.

The girls' emphasis on using their mentors for help in increasing their abilities to perform at acceptable levels academically might have developed later because their classroom teacher did not begin pointing out the necessity of scoring well on the Iowa tests until after the drive to pay for the class trip was well underway; or those kinds of feelings might always have been there but only surfaced once the primary need to find financial assistance for the class trip was out of the way.

Only after the girls were assured their trip would be subsidized, and only after their teacher began to stress the need to achieve grade-level scores on their standardized tests, did they look to their already-in-place mentors for help with academics. They also did not approach their mentors about personal problems or concerns until after the mentors had begun tutoring them.

Were the children so enthused about learning to read and perform mathematical computations that they willingly sought out people with whom to work in these academic areas? Or, were they so unsure of their abilities to score well on standardized tests that they felt they needed to find mentors to help them sharpen the skills (decode the tests?) on which they were to be tested? Were they using mentors to help them learn more, learn better, at a more individualized pace than was possible in their classroom? On the other hand, when the children asked their mentors to help them with academic subjects, were they expressing a lack of confidence in their teachers and the educational system?

I find no evidence that these children suffered from lack of confidence and trust in themselves and in others in their social environments solely because they were African-Americans. I wonder whether the characteristics Taylor (1989) ascribed to African-American adolescents would not be equally applicable to all adolescents. When the children set out to find mentors, they had no doubt they would locate people who would be willing to help them in whatever ways they needed, whether it was with money, tutoring, time, or all three. Did not their actions reflect confidence and trust in themselves and others? Is this kind of confidence and trust in adults all that unusual for adolescents?

Taylor (1989, 159) spoke to the idea that African-American adolescents (all adolescents?) normally chose from two kinds of role models. One is a symbolic model, the other, behavioral. Symbolic models represent "particular values, ideals or ideological systems. . . . Such models are personages with whom the youth may feel a certain unity and pride" (Taylor 1989, 160, citing Klapp 1971). Symbolic models are also "a set of attributes or ideal qualities which may or may not be linked directly with any one person" (Taylor 1989, 159).

The children all classified their mentors as "successful" people. Ed described his mentor as worthy of admiration because she had succeeded even though "when she was little, she didn't have it good." The boys likened their mentors to brothers and mothers, whose help and support can be assumed because of the family ties. The girls referred to their mentors in the same category as godmother. Tatiana described a godmother relationship as similar to having a "second mother." That the children admired their mentors and attributed to them a commonality of ideological worldview and values such as one would find in a family member was evident from their conversations about their mentors.

I wonder, was the symbolic election of mentors to family status a recognition of shared worldviews and value sets or, as with fictive kin, a transposition of a social system with which the children were familiar to a different setting? Did the children choose mentors whose values were consistent with those they had already been taught or with values they wanted to learn?

Taylor (1989, 158) wrote that African-American adolescents (and, I suggest, most likely, all adolescents) search for useful behavioral role models in whom to have faith, whom they can admire and turn to for guidance. Mentors can serve as exemplary models, providing "practical knowledge, skills, or behavioral patterns which may be utilized by the youth for developing behavioral competence" (Taylor 1989, 160). Lemar's comment about his mentor helping him with his "attitude" demonstrated how valuable a role model can be in helping an adolescent develop behavioral patterns appropriate to different contexts, a topic Rhone (1992) has explored.

However, Lemar's comment also showed that children can be acutely aware that they need assistance in making sense out of what adults require in terms of appropriate behaviors in specific contexts. Lemar never understood what it was that he did in class to bring down his teacher's wrath. As far as he was concerned, he was actively engaged in whatever lesson was being taught. He often tried to interject comments or add information to enrich classroom discussions. However, he frequently forgot to raise his hand before talking or held conversations with his neighbor that rivaled the teacher's in terms of loudness. When he was reminded to raise his hand or asked to stop speaking or even, as sometimes happened, when he was ignored, he frequently became visibly upset, slammed around the classroom and demonstrated what the other children and his teacher labeled "an at-ti-tude."

Hare and Castenell (1985, 211) listed problems African-American boys face in other classrooms where the teachers were Caucasian females that are similar to those Lemar faced in his interpersonal relationship with one of his teachers, even though she is African-American. These problems include more frequent trips for the boys to the principal for discipline than for girls, and *a priori* assumptions that African-American boys are harder to handle than girls, disinterested, and, for any number of reasons, typically underachievers. Perhaps it is not ethnic bias but gender or class bias that lies at the root of many of these kinds of prejudices.

Many times following a castigation, Lemar protested to me, "What I do? I didn't do nothin', so why she on me?" He took those upbraidings to heart, even though he did not understand why what he was doing in class had been labeled "wrong." He sought a mentor whom he hoped would help him understand what he was doing wrong and whom he directed to help him develop the kind of "attitude" that would help him avoid trouble with his teacher. I wonder whether the other children's choices of mentors were not also part of their conscious attempts to "make themselves" in ways that were socially acceptable (Appiah 1994, 158).

Unlike the somewhat older inner-city adolescents about whom Taylor (1989, 167) wrote, these seventh-grade children did not appear to suffer from "a lack of commitment to a set of self-definitions, values, and plans for the future." They had extremely clear ideas about what they wanted and needed to achieve with their mentors' help, although attention to specific needs (money, academic help, or personal problems) shifted through time. They had vague plans for their own futures, but those plans included hopes for continued contact with their mentors.

That these seventh graders and their mentors invested so much of their time and efforts into maintaining and fostering their relationships is worthy of note. The mentor-mentee relationships lasted well over twelve months and spoke of a two-way commitment, so one can only assume that they were tested and found mutually satisfactory.

However wrong these particular children might have proved Taylor to be about all African-American inner-city adolescents, they did prove at least a portion of his assertion, on page 169, that how a

> given model is perceived to be depends largely upon the dominant concerns of the youth at some given point in time. The youth who is preoccupied with the problem of choosing and preparing for a career, developing interpersonal or 'survival' skills, . . . is likely to be drawn toward those environmental models perceived to be relevant and useful in resolving those concerns.

And so, Lemar's seeking a mentor to help with his attitude might actually have been his attempt to learn survival skills insofar as "living in the classroom" was concerned. However, the truth of Taylor's statement, and the applicability of the cultural shopping model with reference to mentors, as well, are more clearly demonstrated in a close examination of how and why the children chose certain adults to help them and the shape those relationships evolved through time.

In 1996, the girls' dominant concern was to obtain money for their class trip. They sought mentors to help them achieve that objective. In 1997, both the boys and girls emphasized working with their mentors to get their standardized scores up and to improve their reading and mathematics computational skills. I cannot say with certainty whether this emphasis arose from the need to improve the percentage of students scoring at or above grade level on standardized tests, which had been mentioned to them so often in class; or from their feelings of responsibility for effecting a change in their school's probationary status; or from a valid assessment of their own felt need to learn and improve their abilities and skills to meet personal goals. I sensed, from my conversations with these children, that it was a little of each of these reasons.

Biggie, echoing what the other students felt, bemoaned the effect that being on probation had had in the school. "Bein' on probation is added to our academics. They more tough on us now, an' it cuttin' our activities mostly, like, we used to have basketball games every other day; we used to go on field trips more; teachers used to be more looser."

Three of the children, Coco, Biggie, and Kay, said they felt it was up to the students to get the school off probation. They were told the school's probationary status was because 15 percent of them did not score at or above national norms on the Iowa Tests of Basic Skills. Coco and Kay both thought that every student should work toward that collective goal (the family model).

Kay spoke for the girls when she said, "Our school on probation an' it's really up to the kids to get it off." Biggie, however, placed that responsibility on a specific group of individuals (the sports team specialist model). "The kids in [a certain extra-curricular program] is 'posed to help get the school off probation. They feel this they responsibility, an' they tryin' to do it."

The children's comments about their own roles with respect to the school being placed on academic probation suggested they were unaware that their teachers and administrators were working to help them increase their scores and their learning at the same time, and toward changing the school's status, too. It is also very likely that the children's comments meant they did not believe the teachers and administrators were partners in their venture, as Kay's statement about how the student body had learned their school had been placed on probation revealed. "[Name of administrator] called everyone together an' explained it. She said that the school could get closed, the principal could get fired, an' the kids might not pass into the next grades, so everybody had to get they Iowa tests up."

The children were told that they each needed to work harder to get their individual standardized test scores up to the minimum required by the board of education; but since this minimum was below national norms, they were also told they really needed to bring their scores up to grade level to help the school get off probation. Every child worked individually for himself or herself at the same time he or she also worked for the collective good, often with the help of a mentor.

Where was the blame placed after they collectively and individually failed to raise the students' standardized test scores high enough to get the school off probation? Would it be fair to say that every failure, social or scholastic, is ultimately the individual's fault? Is each success the result of individual endeavor(s) or could it also be the outcome of collaborative effort? Does working with a mentor qualify as a collaborative effort? Are there other documented cases where "school learning, on the whole, . . .a matter of individual study and competitive display before the group" (Labov 1982, 168–69), includes working toward group success?

Biggie indicated he had thought about similar questions.

> I think a good experiment would be to compare the kids that have mentors with those that don't, an' see how they do schoolwise, socialwise, at the groupwise, like when we have cooperative groups, see how they get along in it. I think, I *hypothesize*, the kids who don't want mentors wouldn't like to work in cooperative groups.

Discussions with the seventh graders about mentors and mentoring revealed there were almost as many reasons for choosing a mentor, ways in which a mentor was chosen, and uses to which mentors were placed, as there were children with mentors. I interpret this variability as more evidence of cultural shopping.

At the risk of belaboring the analogy, it appears that "mentor-shopping" may have been first publicly suggested by the seventh-grade teacher. Obviously, Twitty did not "buy" the idea she should have a mentor or want to accept the mentor her teacher had selected for her. The other children, however, were eager to see what was available in the mentor mall. Although the children's choices for mentors were somewhat limited by the number of adults with whom they came in contact, they returned from their collective shopping trip for mentors with people who fit their individual needs of the moment. Having a mentor started a trend.

One might argue, then, considering that the students apply the cultural shopping model to their behaviors, that in this school, among these adolescents, the variations that evolved with respect to the definition of mentoring, the numerous different reasons why mentors were chosen, and the myriad of uses to which mentors were placed over time—the mentoring concept's complexion—should not have been unexpected. As Kohlberg and Gilligan (1971, 1051) point out, "the features of adolescence seem to be acquiring unique colorings in the present era in America."

Chapter 4
Play

In 1998, brightly colored playground equipment with a padded substrate was installed at the back (north side) of the school property. The play set did not include a basketball hoop or swings. For the most part, younger students climbed around it before school began. Older students rarely approached it unless they were supervising or playing with the younger children. Sometimes, not-yet-school-age children, watched by their mothers, scrambled on and around the equipment.

Before installation of this play set, the children's school had no real playground. Then, as now, before school, the older children gathered to talk, jump rope, play tag, and mill around in an L-shaped asphalt parking lot shared by the corner church and the school. The parking lot was always crowded even if there were no parked or parking cars. At the back of the church sat seven dumpsters, five of which usually overflowed with bagged garbage, despite a weekly Wednesday pick-up. Pigeons strutted around the lot, bobbing and flapping, pecking at spilled pieces of trash. When a church function, a funeral or service, was scheduled, the side lot filled early. The children were forced to relocate their activities toward the back of the school. The movement to avoid the cars was amoebic. There was no leader. The first person to notice a car coming in tapped another child to alert her or him and shouted, "Hey, move!" Then, the group oozed to another spot out of the way.

At first glance, the sixth- to eighth-grade children's activities prior to classes appeared, by and large, to be gender-separated. Boys played "dodge" with the boys (without a ball), chased pigeons singly or with other boys, or stood around in clumps with other boys, talking or poring over a sports magazine some boy had unrolled from his pocket or backpack. The girls, some with younger siblings in tow, chattered with other girls, fussed with their hair and clothes and those of their siblings, or jumped rope, usually in the section of the lot that sits behind the school.

Sometimes, boys would come around while the girls were jumping rope. More than once, I saw a boy disrupt the girls' rope game by attempting to "jump in." He usually "messed up" the rhythm. The first time any boy did this, the girls simply threw the offender out of their game by pushing him toward the periphery, while shouting, "Hey! Get outta here! Go 'way!" If he tried again, the girls might turn as a group and "play attack" him. If, instead of running away, the boy wheeled around and tapped one of his chasers on the arm, calling "It!", a game of tag usually developed. Jasmine explained the rules for tag: "The boys chase the girls. They play that boys chase you an' if they catch you, you're on their team, an' then you run an' catch the girls."

Sometimes the play turned a little rough, but it never escalated into a real fight. Clothing might be inadvertently torn during the play, but the rippings never engendered hard feelings as far as I could tell, only a search for safety pins once the school day began. If the boy who disrupted the rope game ran back to his group of boys without giving the signal for tag, the rope game resumed. In any case, some kind of play continued until the bell rang.

When the weather was nice, the older girls spent a lot of their time before school playing hand-clap games or, more often, jumping rope. The ropes were typically pieces of plastic-coated clothesline, sometimes twenty feet or more in

Chapter 4: Play

length. Two girls twirled hand over hand while one or more girls jumped the double ropes. Jumpers jumped, pacing themselves by reciting the rhymes under their breath; twirlers chanted, and other girls (and sometimes boys) watched. I had always called the twin rope jumping *double Dutch*, but the girls said, "No, not really, double Dutch is the rope, *an'* how you turn. When you turn the [doubled] rope in one direction, hand over hand [toward the center], it call *double Dutch*, an' it call *French* or *Irish* if you go in the other [direction], an' it harder to jump."

The girls once tried to show me how to twirl the ropes. It became quite evident that a lot of concentration, coordination, rhythm and practice were required to get the doubled rope segments going at the same pace and with the same arc.

While turning, the girls chanted a rhyme, such as:

> H-E-L-L-O, that's the way you spell *hello*.
> Do your mon-goes like this—[Step, step, alternate feet].
> Do your pop-a-goes like this—[Jump up and down].
> Do your tick-tacks like this—[Cross feet, jump].
> Do your beat-a-beats like this—[Toes pointed in, then out, triangle-shape while jumping].
> Do your one-legs like this—[Jump on one leg].
> Do your mon-goes 1 [2, 3, etc.].
> Do your pop-a-goes 1 [2, 3, etc.].
> Do your tick-tacks 1 [2, 3, etc.].
> Do your beat-a-beats 1 [2, 3, etc.].
> Do your one-legs 1 [2, 3, etc.].

When a girl missed the beat and tangled herself in the rope, another girl took her place. Sometimes, a girl was "goin' real good," and another tried to jump in, so (theoretically) both of them would be jumping at the same time. The twirlers determined the rhyme that was used, and matched their turning to the rhyme's syllabic beat. I never could figure out who decided when the rhymes would change. Some days, the same rhyme was used for everyone who jumped. At other times, each new jumper had a different one.

> My ma-ma had a ba-by. His name was Ti-ny Tim.
> I put him in the bath-tub to teach him how to swim.
> He drank up all the wa-ter. He ate up all the soap.

He tried to eat the bath-tub, but it would-n't go down his throat.
My ma-ma called the doctor. My ma-ma called the nurse.
My ma-ma called the lady with the al-li-ga-tor purse.

Interestingly, when I checked out jump rope rhymes, I found this rhyme extraordinarily similar to the "rude verse" quoted in Opie 1994, page 145, which begins: "Lulu had a baby, His name was Sunny Jim, She stuck it in the bathtub, To see if it could swim. 'E swam to the bottom, 'E swam to the top . . ."

A close cousin to a rhyme these girls used for rope jumping is British handclapping rhyme of the same genre: "Under the bram bushes, Under the sea, Johnny broke a bottle, And he blamed it on me. I told my Momma, I told my Poppa, And Johnny got a whacking on his—Oooh ah cha cha cha" (Opie 1994, 147).

The girls' version was:

> Johnny on the ocean. Johnny on the sea.
> Johnny broke the bottle and blamed it on me.
> I told ma-ma. Ma-ma told pa-pa.
> (An') Johnny got a whuppin' on one foot, one foot;
> Johnny got a whuppin' on two feet, two feet;
> Johnny got a whuppin' on three feet, three feet
> [jump with both feet, and touch the ground with one hand];
> Johnny got a whuppin' on four feet, four feet
> [jump with both feet and touch the ground with both hands];
> Johnny got a whuppin' on his Oooh-a-chie-ca-chie [turn around].

Since I had grown up in a neighborhood singularly devoid of children, I had never heard any of the jump rope rhymes the children chanted before. I asked the girls about the spelling and the meaning of *mon-goes* and *pop-a-goes* because I thought the words might be *Mom-goes* and *Papa-goes*. They corrected me, asserting that what they chanted was correct; but at the same time, they denied knowing what the words were supposed to mean. Later, when I recited the rhymes to a friend of mine, she said she remembered many of them, adding she never knew what some of the words meant either. She suggested that the couplets included "nonsense words" inserted to drive along the beat needed to pace the

Chapter 4: Play   *89*

jumper's jumps. I suspect, rather, that the original words may have simply been forgotten through time and that similar words with the same numbers of syllables have been substituted. None of the girls I asked knew the derivation of the jump rope rhymes they chanted either, although DeDe offered that her mother "tol' me most of 'em old." (For comparisons of jump rope rhymes, see Abrahams 1963; for a dictionary of rhymes, see Abrahams [ed.] 1969).

    The girls were amazed when I confided that I had never jumped a double rope but only a single "skipping rope." They asked, as if I were still doing that regularly, "How fast can you jump? Can you jump backwards?" They encouraged me to try jumping a double rope. "Come on, try! Come *on*!"

    I protested, "Oh, no, I can't! I could never get my feet going right!"

    Towanda chastised me, "Don't you never say *never*! You know better 'an that!"

    They began the rhyme, turning the rope in time: "My ma-ma. . ." I tried to jump in; I failed. "Wait for the beat!" They began again. "My ma-ma sent me. . ." I waited for the beat; I managed to get over each rope once. Jumping rope was not as easy as the girls made it look. We all had a good laugh, and they applauded my effort.

    The next girl to jump made it through an entire rhyme without missing a step:

> My ma-ma sent me to-the-store. She told me not to stay-out-late.
> I fell in love with the grocer-boy, who took my-heart-away, Hey! Hey!
> Who's the mo-ther? I am.
> How's the ba-by? Jus' fine.
> Who's the dad-dy? None 'a you' business
> [or the name of a boy liked by the jumper].

Adding a boy's name usually meant the jumper laughed and missed the beat. When one girl jumped out of the rope, another girl jumped in. The twirlers did not pause.

> Twelve times twelve's one hundred an' for-ty-four.
> When the bed breaks, do-it-on-the-floor!
> Do your mon-goes like this. Do your pop-a-goes like this . . .
> [The remainder of the rhyme was the same as the counts in H-E-L-L-O].

The girls played hand-clapping games much less frequently than rope. Clapping games were begun when there were two girls, and the space in which they stood or sat was small or inappropriate for jumping rope or when neither had a rope. The girls typically clapped to two rhymes, both of which I recalled from my school days. If they clapped to others, I never heard them. The hand positions they used were identical to those I had learned. The rules of play were also the same: If you missed connecting with your partner's hand(s) anytime during the recitation, game, you had to start from the beginning. The clapping pace picked up on the second and subsequent recitations. One girl generally began the rhyme.

The most frequent clap was: "A sailor went to sea-sea-sea, to see what he could see-see-see. And all that he could see-see-see was the bottom of the deep blue sea-sea-sea." Left and right hands clapped together on "a"; the right hand crossed to the partner's right, with a clap on "sai—"; left and right hands were struck together on "—lor"; the left hand crossed to the partner's left with a clap on "went"; left and right hands were clapped together on "to"; then both hands were clapped three times with partner's hands on "sea, sea, sea." Repetition was the norm.

Take Me Out To The Ball Game was the other "clap." Each girl held her hands out with one palm up, the other down. The partners clapped on "take." Then left and right hands were struck together on "me"; right hands were cross-clapped on "out"; left and right hands were brought together on "to"; left hands were cross-clapped on "the," and finally left and right hands were struck together on "ball game." Then, provided there had been no missed claps, the rhyme was repeated faster. Jasmine and I clapped together on two occasions.

Chapter 4: Play

Biggie, Fred, and Lemar told me that boys and men play hand-clapping games with babies but never with each other. The clapping game they mentioned was *Patty Cake*, which I had learned as *Pat-A-Cake*. The boys accompanied their demonstration with the appropriate hand gestures. They said adults had played this game with them when they were young, and that they have played it with their siblings or other babies. There were slight differences between their version and the one I had learned. The words I learned appear in brackets.

> Patty cake [Pat-a-cake], patty cake, baker's man.
> Bake me a cake as fast as you can.
> Roll it and roll it [prick it] and mark it with a *B*,
> And put it in the oven for baby and me.

When the bell rang for school to begin, the girls started for the door, walking and talking, and bouncing along as they braided their ropes to keep them from tangling. Some of the girls twisted their ropes instead. Either way, the result was a large, heavy mass of clothesline approximately one foot in length that had to be stashed somewhere. During the day, ropes were typically stored in lockers or stuffed in backpacks, unless the physical education teacher had told the girls they could bring their ropes to gym class. In that case, the ropes were shoved into the girls' desks until after gym. Once, when Shanita left her rope downstairs in the gymnasium, she became almost hysterical. She begged me to go down to find it. The rope had disappeared between the end of gym class and the time she remembered. It was a good rope, a long rope, and she did not know when she would get another.

Jasmine informed me:

> Most girls learn to jump 'bout six, six an' a half, goin' on seven, like me, an' I been jumpin' ever since. I think I be jumpin' for life, but most girls, when they grow up, they forget 'bout jumpin' an' they get into boys. I start jumpin' when the snow melt an' I stop when the snow come down.
>
> My favorite is *Peach-Plum*. *Peach-Plum* [is] a new rhyme. Thassa only one I know new. I hear Keesie sayin' it, an' then everybody start sayin' it. It go:

> 'Peach-Plum.
> Peach-Plum.
> Pocket full a' bub-ble-gum.
> Don't like it, don't take it.
> Take it up; Take it down;
> Take it alla-way a-round.
> Hot-dog, Ba-by. Chick-en-in-the-gra-vy.
> Here come [jumper's name] with ['a nappy-head,' 'a bald-head,' or some boy's name, depending on the jumper and how much the twirlers want to tease] ba-by.
> 1, 2, 3 [up to 10].
> Ice cream so-da, gin-ger ale, pop.
> Step on the let-ter of your sweet-heart.'
> [The letters of alphabet are called out until the jumper stumbles.]

When school let out for the day, and the weather was nice, the girls did not congregate in the school parking lot to jump rope. They moved their locus of activity across the street to one of the cement play areas between project buildings. The lot where I observed "rope" happening most frequently is a vacant, open area where the rusty bones of a swing set sit in the middle and a single bench has been placed to the side. Biggie told me, "But, see, we missin' our swings. They no more swings there." Moochie continued, "If you wanna swing now, you gotta climb up, get the chains down, let 'em down, an' put up a board right there." The swings may have been a great loss to the boys, but the girls never mentioned them. They did other things in the play lot than swing.

The girls who did not first stop off at home ambled toward the lot in small groups or singly. Some had younger children of both sexes (siblings?) who attended the school in tow. Usually, more than one girl carried a rope. When three or more girls had gathered, whoever had the rope asked: "Who wanna play rope?" and they started jumping.

I noticed that adults supervising younger children occasionally glanced at the jumping girls. Sometimes, older girls, perhaps fourteen or fifteen years old, rather self-consciously laughing, jumped in as the rope twirled. A few boys who walked by sometimes stopped momentarily to observe. Some called out to one or more of the girls, but most strolled past going on about their own business.

Goodwin (1990, 36), Lever (1976), and Gilligan (1979, 435) all classified jump rope as a traditional female activity. Jasmine disagreed.

> Some boys do jump rope. They jump single, [but] some jump double. It depend on if the person can jump. Boys don't usually do it 'cause the other boys would think they gay when they jump. Mostly, it just sissy boys that jump. 'Course if they little, it don't matter.

When I asked the boys whether boys jumped rope, Fred said, "Sure, boys jump double Dutch. Our sisters taught us, but mostly boys jump single. Double Dutch, it mostly like, a girl thing."

Twan immediately protested, "No, it ain't." Biggie concurred. "It really ain't. Boys jump rope, but mostly single, so's they build theyself up." Tatiana clarified the contexts under which boys typically jumped rope: "When everybody playin', the boys jump. The girls teach 'em."

However, the boys did say they never carried ropes around like the girls. Jasmine confirmed this was true. "Nope, no boys carry ropes." Apparently, among these children, rope was one of the girls' preferred and primary play activities until at least age thirteen, whereas for the boys it was simply an activity in which they could, and did, participate *with* the girls less frequently as they became older.

What purpose did jumping rope serve in these children's lives? Was "rope" something more than just a child's game? For one thing, it falls under the broad classificatory category of recreational activities, and, as such, "is recuperation of energy" (Dewey, 1916/1985, 213). Jumping helps develop coordination, as I can personally attest. It is also good exercise, especially if one is an accomplished enough jumper to make it through an entire rhyme. And, jumping is cheap entertainment. All you need is a clothesline and, ideally, three children. If you are short one person, you can still jump if you tie one end of the rope to a fence. In a pinch, as Jasmine said: "If you single, you can jus' turn the rope you' own self with nobody jumpin'." In fact, you do not even need a rope to jump. I once jokingly asked Wynona, whom I noticed hopping around and shuffling her feet while standing in line, if she were tap-dancing. "No," she replied quite seriously, "jumpin' rope." Girls can also ask boys to turn the rope for them. Twan told me, while demonstrating the hand movements for double Dutch, "I can turn a rope easy."

Rope was focused interaction for these children. "In order to coordinate their behavior with that of their co-participants, human beings must display to each other what they are doing and how they expect others to participate in the activity of the moment" (Goodwin 1990, 1). Younger children observed older children jumping rope long before they were physically capable of the coordination required to perform the actual twirling and jumping. Princess said, "You learn to jump, I guess, by watchin' other people." The children learned the rhymes by hearing them repeated long before they actually used them for timing the rope twirling and their jumps. Older girls began teaching the art of rope to six- and seven-year-olds, including their brothers and other boys.

Teaching younger girls and boys how to jump rope was an activity that served different functions. In this school, rope provided opportunities, primarily for the girls, to switch being teachers, learners, group members, and leaders. An older girl maximized her chances of putting together the preferred triad for rope when younger learners were around upon whom she could call to turn the rope or coach in jumping. The younger girls and boys learned or sharpened their skills at jumping rope and twirling to a beat. At some later date, they could and did teach those skills to others. And, the older children—again, most often girls—were able to demonstrate their prowess at rope.

All the girls and boys, by virtue of watching and being actively taught, learned new techniques and rhymes and had opportunities to practice them. The girls demonstrated a new way (or new to them?) to jump rope to the counting chant called "1-2-3, sa-la-mi." The twirlers turned a single rope at normal chest

Chapter 4: Play 95

height for the numbers, but lowered the rope fast to waist height on the word *salami*, forcing the jumper to duck. If the rope hit the jumper, or he or she stumbled, the child was "out." If the jumper avoided being hit or stumbling, the rest of the rhyme was chanted: "4-5-6 salami! 7-8-9 salami! 10!" (The next set of jumps was performed to "1-2-3 bologna," etc., then "1-2-3 cheese," etc., then ham, turkey, and finally bread). Jasmine hated to jump to this rhyme because, she complained, she was so tall that she was unable to duck low enough to avoid being hit by the rope.

When I first heard the girls chant this rhyme, they were saying "1-2-3 salam-mee." I asked them to define *salammee*. They shrugged, indicating they did not know what the word meant. After hearing the rest of the rhyme, I asked if perhaps the actual word might be *salami*. Tatiana and DeDe agreed this pronunciation was more likely correct "seein' we makin' a sandwich." The girls subsequently changed their pronunciation of *salammee* to *salami* when they chanted this rhyme. I wonder which pronunciation will be passed along.

The girls with whom I talked about rope confirmed that "jump rope is another game which, although not inherently competitive, allows for clear distinctions among group members" (Goodwin 1990, 42–43). However, Princess said, "There no class for who the best jumper." The reward for being best on a particular day, according to DeDe, was "Whoever get the farthest don't have to get on the end [of the line]." The boys said they never ranked any boy who jumped rope at all. I also never overheard anyone ridicule a child who could not jump well.

Rope was very much a collaborative activity that reflected how these children ordered their social interactions when free from adult constraints. There were twirlers, and there were jumpers. Each person had a specific job that he or she had to perform as part of the rope unit for the duration of the set, the length of which was defined by a jumper's skill. Turn taking was part of the rules of play in rope. The initial order for jumping turns was determined before the game began. The children called out numbers (1, 2, 3, etc.). According to Tatiana, "Before you start, everybody call a number, like 'First,' 'Second,' 'Third.' Kids call 'em theyself. If somebody call the same number, somebody gotta pick a new one." The particular child who began each new set shifted as the play progressed. For example, if a child who originally had been third to jump managed to make it farther than anyone else jumping in that set, that third jumper took the other child's place at the start of the line for the next "round" of rope. A child's turn lasted as long as he or she did not stumble or get hit by the rope while jumping. Goodwin (1990, 45) found a similar pattern among the girls on Maple Street and pointed out that this was at odds with Lever's (1974, 192, quoted in Goodwin 1990, 311) middle-class girls' data where "no one keeps track of the jumps made but the jumper herself."

The boys I observed rarely mentioned basketball other than to refer to it as something they did in connection with the after-school sports program or at the Boys and Girls Club. This might be because the single hoop near their homes was bent and rusty, because their school team record was 1 for 7 during the entire 1997–98 season in competition, or because the boys were generally involved in things other than basketball when they were with me. I did attend, at their invitation, two school games, both of which they lost.

Once, in early April 1998, I ran into Fred and Ed carrying a basketball. They asked if I could drive them over to the outskirts of their housing project where there was a serviceable basketball hoop, so they could shoot a few baskets. This request immediately followed Fred's winning the Most Valuable Player trophy for basketball at the Boys and Girls Club. It also turned out that Fred liked a girl who lived next door to where that hoop was set up, and he was hoping to see her.

When I spoke with the boys about basketball and their school team, they said they used to have games almost every other day after school before their school was placed on academic probation. They also said they wished some of the taller girls in their class were on the school team so they could win more games when they did play other schools. The boys added that no girls had joined the after-school sports program to play basketball for some unknown-to-them reason. Perhaps one of the reasons why the seventh-grade girls did not join the basketball programs at the school or the Boys and Girls Club was because their leader, Tatiana, did not want to participate in those particular kinds of activities. When I asked the girls if they ever played basketball, I received negative replies all around. DeDe advised that she "don't like basketball, but I do like volleyball," and added that the children only played volleyball at school, again because that was where they had access to a net and ball.

Playing basketball was never one of the reasons the boys gave for wanting to come out to my house, although they knew I had a backboard, net, and ball, purchased on one of Biggie's and my shopping expeditions and installed with more luck than skill on the garage. On three occasions (March 1997, June 1997, and April 1998), when we were together, the boys indicated they wanted to play basketball. However, the suggestions to "shoot a few baskets" came after they had completed downloading hip-hop rap lyrics from the Internet, typing school assignments, and playing Megarace on my computer.

On the first occasion, Fred, Art, Biggie, and Ed began simply shooting baskets without keeping score, trading off the ball following a missed shot. They were practicing their "specialties" rather than playing any kind of game with rules. As they bounced around after the ball and each other, they told me their specialties. Fred did not like to shoot hook shots, although he claimed he was good at them. Art was great at free throws, Biggie "play[ed] the net," while Ed was known for his three-pointers. Even though Fred maintained he did not like to make hook shots, when I saw him play, he jockeyed Biggie for a position at the side of the hoop where he could make such shots whenever the ball came to him. Ed hovered at the perimeter of the driveway "court" where he could try for a three-pointer, while Art ran around trying to steal the ball.

On the second occasion, Twan, Fred, Biggie, and Lemar included me in their play, first as a player, then as a referee. They gave me pointers about how to shoot

("Hol' your arms up like this an' hol' the ball, aim, an' let it fly. You don' gotta throw you'self after it") and dribble correctly ("Move the wrist side to side, not up an' down. Use the arm to control the ball, not bounce, bounce, bounce by the wrist"). They laughed along with me at my efforts. At one point, Twan and Fred actually knelt down to shoot baskets from the free throw line in order to disprove my contention that I was too short to sink one.

My husband and stepson were then pressed into service for an informal game. I was designated referee. Because I was almost useless in that capacity, the boys—and I include my husband and stepson in that category—effectively monitored their own play. They coached me about when to call another player for a foul, holding, or traveling. "Com'on, ref! Call the foul!" However, no one formally chose sides or formed a team even though there were enough players for two teams of three. Each player was a team unto himself, shooting when the opportunity arose, guarding and blocking when another player tried to take a shot.

On the third occasion, I asked Biggie, Twan, and Fred whether they knew how to play *Horse*. They said "yes," and immediately switched from not keeping score to counting baskets (one letter added for each miss; one letter subtracted for each basket made, until the individual tally spells *horse*). Despite their coaching about how to "set up a shot," I quickly racked up all the letters in *horse* by missing five straight attempts and was relegated to the sidelines to watch. I stood next to Moochie who never did like to play basketball.

The boys did not keep score out loud until I introduced the idea of Horse, although I am reasonably certain that, while they played, they monitored their own baskets even if they did not tally them. However, there never was any indication that "status" was confirmed on the boy who had scored the most points, either during or after these games. In the few instances where I observed the boys playing basketball, each boy appeared to be competing against himself.

When I tossed the ball out to the group of boys, whoever caught it shot first. After a shot was attempted, whether successful or not, the ball belonged to who-

Chapter 4: Play

ever ran forward and caught it. In the event that it became a loose ball, whoever stopped it was entitled to shoot next. Scoring a basket in this version of basketball did not mean that a boy who had already shot once could grab the ball and shoot again.

When the boys played informal games, such as the one during which I was referee, whoever had the ball tried to shoot a basket. The others jockeyed for position somewhere near the basket, while one or more boys typically guarded the shooter. When the boy with the ball was too closely guarded to attempt a shot, he would try to pass the ball to anyone who was "open." Since there were no teams, it did not appear to matter to whom the ball was passed. I assume the object of this version of basketball was simply to keep the ball in play. Each boy took his specialty shot as opportunity, and the ball's bounces, permitted

I found it interesting that until I introduced the idea of tallying scores for baskets in Horse, there was no recognizable comparative or competitive component in the boys' basketball playing. Although I observed no other spontaneous examples of the children playing what are usually classified as team sports, the noncompetitive nature of play during these informal basketball sessions led me to wonder how much of the competition in children's adult-supervised play might be the direct result of an adult's structuring of the game rules or of adult intervention (intrusion?) in children's play.

Some of the seventh-grade boys (Moochie, Waldo, Terrell, and Ken) who were especially interested in nature went up along the railroad tracks that run behind their buildings. This is not as difficult or as dangerous as it sounds. The tracks are easily accessible simply by walking up a slight slope that abuts a sidewalk near a railroad overpass. There are no gates or barriers. At the top of the hill, the railroad land is broad and flat. Two sets of tracks have been laid there. On a clear day, you can look down the line toward the city and see the switching yard and any train that might be coming from miles away. From atop the tracks you can peer down at various structures: a stable for the carriage horses that give buggy rides downtown; a car parts yard; and a huge, open-door Quonset hut used as a temporary garbage dump. Commuter and freight trains whiz by, but as Moochie explained, "You stay away from the tracks, you stay along the side. There's a big brick wall [actually stone and cement blocks that shore up the hillside] over there, an' everybody can stay away from the trains."

The track area is weed-choked and riddled with holes. Old boards, tires, and unidentifiable metal parts lay strewn over the landscape. There are discarded adult-sized shoes and liquor bottles, too—evidence that not only these children frequent the tracks. The single time Moochie took me up to show me around, he took pains to help me navigate through the weeds and around the holes. "Watch out! You fin'a kill you'self!" He added *sotto voce*, "Cain't take you no place—trippin' an' fallin' alla time."

Moochie told me that "girls who live up by us, 'round our age [thirteen years old], only not in our school, be goin' there doin' the same thing [as the boys], but no girls from here [go]."

Jasmine corroborated his statement.

> Mostly boys go up on the railroad tracks. They skip rocks or they watch the trains go by. It fun, I guess. If they be up there, they catch bunnies an' keep 'em. Terrell look for snakes there. They lotsa rats up there. Sometimes they say people on the trains will shoot at 'em, but I disbelieve that.

She also claimed to speak for all the seventh-grade girls in her school with regard to the tracks when she asserted she would never go up there because "they's wildlife there, an' I don't like no wildlife." (See Kotlowitz 1991, 5–7, for a similar discussion of the tracks, snakes, and reported shootings).

"Going up on the tracks" was often synonymous with "going hunting." Rabbits, garter snakes, bugs, and feral dogs live and roam along the tracks. The boys went up there frequently during the spring, summer, and fall to locate animals, observe them, pet them, and sometimes "live capture" them.

Moochie said he occasionally took a captured rabbit home to watch for a few days, then released it back to the "wild" on the tracks. The snakes they found in the grass near the tracks were described as "havin' long stripes down they bodies," and the boys have identified them as garter snakes. Terrell maintained he had learned a lot about snakes from observing the ones that lived along the tracks. However, I suspect that he was thinking about other kinds of snakes when he told me, "Like a snake when it attack you, it can't see the motion, they sense the vibrations." Moochie believed "they [the snakes] come in with the trains." He even boasted about having caught a few of them. He scoffed when I asked him if he used a net. He explained, then demonstrated, how his uncle down in Mississippi taught him snake-catching techniques.

> First, you see the snake—you walk up easy, they don't move—you look at him. An' then you put you arm down with you hand open, an' they move, an' you grab 'em by the head, right here (pointed to his jaw), so it hold the mouth closed, an' just keepin' your hand like this, don't let it get at you!

He offered to bring me a snake for my garden "'cause they's good for keepin' down the bug population."

The tracks are home to "all kindsa bugs." Moochie was excited when he trapped an albino moth up on the tracks in August 1997. He put it in a plastic container where it promptly laid thousands of minute orange eggs and then died. He pinned its wings down to cardboard, after we consulted about how best to preserve it. He wanted to know about albino moths. Why were they albino? How did they get that way? Were the babies going to be albino? We read up on the British peppered moth data and discussed the study. He was absolutely certain the eggs would hatch, and he wanted to have the correct kind of food for the larvae when they emerged. So, we consulted the Internet for information about the care and feeding of moth larvae. As late as December 1998, he was still waiting for those eggs to do something.

Going up on the tracks was sometimes only for wildlife "observation." Moochie especially liked to look at rabbits and their babies. Terrell described the rabbits near the tracks as being white, black, and mixed colors, most likely the descendants of domesticated rabbits. He claimed that some of "the kids, they go an' catch the rabbits. They sells 'em, or they eats 'em." The boys said they have noted differences between adult rabbit and baby bunny behaviors. They noted that adult rabbits simply hopped quickly away when they sensed danger, while baby bunnies, "they jus' stop shock-still [stock-still] an' then they jump straight into the air, come on down, an' *then* they start runnin'." They told me that the summer was not a good time to look for rabbits because "they out hoppin'" and winter was no good "'cause they in they burrows."

The dogs that live up on the tracks are mixed breeds and some "pure bloods." Terrell reported, "We—me an' Ken—look for dogs there, too. They—some peoples—left they dogs out, an' we see pit bulls, an' one time I seed a big black police dog, an' he was real friendly." None of the boys ever mentioned that they captured the dogs, although they did confess to petting some of them, and checking out their paw prints in the mud. Moochie, Ken, and Terrell all maintained that they want to be scientists, biologists, or animal behaviorists when they grow up. Terrell told me, "I want to do animals. In my future, I want to study animals—communications an' they movements."

Going up on the tracks was evidence of the boys' current interest in wildlife and nature. The tracks were a science laboratory they could freely explore, learning about science, biology, botany, and ecology; sharpening their observation skills; raising questions they could pursue; testing what they had heard or read. Time spent on the tracks was good, early preparation for the careers the boys hoped to have when they grow up, and it was free.

Goodwin (1990, 50) stated that an activity made into "exclusively male undertakings constitutes one way in which the boys attempt to critique girls." However, I found no evidence that these boys had designated going up on the tracks as strictly a "boy" activity. Going up on the tracks was simply nothing the girls in this school ever did or expressed any interest in doing. The boys never said that girls could not or should not go up on the tracks simply because they were girls. They never forbade their female classmates to come along with them. Nor did the boys ever indicate they resented the girls who did go up on the tracks for going there. They made no disparaging remarks about those girls, like calling them tomboys, and never implied that they felt those girls were intruding on traditional "boys' territory."

Going up on the tracks was a single, dyadic, or small group activity these boys did with boys, and they said that it was something the girls who went there did the same way. Moochie never mentioned "hooking up" with those girls in any way, either in terms of going up on the tracks together or even of happening to be up on the tracks at the same time. This public space, the area up near the tracks, was simply where gender-separate, but parallel, activities and play occurred.

During the time I was doing my observations in 1996, the boys called two Toy Feasts. Although I thought, and still think, the words *Toy Feast* might have sprung from some mis-hearing or misunderstanding of the word *fest*, its designation as a feast was actually correct. I gathered from conversations with the boys that they believe they invented this activity.

The Toy Feasts I observed were held outside in a public space, on the cement area in front of one of the buildings, close to the entrance but far enough away so that adults coming and going could get through. They took place in nice weather, after school or, as Moochie told me, on weekends. Toy Feasts were never held in a child's house or apartment, but they could sometimes be held in apartment building hallways. Because the outdoor feasts were in a public space, they sometimes became a mixed-gender activity, but one with a twist.

One child, usually an older (sixth- or seventh-grade) boy, organized the feast. He told other boys he saw, who then told their younger siblings and friends to come. Children rushed into their buildings to get a toy and, perhaps, a friend to bring to the feast. The toys were placed in a pile, close to the brick wall of the building, if they were not taken out of the owner's hands as he or she came to the feast. "Ooh, lookat that!" "Lemme see!" "Whassat?" "Whatcha got there?" Children sifted the pile even as new items were being added. The contents of the pile changed as toys were added and taken out. Exchanges occurred all the time during a Toy Feast. "Can I see that?" "Here, lemme have it now." "Com'on, Man!"

Biggie said, "We have a Toy Feast. It like, when all of us bring out our toys, an' like, we play with our toys."

Moochie elaborated, "Toy Feast is like, I bring out the toys I wanna play with, he bring out the toys he wanna play with, we play with 'em, an' then we [ex]change 'em."

There was parallel play by gender but not always by age at these feasts. I saw boys showing other boys, their same age or younger, the intricacies involved in changing a Transformer toy from an insect or robot to a car or truck or plane.

Moochie and Biggie updated my vocabulary by telling me that these toys were now called "B[ug]-Bots" or simply "'Bots." I saw an older boy explain to a younger one that the toy turned into a gun; then he demonstrated the order in which the parts had to be turned, twisted, and clicked to effect the change correctly. The younger boy worked with that toy alone for a while, clicking and reclicking the parts, until he got it right.

The older boys and older girls played in separate groups and frequently exchanged toys between members of their same-sex group rather than going back to the pile for a new toy. "You finish with that yet?" "Wanna play this?" The boys typically played with other boys and with "boy toys" like 'Bots or, less frequently, with board games. The girls, always fewer in number at the feasts, played with girls and "girl toys," or board games. At Toy Feasts, younger boys and girls sometimes also asked an older boy or girl (cross-gender, older-to-younger instruction) to explain the rules of some game.

Chapter 4: Play

Biggie said, "Like, if I brought out my *Wari* set, you might get people playin' with it."

Moochie added, "They might do that on the playground [directly north of the building where Moochie used to live]."

Wari, also known as *Awari* and *Mancala*, was the one board game I found I could always interest the children in playing. It is an African game involving a set of opponents who move different numbers of stones from cup to cup in an attempt to capture and amass the greatest number of those tokens. In Africa, Wari is played using either a game board with shallow cups in parallel rows or by using two rows of holes that have been dug in the dirt. The children learned about the game in their African Cultures class. It looks deceptively simple to play.

During Toy Feasts, if a child tired of playing with a specific toy, he or she found another, stood observing play in progress, or went home carrying the toy he or she brought. The toys were never permanently exchanged or even loaned out for overnight, I was told. My suspicions are that it was a factor of toy ownership, an owner's attempts to make sure his or her toy did not disappear during the feast, and toy type (so-called boy toys/girl toys) more than of ritualized behavior, proscription of cross-sex interaction, or a desire by either the girls or boys to play separately. According to Biggie, "Toy Feasts—they last 'bout an hour or two."

Moochie added that when the weather was bad, or "just sometimes," he and a friend or two sometimes held Toy Feasts in the hallway outside his old apartment. He told me that these feasts were "the same thing" as the ones held outside. However, his recounting of what occurred at the indoor Toy Feasts showed that, although the activity might have had the same appellation as and elements in common with the larger, outside feasts, indoor feasts were more serendipitous. These feasts were not "called" but emerged when two or more boys who ran into each other somewhere close to home decided that they wanted to do something together for a while. From Moochie's description of the indoor feasts, it appears that they were nothing more than what I would classify simply as children playing together.

While there were outside activities, and outside activities that could be carried on indoors, there were also exclusively indoor activities, such as playing house or school.

DeDe claimed, "You play house inside, never outside."

Tatiana added, "You play with sisters, cousins, an' you play 'til you get bored or tired."

Almost all of the seventh-grade girls I asked said they still played house sometimes. Tatiana and DeDe were the exceptions. DeDe claimed, "I quit just now, when I turn thirteen." Tatiana advised, "I quit when I was ten. My mama tol' me, 'Quit playin' with baby dolls,' so . . ." The girls said that playing house was never solely a girl activity. Coco explained, "No, it not only with girls. Some did. Some didn't. You could play make-believe boyfriends." Playing house could involve any number of imagined locations and situations. As DeDe said, "We used to have our own house. An' I cut my doll's hair off an' permed it. I put peanut butter all over her head an' 'tended it a perm."

Kay explained, "Sometimes [the person] who is the mother tell [those] who [are] the other people what to do"

"Like goin' shoppin'," DeDe said.

Coco, with a laugh, added, "Like goin' to bars."

"Or play goin' to school," Kay commented.

Said DeDe, "Like, when you play school, you go to school, have lunch, be 'bad,' play 'gettin' the teacher' . . . "

Tatiana explained that "the oldest person in the play group always the teacher [when playing school], an' the baby is the youngest, when you play house."

"Or you can use a baby doll," DeDe added. "I still have my baby doll I got last year."

Chapter 4: Play

Coco giggled. "Or you can use a teddy bear. Sometimes, we play pregnant with puttin' a bear up under our shirt—or [pause]—a balloon. We play [that] we moanin'; we tired, an' then we get a baby."

I asked Jasmine what would happen if, when playing house, a really bossy person were the mother. She said, "Well, I'll be the grandma, or the auntie. That way I can always go home." When I pressed her to elaborate, she said, "Well, if you the grandma, the mama gotta do what you say, an' if you the auntie, you have you' own babies, or else everybody have they own babies."

Then I asked what would happen if a "bossy" person were the teacher when the children were playing school? She said, "Whew, I wouldn't wanna play. I'd be gettin' detentions an' homework an' all that! I wouldn't play if like, [name of a well-known "bossy" girl] was teacher."

For the most part, whenever I mentioned that the girls still played house, the boys snickered. They talked about playing house in the past tense.

Ed said, "When we little, we play house. We had a house in Head Start. Now we got a clubhouse where, like see, we get this blanket, an' you put it up, an' you pull it down. We quit playin' house an' 'play-school' with baby dolls 'round when we 'bout seven or eight."

Twan interjected, smiling, "I'm still playin'!" The other boys scoffed, but Twan insisted he still played house. "I do!"

Biggie explained why he believed most of the boys have given up playing house: "'Cause you find somethin' else—you be movin' on."

When Jasmine, Kiki, and Wynona were at the Workout World, they discovered a play area set up for house. There was a doll bed, a high chair, a changing table, a rocking chair, a doll blanket, and a baby doll. Jasmine was particularly thrilled. "Oh, look! Let's play house." She picked up the naked doll and directed Kiki, "Find the clothes." Kiki dutifully went off to locate the doll's clothes that had apparently been removed earlier in the day. Jasmine then instructed Wynona, "Now, you go fix the baby's food an' I'll change her." Wynona trotted over to the play kitchen area around the corner and began "pretend" cooking. Approximately two minutes later, she returned holding a dish.

Jasmine, meanwhile, had gone to the changing table and diapered the baby. As she worked, she talked to the baby: "We fin'a get you all fixed up, don' worry. You'll be havin' you' food soon enough." When Wynona came over, she said, "Here's the food." Jasmine told Wynona to carry the food over to the high chair "an' then bring me that blanket." Jasmine then wrapped the baby up in the blanket, placing it in the high chair.

At that point, Kiki returned with the doll's nightgown. "Found it!" Jasmine turned to her, saying, "Put it there. Doncha see, I'm busy with the baby?" Kiki placed the gown where Jasmine had indicated. When it became clear Jasmine was involved in solitary play with the baby doll, Kiki wandered off with Wynona to explore a nearby exhibit. Jasmine, however, took no notice of their departures. She cajoled the baby doll, "Here, open you' mouth an' eat. It's good."

When I asked her what the baby was eating, she replied, "Mashed peas an' carrots." After a few more minutes of pretend feeding, Jasmine announced, "All done!" She lifted the baby out, scooped up the clothes and blanket, and took them all over to the changing table, where she put the nightgown on the doll, threw the blanket over her shoulder, and burped her. She then took the baby doll to the rocking chair, where she sat and rocked her for a minute. Then, still talking to the doll ("Shhh, shhh, we goin' to sleep now"), she walked a few steps to the bed, placed the baby on her tummy, and rubbed her back while repeatedly telling her, "Go to sleep." Then she turned to me. "OK, whatcha wanna do now?"

I asked Jasmine where she had learned how to take care of babies. She replied that she frequently baby-sits for her younger twin sisters and occasionally helps her mother out by taking care of the children for whom her mother provides home day care. She added that she enjoys doing this, unless the children are sick. "Once my mama had this baby [she was watching], an' he didn't have no medical card yet. He couldn't go to no clinic, an' he was sick. So, what I did was I just gave him the Tylenol® and prayed." Part of the reason that Jasmine was still very much involved in playing house at an age when it has become a peripheral activity for other adolescents might have been because her younger sisters were frequently in her care. She amused them and herself by playing house.

These children's play, in some ways, was at odds with the data collected by other researchers. Although the games' names were the same (rope, tag, dodge), in many cases, the rules governing who played and the participants' interactions during play were slightly different. Local traditions might have accounted for some of these differences, as Thorne (1993, 108–9) has suggested. Adaptation(s) to local (ecological, socioeconomic) situations, or changes over time, much as Opie (1994) found among the people in her playground, could account for others. Differences might also have been a factor of the specific times when all of us researchers made our observations, or they might have been because of the varying ages of the children we observed.

In a child's world, things have a short shelf life. Activities may be done intensely for a while and then dropped, never to be picked up again, or dropped and reintroduced months later. For example, when I asked Moochie in November 1997 if he were still going to Toy Feasts, he said, "Not really." I asked, "Why's that?" He simply shrugged. Biggie suggested a possible reason: "[Moochie is] movin' on."

Goodwin (1990, 49) found the children on Maple Street "joining with and separating from each other for various activities." Based on my observations of these seventh graders at play, she was right; such "fissions and fusions" do and did occur. Many of the children's activities, whether gender-separated or mixed-gender, seemed to reflect an "informal arrangement between the sexes" (Goffman 1977, quoted in Goodwin 1990, 49) and appeared to be based on variables other than gender, rather than on any hard and fast rules against interacting with opposite-sex children.

Goodwin (1990, 46–47) also characterized the Maple Street girls' group as egalitarian and the boys' group as hierarchically organized societies. "While the actions of the boys make a visible hierarchy, the girls' actions display an orientation less toward explicit ranking than toward similarity among group members" (Goodwin 1990, 45). She claimed that there was a correspondence between these girls' social structure (i.e., each had the same social status and the group had no permanent leader), and that of the anthropologically famous foraging people of the Kalahari desert in southern Africa, the !Kung bushmen (Ju/'hoansi), described by Lee (1974).

However, she also admitted that her data had been gathered only during observations of the children at play. She did not attempt to discuss what she thought she saw or heard during the children's interactions, nor did she ask them to clarify exactly what they were doing, or attempt to verify that her assumptions about the underlying rationale for their behaviors were correct.

Goodwin (1990) found, moreover, that "bald" imperatives were unusual because the girls on Maple Street more typically issued directives that included themselves, left the time frame for the actions open, and showed concern for the well-being of the directive's recipient. The girls I studied did use inclusive terminology when talking to the other girls, but if those took the form of directives, they were generally initiated by the girls' leader. For example, my videotapes were replete with commands that stressed immediacy given by whoever was the girls' leader on the trip ("We gotta go!" or "Let's go!" or "Com'on, y'all"). I have documented no instances in which any given directive left the time frame open.

The difference may be because the contexts in which I gathered data were slightly different from the context in which Goodwin (1990) operated. My data came from informal field trips, essentially child-directed but adult-supervised, and from in-school interactions, essentially adult-organized and supervised, whereas Goodwin gathered her data from children's interactions in unsupervised play contexts. I also asked the children I observed about what they did, why they did it, and the reasons behind their behaviors. Goodwin (1990, 23), on the other hand, "chose to ask as few questions as possible," being more "concerned with the indigenous organization of children's talk and activities than with accounts of their activities to an outsider."

The benefits of asking the children what they were doing and what they meant in order to reach a better understanding about "their ways of looking at it" (Schubert 1993) became extremely clear when I was recording the girls engaged in what I had already mentally classified as gossip. I asked them why they were gossiping. My question led to the following discussion.

"It ain't gossip 'cause you family," Coco said.

Tatiana offered, "We all family here."

"Well," said Keesie, "if it [the subject under discussion] true, it ain't gossip anyways."

"*Gossip* is when you tell somethin', an' you don't know somethin'," Tatiana clarified. "*Truth* is when you actually there, an' you *know* what went on; an' *lies* mean you too scared to tell the truth, like when they gonna hurt you."

DeDe countered, "If you tell a lie tryin' to keep someone from bein' hurt, it not really a lie."

"It may be a lie; it depend," Tatiana said.

Jasmine noted, "Like, my mama don't like her job 'cause they be playin' 'he say-she say' alla time. That gossip."

My data, gathered from observing and interacting with the seventh graders in a variety of situations including play and then discussing their activities with them, led me to a slightly different interpretation of the girls' and boys' social structure in terms of macrosocial models. My framework can be used to reinterpret Goodwin's (1990) and Lever's (1976) data. It also provides a way to reconcile some of the differences found in those studies, specifically the differences that Goodwin and Lever attributed to social class.

In this group of girls, Tatiana was most often the leader and organizer of their activities. Frequently, she was the one to initiate "rope" or other games. Many times, she mitigated disputes. She was the one who was said to be the teacher's pet, who often got away with behaviors that others did not, on whom much responsibility was placed as class president, and who customarily spoke for the girls.

The children perceived Tatiana as having a great deal of power. When the teacher left the room, or the children changed classes, Tatiana was generally placed in charge of monitoring everyone's behavior and reporting back to the teacher about offending individuals. The boys complained that she infrequently wrote down the girls' names, even if they had been "acting up." Both boys and girls, alike, complained that Tatiana gave preferential treatment to Twan, who could "get away with anything" when she was in charge. Tatiana maintained that, as class president, one of her responsibilities was to make certain that the other children were aware of their homework assignments. She also claimed she was expected to remind them to do their work. Not all of the girls followed Tatiana in everything, however, but those who did follow her deferred to her.

Instead of being an egalitarian model, then, these particular girls' social organization more closely resembled the type found in a ranked society that relies on kinship as the framework for social and political life. Among the seventh-grade girls, being female served the same purpose as being related by blood or fictive kinship ties. Ranked societies provide relatively egalitarian social relations but may also have a "chief" who is accorded more prestige.

The seventh-grade boys' social organization was the one that more closely resembled Goodwin's proposed egalitarian model. The boys had no single, acknowledged leader to whom they consistently looked for directions or structuring of activities or to whom they deferred. Leadership roles changed according to whatever activity was happening at the moment, much like what happens in band-level groups. In band-level societies, labor is divided by age and sex. Band-level societies have informal and situational leaders. Situational leadership falls to those with special abilities or knowledge, but the role carries no permanent prestige.

To illustrate, Moochie was informally known for being "good in science," so when the boys were involved in something classified as scientific, they deferred to Moochie's expertise. Ed was "the best reader," so when the situation demanded, he was consulted. However, no boy's expertise in a certain area carried permanent prestige. Success in an individual venture, whether academic or athletic, was acknowledged by a "high five" or other accolades whenever the situational leader(s) and follower(s) achieved their goals.

Goodwin (1990) and Lever (1976) designated "rope" a girls' activity. In a somewhat tautological argument, they used the rules of rope to justify classifying the girls' social structure as noncompetitive and egalitarian. If they were aware that rope was also a mixed-gender activity, at least up to early adolescence, would they still have classified it as noncompetitive and egalitarian? Many of the differences in the structures and forms of play among Western adolescents noted by various researchers have been attributed to ethnicity or social class. Could these differences be better explained if the data were analyzed according to the gender-specific macro-societal models I have proposed above?

Play, as a general category, serves a number of different functions, not the least of which is social. What most of the data on play and children's games have demonstrated is that "play is serious business" (Bruner 1975). As Dewey (1916/1985, 211, emphasis in the original) pointed out, "Persons who play are not just doing something (pure physical movement); they are *trying* to do or effect something."

But what were the children trying to do when they played games? When the children played house or school, were they rehearsing for the real world? Were they learning how to act within a specific social order, as Mead (1934), Piaget (1932/1965), and Gilligan (1979), among others, have suggested? If this were so, why was their play so plastic? Why was there no "script" that set forth how the play was to progress and end?

Bateson (1971, 261–66, and 1972, 177–93, quoted in Schwartzman 1976, 317) believed that children were "learning to learn" when, and as, they played. When they were playing, these seventh-grade children were learning, and they knew it. Just like they found mentors to help them learn, they participated in games and play activities to help them learn. They heard or learned a few simple rules and acted them through. They invented, eliminated or modified a rule, played the game through again, then assessed the effects of the new rule, the change or modification.

Play activities and games permitted them to experiment with different possible outcomes by "playing at doing," and then to reflect upon the ramifications and implications of their actions within a play situation or game structure. In this sense, the children were creating, trying out, and "shopping" for different organizational techniques that would work within the parameters of their pre-existing social structures.

A very different picture of the children's play emerges if one adopts the perspective that the children are learners and that they learn by trying out different activities, testing different roles, and constructing different models. They are gathering information about, exploring, sampling, trying out, practicing and learning a variety of different behaviors and skills during play, with the desire to learn driving all of the other behaviors. Each child learns from "the interplay of the multiple contexts in which he or she moves. . . . [These contexts] give multiple dimensions [to the child] . . .and situate meaning and circumstance" (McLaughlin and Heath 1993, 213).

The games and play activities allowed the children to act both as play object and play subject within the framework of a social event, the structuring activity (Ehrmann 1968, referenced in Schwartzman 1976, 303). All the children's games had rules and the children learned them from watching, direct instruction, and participation. The children were learning that rules can and do change and learning the ways in which changes could be effected. They were also learning which changes were good and which changes were not.

The children's play activities required an initial willingness of the individual participants to accept their roles within the activity's traditional structure. However, the children adapted to the immediate situations that the game participants, including themselves, set and worked through "what if . . ." scenarios.

The children might have been learning the appropriate sex roles and skills for adulthood when they played house, but then what were they doing when they played school? House and school, in particular, appeared to be modeled after the institutions with which these children were most familiar and with which they had had the most experience. Were the students imitating adults with whom they have come in contact when they played house and school? If so, why did I never see or hear about the children playing "church" or "gangs?"

How does one explain the role reversals in tag by either the rehearsal or imitation model? Could "rope," instead of being interpreted as reinforcing noncompetitiveness and egalitarianism, behaviors considered to be ill-suited to professional success in corporate America, be more correctly interpreted as a cooperative activity that rewards individual success, both of which are highly valued in the business world today? Are mentor-mentee behaviors, greatly valued in the business world and academia, being developed, learned, imitated, and taught during Toy Feasts? Would the application of a sports team model to these boys' social structure with their situational specialists affect the interpretation of their activities?

As Dewey (1916/1985, 214) pointed out, skills and information gathered during games and play can be freely transferred to work. I wonder if a classroom teacher could take advantage of the various kinds of behaviors that children employ during their games and play activities to structure more effective pedagogy and classroom activities and form cooperative and peer tutoring groups up and down the grades?

CHAPTER 5
SOCIAL STRUCTURE

In July 1997, I videotaped two sets of students, Coco, DeDe, Tatiana, and Jasmine, then Biggie, Art, and Moochie, talking about what they thought they had learned during the past year and why they thought those things were important and worthwhile. The children had been so many places and had done so many things, both in and out of school, I was curious to discover which kinds of experiences they thought had been particularly valuable and why they thought so. I also wanted to find out whether their comments would reflect gender differences. The girls started the discussions with school subjects they had learned and felt were helpful.

Jasmine began, "Like, it [school subjects] was valuable in a way. We had went over a lot of things [that later appeared] in the Iowa test."

"Percents," Tatiana gave as an example.

"Math," DeDe offered. "When you go to a store, you gotta make sure they ain't cheatin' you."

"Like one-halfs," said Tatiana. "You gotta know if a shirt cost twenty dollars so, when it half-off—so, one-half is ten dollars."

Corroborating the practical value of this lesson, DeDe noted, "An' they have lotsa half-off prices at Venture an' K-Mart."

Tatiana switched tracks. "It's really good we had the Constitution in seventh grade. It's really good to learn 'bout the Amendments, an' because it the law, to tell you 'bout the United States.... Then when we get to high school, we don't have to take it in high school!"

The conversation veered off into what the girls felt they had not learned during the past school year. DeDe stated, "We didn't do writing an' composition, an' we be needin' that."

Jasmine observed, "What we didn't learn—our teacher always tell us do more comprehension, but I should know what comprehension is, 'cause we 'posed to do certain things to get our comprehension."

"Or science, plants, or animals," Coco added. "You might get bitten by an animal. You have to know the study of an animal—where do it get the different diseases the animal could catch. What they tryin' to kill me with is, they be tryin' to get us ready for high school, an' we not goin' to high school just yet. We just be goin' to eighth grade!"

Jasmine lamented, "We haven't gotten all the seventh-grade stuff that we need in seventh grade."

"It take more than two days to understand like, algebra," Tatiana explained. "Like, we jump to each subject an' there's not enough time. Each subject should have a day, like there's five days an' five subjects. Monday, math; Tuesday, readin', then, Friday, we can go over the stuff we didn't understand. Friday, we get in a little group an' talk about it."

Later, she added she thought more time could have been devoted to teaching the students how to type. "I want to learn how to type, 'cause that is the major thing in my life now."

I then asked Biggie, Art, and Moochie the same question. Instead of subject matter, Biggie mentioned a tool the teacher had provided during the year. "My learnin' log—for recall."

Art picked up on the topic and elaborated. "I think it [the learning log] help with comprehension an' writin'. I mean sometime I don't write in it, but I go home an' think 'bout what I learn, an' then I write. Like, this week, I wrote a whole lot—a halfa page."

Moochie, also mentioning tools, said, "I learned a lot—Venn diagrams, graphs. I can use these in my career, an' they help me with my homework, now." He chuckled. "Out of school, I like, chart the days of the things I have to do: [such as] Monday through Friday, I work at the [Boys and Girls] club; Saturdays, I help Suzette on the mural [at the Boys and Girls Club, work for which the children were paid]."

Only Art had a complaint about what he thought he might like to have learned but did not. "Well, [name of program] wasn't a lot of help 'cause the teacher sat there. How we 'posed to improve our readin' without nobody helpin'?"

Kay's comment that "most of education isn't at school; it's everywhere" was shared by all of the children with whom I spoke. Jasmine affirmed that she learned "valuable things inside school—outside school." Moreover, all of the students with whom I spoke said that they saw some connections between and among what they learned in school and activities and things they did outside of school. Yet, perhaps because of the school's probationary status and the renewed emphasis on acquiring the skills required to take standardized tests, many of the students have come to see their school as the central place where they will learn not only "how to" but what they need to know to pass those tests.

Unlike the Bostonian ten- and eleven-year-olds who had difficulty figuring out how to fit school learning into their social life outside school (Dewey 1901/1991, 236), the girls had few problems seeing immediate applications for their academic subjects, including arithmetic. The girls' emphasis on the use of mathematics in the context of shopping, was fully in keeping with their roles within the family, both currently, from what they told me, and possibly in the future. The girls said they accompanied their mothers shopping. They also said they were frequently sent to the store to make purchases and were instructed to comparison shop for the best values. The girls were interested in learning the subjects and techniques that would permit them to exercise their responsibilities well.

To illustrate, on the day I took care of Jasmine and her twin sisters, their mother gave Jasmine ten dollars to buy lunch. Apparently, she had directed Jasmine to bring her change. Jasmine read the overhead menu at the restaurant, quickly calculated the cost of three cheeseburgers, three French fries, and three small drinks. She decided that she had enough money to pay for those items, and receive approximately one dollar in change. She told her sisters what she was going to order and, when we reached my house, called her mother at work to report she only had thirty-eight cents left. Jasmine either had forgotten or had not realized that she needed to calculate the sales tax. Later, at the grocery store, when we were working out which purchase was the best buy, using a calculator and "cents-off" coupons, Jasmine calculated each item's cost plus tax.

On the other hand, the boys mentioned tools, which are really organizational or strategizing techniques, as being the most valuable things they had learned in school. One reason for this might have been that the boys were more involved than the girls in activities outside of the home and family to the degree where tools—especially organizational ones—rather than actual academic subjects, were quite useful. Another reason might have been that tools, and the mastery of them, permitted the boys to become "experts" in specific activities and also allowed them to perform those roles more efficiently. However, both the boys' and girls' frustrations, documented here and in following chapters, stemmed from a commonly held perception that they did not think they were always receiving the kinds of, or amount of, academic material, tools, and instruction in school that they believed they needed currently and for the future.

Many of the seventh graders I studied attended some church, although the denominations were different. The large number of church attendees identified among this group of children was not unusual since a 1987 Gallup Poll found approximately 78 percent of African-Americans consider themselves "churched," claiming church membership and attending church within the last six months (Lincoln and Mamiya 1990, 180). Most of the students had no difficulty identifying the church as an institution they felt could teach them worthwhile lessons and as a place where they could learn outside of school.

Just as the children were not particularly forthcoming about what they really felt about school, their teachers, or gangs until we had known each other for almost a year, they only reticently admitted they went to church. Only three of the children talked at any length about church and their involvement with those institutions.

It became obvious the longer that I interacted with Biggie, Moochie, and Jasmine that church teachings and church activities were part of the social fabric of their lives. They peppered their conversations with paraphrased Biblical quotations. They sometimes sang snatches of Gospel songs while they worked. They assessed their classmates' behaviors using church-based standards.

Moochie went to church less often after he started attending pottery classes at the local Boys and Girls Club, began working Monday through Saturday, and became involved in after-school sports. One conversation we had concerned the necessity of actually attending church. His argument suggested he had given the issue some thought. "I think you don't really need to *go* to church. I think you can read the Bible at home same as in church. Don't it say 'the Holy Ghost is always within you'? So, why you got to go to church to get the Holy Ghost?"

Yet, Moochie had attended Bible camp for three weeks during the summer preceding his entry into seventh grade. The camp was out in the country, away from the city, and a place where he learned something about God. He regarded the experience as both positive and negative. The good aspects were that going to a camp where "African-Americans an' lotsa Hispanics learn 'bout Jesus" afforded him a break in his routine, released him from household chores, and provided opportunities to explore the wildlife in a different area. The negative aspects were that the structure of the camp day did not allow him enough free time to pursue his own interests. He said:

> First thing you do, at the top of the mornin', is church, break, church, an' then you have like a half-hour or whatever. An' at church you spend like three hours in church, right? Then, next time, you have 'bout a half-hour free, an' then the next time, then it be lunchtime, an' then you eat, an' then you go to church for another three hours. You come back, an' then you eat dinner, an' then you go to church again for another three hours, an' then, it's lights out 'bout eleven o'clock. By the time you get out it's like nine o'clock. I go *nine* hours a day!

Biggie, on the other hand, found no negatives in the amount of time he spent in church or at church. He talked about his week that revolved around his church activities.

> Well, we go to church, an' I go Monday, Tuesday, Wednesday, an' my mama goes Thursday, an' Sunday, an' sometimes, some Saturdays for me. In my church, sometimes the minister goes overboard, sometimes he don't, but we get out on time, 'bout one o'clock. I go to Sunday school, then go to church.

Biggie began attending Saturday morning tutoring sessions at his Missionary Baptist church where he worked with a certified teacher to increase his reading comprehension. His mother told me that she and other parents in her church had organized this free tutoring program for neighborhood children because they believed the students needed help with their reading skills. (See Lincoln and Mamiya 1990, 150–57, for a list of and discussion about community outreach programs typically sponsored by different African-American urban church denominations. Baptist denominations, in particular, have a long history of social outreach programs).

Biggie was also the Youth Bible Studies Leader and taught the weekly Bible lesson to younger children. I asked him whether he read the lesson he taught from the Bible. "No, my mama go over it [the lesson] an' break it down for me, an' I break it down further [for the children]." He related that the Bible lessons lasted

Chapter 5: Social Structure 123

"'bout an hour, an' then we get back together an' talk 'bout what we learned." Biggie met his mentor in church and interacted with her approximately four days each week at the church. He also met a girl he liked at his church, a fact that meant he *really* enjoyed going to services. He helped his mother, who was president of the Auxiliary Association, plan and cook for church socials. He said, "My specialty is side dishes." He walked over to his church to attend services three nights each week following dismissal from the after-school reading program and after-school sports program. On those nights, he did not return home until after nine o'clock. He was taught "to treat people right an' to love everybody." He considered this kind of conduct part of learning "how to be a successful young man."

After she moved, Jasmine stressed the need to find a neighborhood church. Her mother found what Jasmine called "the family church." When I asked her what she meant, she explained, "My family go there, my auntie an' my cousins, an' her sister, an' lotsa families go there, so it 'the family church.'" Approximately three months later, she confided:

> I don't go to the 'family church' no more. My sisters go, but they [parishioners] act funny at that church. It seem like they don't like me or somethin'. Okay, lemme tell you how it is, okay? I come there, right? An' sometimes the preacher, he talks, an' he be talkin' 'bout people toes, an' then he be talkin' 'bout the women come up there with little bitty skirts on, an' they gotta put a towel over they legs so can't nobody see ' em, then he talk. It funny.

Biggie, who was present when Jasmine was talking, chided her about her interpretation of the minister's lectures:

> Respect—respect of God's House. I can see it. If you gonna come up in church, don't be wearin' that tight stuff. You respect that this is the House of the Lord. Don't come to the Lord with tight stuff, stuff that hug you. That for the world. It's just like if we [males] come in with shorts, that ain't no kinda respect!

Jasmine shrugged and commented that, nonetheless, she still thought the minister preached "funny" sermons. In December 1997, Jasmine related that she and her mother had found another church where they can sing in the choir once they show their commitment by attending services for one month. She was eager to sing and reported that "I believe this church is better, even though they don't believe in no Holy Spirit." She felt that it was important to go to church to learn about God and "how to live right."

The students were also involved in activities that, according to some of them, helped them "experience the world more better." They went on school-sponsored field trips. Every school-organized field trip had some connection to the formal curriculum in school.

Biggie thought field trips and watching documentary-type videos were good ways to learn.

> [We need] field trips, educational field trips, I mean, an' movies that talk about our heritage. The museums, an' different other kinds of educational trips, 'cause [name of museum] shows a lot of exhibits 'bout our heritage. You just can't go one time, an' get everything. You gotta go like, many times to really understand what you're looking at.

In 1997, the seventh and eighth graders took school-sponsored trips to a museum and a leadership conference. They also went on an architectural tour. Then, toward the end of the school year, they went on class trips to Springfield, Illinois, and Washington, D.C. The trip to a state capital is not an unusual destination for seventh and eighth graders. The Washington, D.C., trip is a fairly standard one for upper-level elementary students to take the year they study the Constitution and the Revolutionary and Civil Wars.

Terrell assessed the Washington, D.C., trip.

> I like everything. I couldn't wait to get outa that cemetery [Arlington], 'cause I was scared. I like the Tomb of the Unknown Soldiers an' what? Which other part? An' the Art Room at the [African] Art Museum. 'Cause we talkin' 'bout 'mask-ees', an' I like the soldiers an' the way they movin' they guns.

> I think I wanna go in the army, 'cause I get money for college, an' maybe I think I don't wanna go to the army, 'cause they act crazy when they get out.
>
> They don't have much up insida there [Frederick Douglass's house]. The Naval Museum, that was fun, too. Mt. Vernon was kinda sad 'cause he got kilt an' his slaves got kilt [?]. I like the mill too. They findin' different kinda 'teeth-ees' an' things. It like explorin'. Is that what you do? You ever been on a search like that? What do you do with the stuff you find?
>
> At the university [Howard], the part I like was the first beginnin' part. It show you what college was. The guy [a student who talked about the university with the students], he want to be a scientist, but now he want to be a doctor. I wanna be a herpe—herpetologist with the reptiles.

The number of field trips the children took during the 1997 school year had, by their accounts, been reduced from previous years. Most of them saw the reduction as directly correlated to their school's probationary status and their teachers' emphasis on academic skill development in the classroom.

Coco said she did not think the reduction in field trips was necessarily something negative. "I'm really glad that [our school] don't go on as many field trips as we used to, 'cause I think we don't get enough work done."

Jasmine and Tatiana said that some of the informal field trips they had taken with me throughout the year, to places they had indicated they wanted to go, had been fun, informative, and useful in ways they had not initially anticipated. Jasmine recounted one of her experiences.

> We went to the Workout World, an' the thing I like, what I didn't know before, is the Five Senses game. We saw a movie 'bout the brain an' seein', an' it show how important [the] other senses is, like hearin', an' then we went to the Five Senses game an' saw what they was talkin' about.
>
> It look like a maze. You gotta go in there with the lights all off. You had to take off your shoes, an' you had to crawl, an' you have to smell your way an' feel your way through the whole thing, but you can't see 'cause the lights are off. An' I got lost! The first time I got through, me an' Kiki an' Wynona. They left me up in the tunnel the second time. I

couldn't get up the ladder part, an' this lady pushed me up, an' then I was followin' them through an' then they got lost, too, but then they left me, so I was in there cryin'.' I—*for real*! The lights was off, an' I was in there cryin' 'help,' an' I didn't even know I was sittin' by the door, an' then I just stuck my foot out. I didn't even know I was by the door.

We went through this house where each room was a fire hazard. 'Case you have a fire, you should know what to do. An' doncha know, the Iowa test had some questions 'bout fire on it?

Tatiana said:

Let me tell you 'bout my trip. We got to see what y'all don't get to see in the [natural history] museum. We was up behind the exhibits. We got to see the actual things that was in the museum when we—It was December or November—an' we got to see what it was up there! Oh, it was so much pretty things. You cannot touch it. If you gonna touch it you gotta put on mittens, an' they're white, yah, an' you gotta be careful if you touch it, when you touch it. It was so much things, we didn't see it all, but *ooh* . . .

I didn't know nothin'—well, not much—'bout archaeology, an' I think it important so's to learn 'bout our heritage, an' that why I think it important to see these things. An' we met an African archaeologist, an' later on, one time, I saw him at [the store]!

As part of my data collection, I videotaped the informal field trips the students and I took during the 1996–97 academic year. While reviewing the tapes, I began to see interesting patterns. The tapes revealed that, although I had good documentation of what museum exhibits or attractions had attracted and held their attention, I had also clearly caught the children's social structure and group dynamics.

These were not focused trips in terms of having a single learning objective. Instead, the trips were designed to facilitate the children's gaining additional information about topics they had said interested them and to afford them time to explore whatever caught their fancies. I anticipated I would get a better idea of how the children went about learning what they wanted to know from museum and zoo materials if I let them lead the way. I also permitted them to film whenever they wished because I wanted to see what they chose to film and what kinds of things and events interested them. In addition, unlike school-sponsored class field trips, we never had more than five children on any trip because that is the maximum number that could fit in my car.

Most often, I took all girls or all boys to a single place. This was not my choice, but was based on where the children said they wanted to go. When the students signed up for our joint informal field trips, it turned out that only girls wanted to go to a haunted house, the Science Museum, Workout World, Lapidary Art Museum, a grist mill, a conservatory, and the Academy of Science, and only boys wanted to go to the aquarium, the observatory, the zoo, and to the physical anthropology laboratory for dissection. Both boys and girls wanted to tour the natural history museum, and the Power Museum.

Not all the children in the class wanted to go on these informal field trips, and some children wanted to go on all of them. Interestingly, best-friend dyads did not pick the same places to visit. I put mixed-gender groups together to take to a powwow and a restored mansion estate with gardens. I asked particular children to go on those trips because much of what they would be able to see, experience, and investigate fit their expressed interests.

I was surprised to discover that the trip tapes clearly documented the degree to which the children's pre-existing gender-based social structures shaped their learning opportunities in a museum. The videos show that if the group were composed of all girls, one of the girls assumed the role of leader. This leader most frequently directed where the group went and what the group stopped to examine. The girls tended to stay close together in the museums and close to me. I wonder whether this was because I am female, too, or because I am an adult. The exhibit was discussed, explored, and commented on, then the group moved on. Less frequently, one girl other than the leader found something really novel or interesting. She then called the others over to join her. No girl ever wandered off alone, and no girl ever left the group and returned to announce what she had found elsewhere. If an opportunity for imaginative play arose, the leader usually initiated the play.

The tapes of the all-boy groups at museums, even if the groups were dyadic, showed that the boys most often explored the exhibits on their own. They met back up with each other (and me) either accidentally, or when reporting on something interesting to coerce the other boy (and me) over to see, or to touch base with me.

The videos documenting the interactions of mixed-gender groups at museums revealed that if the group consisted of a single boy and a number of girls, the girls would follow the boy to specific museum exhibits. I never observed any boy either encouraging or discouraging the girls from accompanying him. I never heard any of the girls ask to accompany a boy or overheard any boy direct the girls to follow or accompany him. The same kind of informal grouping occurred if there were one or more boys and two or more girls. One boy would go off on his own, perhaps with a girl or girls in tow, while another boy would go somewhere else, either alone or with girls accompanying.

Four girls, Shanita, Sierra, Coco, and Lavinia, went to the Science Museum—a huge place with a number of different exhibit halls dealing with science and industry. The exhibits include a coal mine; a replica of an aircraft carrier; a real dry-docked submarine; mock-ups of an airplane, train, and mechanized farm; exhibits on petroleum, health, images, communications, and nutrition; and a gigantic doll house, among others.

The video of the girls at this museum begins in an exhibit area that contains Rube Goldberg-type gravity machines. Shanita, who struggled with Tatiana for a leadership position among the girls in the classroom, simply assumed the leadership role with this particular group of girls. Sierra pointed and yelled, "Hey, Shanita, the Yellow Submarine, right there!" Shanita and the rest looked where she pointed, and the entire group went over to the case. Shanita began singing *We All Live in a Yellow Submarine*, a song the children had learned at school in their

Chapter 5: Social Structure

music class, and the rest of the girls joined in. At the end of the song, Shanita turned to Sierra: "Shall we go, now?" She replied, "Yah," and the group moved off.

They next traveled to the naval exhibit. Telephones were set up so four people can listen to four separate "officers" talk about their jobs aboard an aircraft carrier. Shanita located the telephones first and called the others over. They pretended that they were holding telephone conversations with the Navy personnel. Then, Shanita said, "Lavinia! Hello!" and they all shifted to holding telephone conversations with each other. They queued up for the plane ride that simulates take-offs and landings on an aircraft carrier, twice.

The way back to the main hall required passing the chicken hatchery that the girls had overlooked on their way to the naval exhibit. Shanita noticed the chickens and stopped. Lavinia was the most enthralled: "Lookit! It fin'a hatch!"

Coco said, "It the heat."

"They crack out! They bust out!" exclaimed Sierra.

Shanita, tapping the glass, said, "It pushin' out!" Coco and Lavinia then tapped the glass, too. Lavinia moved over to the other side of the glass case, and spoke to the chicks. "You' food over there. Go eat!" The others moved along with her, tapping on the glass and commenting on the chicks. Shanita's reading of the sign about the chickens signaled the end of chicken-watching.

When Shanita announced she was hungry, the group trooped down to the museum basement to the Pizza Hut restaurant located there. After lunch, I suggested they visit the dollhouse exhibit. There are telephones there, too, with a recording about each of the rooms in the house. The girls picked up the telephones and listened. Because there were only enough telephones for the girls, Coco advised me, "They tellin' stuff about the castle." Then, Shanita began "talking" with Lavinia again. The other girls picked up the game, too. Shanita said, "My phone went dead! I guess the bill was late!" The rest of the girls giggled.

Shanita consulted her map of the museum and said, "Let's go up the elevator." Then, forty minutes after their first visit to the hatchery, they were off to reinvestigate the chickens.

After watching the chicks and commenting about them again, Shanita looked around and directed the girls toward a step-on scale. She weighed herself first, then Sierra stepped on, then Lavinia, and, finally, Coco. Each girl noted how much she weighed. The nutrition exhibit attracted their attention next. They rode bicycles that showed how many calories they were burning. They checked out the components of a balanced meal and looked at the "fake" pies and cakes. They discussed which pies and cakes were their favorites and which ones looked "real" or "good."

They took off to the adjoining hall where they pretended to be mail carriers and mail sorters. Shanita was the first to stick her head through the life-size cutout of a 1910 letter carrier, and the others followed suit. Coco soon discovered a keyboard where she could address letters to herself, so the girls watched as she typed. I took them over to the coal mine exhibit. Shanita said, "We gotta wait in line. Let's go." I convinced them to stay despite the wait. They did. After the tour, Shanita directed us all over to the petroleum exhibit, explaining, "I wanna come in this exhibit 'cause they talkin' 'bout rocks."

When I took Kiki, Jasmine, and Wynona to the Workout World, Jasmine became the girl in charge. The videotape shows her consistently walking out in front of the other two girls. It documents five separate times when she said "Com'on, y'all" to move them to other parts of the museum to see a different exhibit. She was the mother in the playhouse area and the driver in a play car. She led the girls through the playhouse designed to highlight fire hazards.

The other two girls never once assumed a leadership role at this museum, although Jasmine was left twice. One time, as the girls played house, Kiki and Wynona went off together to find something else to do when it became clear that Jasmine had no further jobs for them as sisters or helpers. Jasmine continued to

Chapter 5: Social Structure

play house, and her comment to me ("OK, whatcha wanna do now?") indicated that she did not consider herself to be playing alone even though Kiki and Wynona had wandered off. Another time, Jasmine was left behind when she became lost in the Five Senses maze, while the other girls did not.

I never documented any girl intentionally going off by herself in any of the museums we visited. However, one time, Shanita, Coco, Lavinia, and Sierra did become engaged with separate exhibits within the same hall at the Science Museum. This particular space is dedicated to high-technology images and imagery. There are convex and concave mirrors, computers that generate facial snapshots for comparison, virtual reality sets, and a heat sensor that casts multicolored images onto a large screen. The video showed each of the girls gravitating to a different exhibit, and trying it out to see what it could do.

Sierra was dancing in front of the mirrors, first one and then the other, to see the difference the mirror shape made in her shape. "Oooh, lookit! It wavy. I look like I got long legs!" This exhibit did not hold her attention long. She quickly looked around to see what the others were doing.

Shanita was moving forward and backward in a virtual forest scene, stepping onto and off the footprints painted on the floor. She was checking which parts of herself disappeared when she took a step left or a step right. She used large, elaborate hand movements to juggle an invisible ball. Her eyes never wavered from the screen that tracked where she was and what she did. "Whew, this hard!" Sierra joined her. They bounced and bumped together.

Coco had stopped at the *Picture This* exhibit. The first time, she followed the instructions: "Position the eye over your eye, then press 'Send'." The next three times, she positioned the eyes, nose, and mouth in different spots, pressed the button, and waited to see the results posted on the overhead screen. She was silently absorbed in pushing the buttons and sending the information. She moved to the adjoining exhibit of a 3-D skull. She looked at the model, pushed a button, and noticed that the button caused the skull to rotate. She pushed another button that enlarged the picture. The last button she pushed blew the skull to pieces along the suture lines. She never read the instructions about what the exhibit was supposed to demonstrate.

Lavinia put on and took off her coat numerous times to see if the coat affected the heat sensitive color image of herself on the screen. She danced, flapped her arms, stomped, and moved her head, sending red, orange, yellow, green, and blue waves of color streaming across the screen. The others joined her. The screen image resembled a huge blue-green blob with erratically moving, multicolored tentacles.

When the boys went through museums or the zoo, I never knew what direction they might take. They always started out with me; but as soon as we reached an exhibit, they took off on their own. The video of Lemar and Terrell at the aquarium showed the boys in the same exhibit room but wandering from case to case separately, at their own pace and in no particular order, checking out frogs. I wonder whether the exhibit makers ever thought their careful arrangements of anurans by size, eco-niche types, and continents would mean so little. When the boys did manage to be at the same case at the same time, it was really by accident.

By the time we were ready to enter the dolphin exhibit, Terrell was far ahead of Lemar and me. He doubled back to announce, "They gots different kindsa whales in that pond up ahead!" We hurried to look. When we were watching the sharks in the coral reef, Lemar was next to me but Terrell had wandered over to the other side to look at something else. The videotape rarely captured both boys in a single frame.

The film of Fred, Moochie, and Art at the observatory showed the same phenomenon. We happened to be there while the museum was hosting Chemistry Day. I noticed some high school students demonstrating the properties of polymers and I directed the boys' attention to them. They stopped long enough to poke holes in balloons and stick their fingers in latex to make "rubber bands." Then, they struck off on their own to investigate. Fred looked through a telescope at the night sky, Art pretended to journey to Mars, and Moochie looked through three-dimensional glasses at a strand of DNA. Art called my attention to a Mars rock, but Moochie demanded that we come over to examine how the glasses worked.

Upstairs at the observatory was a large exhibit hall where early stargazing instruments were displayed. Moochie was filming. He panned one particular room from every possible angle. The video recorded no people, only distant, disembodied voices, because Moochie was filming in a different room from the one where Fred, Art, and I were checking out the early astronomers.

I took a mixed-gender group of students (Ed, Biggie, DeDe, Tatiana, and Kay) to the natural history museum. This museum has numerous halls with plants and animals; huge exhibits dealing with Egyptian, South American, North American, Central American, and African cultures; and dinosaurs, among other things. The Egyptian exhibit is a mock-up of a pyramid. The videotape begins with Ed, Tatiana, Kay, and DeDe looking at sea birds. The tape documented Ed and the girls talking about the effects that pollution and oil spills have on birds. Ed mentioned he learned about how tar can kill birds from the *Free Willy* movie. Ed, DeDe, and Tatiana discussed how this particular exhibit had been constructed.

"These was real animals once," said Ed.

"An' this glass—" Tatiana mused.

In addition, DeDe noted, "This special wax here."

Biggie was not in this part of the film. He had said he wanted to look at "flamingos an' they babies." He returned to the group, then escorted them over to look at the flamingos and pelicans. Ed disappeared. He had wandered off to look at a different case. The children meandered out to the central hall and headed toward Egypt. They stopped in front of the Africa exhibit, which none of them wanted to see. However, the girls heard music coming from the exhibit and started dancing. They all piled into a "pretend" bus to watch a video. Tatiana explained for the benefit of the videotape, "We lookin' at Africa." Ed, not content to wait for the end of the video, quickly walked off somewhere. He returned just as the Africa video lost its attraction for the others. They headed toward the Egyptian exhibit. Biggie was fascinated with the naturally preserved mummy on display. "This real?" he asked. I explained a bit about natural mummification and artificial mummification; and the group, except for Biggie, moved into the mock-up of an Egyptian pyramid. He stayed behind either to read the sign or to look at the mummy longer.

Inside the pyramid, Kay passed along a superstition. "If you step on this," she said, referring to a clear floor panel through which a mummy was visible, "an' stomp you' feet three times, the mummy will come alive!" DeDe and Tatiana explored the slit they discover in the tomb wall. "I see a big eye!" DeDe exclaimed. Tatiana said, "I never knew we could look in here." Ed examined hieroglyphics with DeDe, Tatiana, and Kay. The film captured Biggie's back as he walked past the rest of the group and through a door.

Tatiana and Ed started down the stairs. DeDe and Kay had to catch up with them because they had spent more time looking the hieroglyphics. We met at the base of the stairway. We located Biggie around the corner, looking at a small model of a mortuary. He pointed out that "they in they drawers, they work drawers." He added, indicating he had gone ahead even further in the exhibit and doubled back, "An' I want all the girls cover they eyes up, 'cause they guys in there, an' they naked." Biggie moved on ahead again while we followed. Tatiana filmed. She panned the cutouts of the naked men. Ed and the girls next looked at and exclaimed over the jewelry. Tatiana asked, "These real?" DeDe, Kay, and Tatiana discovered Biggie filling a bucket with water and emptying it. The video showed disembodied hands filling and dumping water, only Tatiana's voice was heard because she was still filming. "Here we are puttin' water in the bucket. An' here [my name] puttin' water in her bucket so she can feed her children, an' give them water."

Chapter 5: Social Structure

Ed wandered off to lie on an Egyptian bed, trying it out for size. The girls lay on the bed, too, one after another. The boys decided they wanted to see the totem poles, so we headed off toward the Northwest Coast exhibit. En route, the children remarked, for the first time, that Biggie seemed to be missing. Ed asked me, "Where Biggie go?" DeDe called out, "Biggie?" And Tatiana questioned, "Where Biggie? That's our leader. Where our leader go?" We found him sitting on a bench in the South American hall, looking very tired. Kay and DeDe plunked down next to him for a moment. Ed jumped into and out of a large wooden canoe from the San Blas islands, while the rest of the group ambled toward the North American hall with a cautionary comment to Biggie not to get in the boat "'cause it break." DeDe captured Tatiana placing her arm across Ed's shoulder while they walked ahead of the rest of the group.

After I had reviewed this tape, I was interested to see if the same kind of dynamics occurred with another mixed-group at a museum. I asked Jasmine, Kay, and Moochie to accompany me to a restored suburban estate that has been opened to the public. I chose that particular estate because both girls had said they liked flowers, gardens, and "pretty houses," and I knew Moochie liked nature. We started off at the visitor's center, which housed oil paintings of the mansion and gardens on the walls.

A ten-foot square section of the floor is clear plastic with a scale model of the entire estate underneath. Moochie was the first to venture onto the floor. He peered down at the model. Jasmine asked, "Is it gonna break?" Then Kay addressed her question directly to me. "How come it don't break?" When reassured the see-through floor would not break, the girls gingerly stepped out onto it and were soon engrossed in trying to locate where I had parked the car according to the estate plan.

On the way to the mansion, we passed through the gardens. Jasmine asked me about rhododendron flower buds: "Moochie say it parta the tree." Kay pointed out they had seen "these [oak leaf hydrangeas] at your house." Moochie demonstrated his knowledge of fruit-bearing trees to the girls. "See they call these 'dry mouth' apples, an' I think these is cherries. Only one way to find out—bust one open an' see if they's pits." He dropped a cherry on the ground and stepped on it. "Yep, they cherries."

Then he saw a reflecting pond and ran toward it, saying, "Be right back!" Kay, dashing after him, squealed, "I wanna go, too!" He yelled back to me that he had discovered frogs. As was typical, Jasmine professed terror of wildlife, saying, "I'm scareda birds 'cause they might attack me!" She stayed on the path next to me, examining the flowers at a safe distance. She commented in an offhand manner that "we need plants for air." Moochie became very involved in watching the frogs jump and dive. Kay was right next to him as he moved around the pond edges. I coerced Jasmine to join them. She protested the entire way down to the pond. Once there, she too looked for frogs, but at a greater distance from the pond than Kay and Moochie and urging caution the entire time. *"Be careful!"* And, on seeing a bee, she warned, "Bees sting you! He gonna sting. You 'bout to die!" Then she noticed a dragonfly. *"Oooh, Lord! We gotta get away!* They fight; they sting; they land on people. I ain't tellin' no stories!" She pointed: "Ooh, frogs!" Moochie counted them. "There's one, an' there's one." He explained what he knew about frogs, but Jasmine was not really listening.

Moochie asked a gardener what he was spraying ("Water" was the reply) and gravitated back toward the mansion with both girls in tow. Moochie talked about how he learned so much about wildlife.

> All those years bein' down in the country with my uncles an' all, taught me how to catch fish with my hands. I know how to catch frogs, snakes, an' I know how to catch birds, too. They taught me. I was watchin' first, then they showed me. After I got done watchin', they showed me how.

We entered the mansion but were required to stay together on the docent-led tour. The children were especially fascinated with the old kitchen equipment. They have seen some of the utensils in their own homes or those of their relatives, while others left them unable to fathom their uses until told.

Chapter 5: Social Structure

We straggled over to the Idea Garden, which Jasmine called "an orchard of flowers." Moochie filmed the statues that lined the long esplanade while the girls walked ahead on the path. In the garden, the girls followed after Moochie as he jumped around touching and commenting on the fishponds and the different kinds of vegetables. Then he was off with Kay to the real orchard to look at peaches and apples. The orchard provided Moochie with an opportunity to discuss fruit ripening and pesticides, a subject about which he had also learned from his uncles. Jasmine was concerned that grasshoppers would "get" her, so she stayed with me on the gravel path. *"Look out for grasshoppers!* I'm scared of 'em. Scared to death of 'em." Despite Jasmine's hysteria over the wildlife she encountered on this trip, the children gave this experience a "thumbs up." Moochie said he learned about cold frames used to protect outdoor plants, and the girls said they enjoyed the flowers and "'specially the old-timey kitchen."

My data from informal field trips showed patterns similar to those I gathered during the children's games. On field trips that included only girls and in games that the girls organized, one girl always assumed a leadership role to initiate, direct, and organize the activities. When these girls interacted, one girl would use an imperative ("Com'on, y'all" or "Let's go up the elevator" or "We gotta get away!") to advance the group's activity, much as Goodwin (1990, 118) discovered for the girls on Maple Street. These girls' use of directives for action ("Lookit this!" "Look out for grasshoppers!" "Be careful!"), to express the requirements of the current activity, was also like Goodwin's (1990, 117) data.

Goodwin found, however, that these kinds of "bald" imperatives were unusual because the girls on Maple Street more typically issued directives that included themselves, left the time frame for the actions open, and showed concern for the well-being of the directive's recipient. The girls I studied did use inclusive terminology when talking to the other girls, but if those took the form of directives, they were generally initiated by the girls' leader. For example, my videotapes were replete with commands that stressed immediacy given by whoever was the girls' leader on the trip ("We gotta go!" "Let's go!" "Com'on, y'all."). I documented no instances in which any given directive left the time frame open.

The difference might stem from the contexts in which I gathered data, which varied slightly from the context in which Goodwin (1990) operated. My data came from informal field trips, essentially child-directed but adult-supervised, and in-school interactions, essentially adult-organized and -supervised, whereas Goodwin gathered her data from children's interaction in unsupervised play contexts. I also asked the children I observed about what they did, why they did it, and the reasons underlying their behaviors. Goodwin (1990, 23), on the other hand, "chose to ask as few questions as possible," being more "concerned with the indigenous organization of children's talk and activities than with accounts of their activities to an outsider."

In school, Tatiana was the recognized leader of the girls and class president for two years running. When she went on a field trip with other girls, as she did to the Academy of Science and behind the scenes at the natural history museum, she merely extended her in-school role of leader to include being the leader of the field trip. The other girls in the group did not object or fight over the leadership position. On trips where she was not present, such as at the Workout World or at the Science Museum, another girl assumed the role of leader. This role might have included directing and legitimizing activities, keeping track of assignments, reiterating what had been said, and pacing all the girls' learning and play. The girls' nondifferentiation of the group members was most clearly expressed through their emphasis on doing things together as a group.

The girls' directives ("Let's go!" or "Com'on, y'all.") spoke of group-awareness. Goodwin (1990) interpreted such directives as indicating the girls' social structure to be egalitarian. Her data and mine were virtually identical on the surface. We differ on the assignment of societal types to these behaviors. My data on the girls' group structuring show there was a girl leader who had power and prestige and whose followers were generally undifferentiated members of the group. The model that most closely approximates how these girls organized their interactions and group dynamics is that of a ranked society, similar to a family.

On informal field trips where the participants were all boys, each boy ventured off on his own. In museums, perhaps because I took boys who were simply interested in the exhibits, rather than taking only the acknowledged "expert" in a particular subject, no one boy assumed the role of specialist for the entire trip. Each boy was an individual learner who, nonetheless, by simply announcing what he had discovered or noticed, motivated the others to go to see it and led the way to it ("They gots different kindsa whales in that pond up ahead!").

I documented that the boys used different structuring language than the girls in play situations. Their imperative commands were most often directed toward an individual, not toward the group ("Com'on, man!" or "Lemme see!"). Goodwin (1990) interpreted these kinds of directives as indicating the existence of a hierarchical relationship. Again, both Goodwin (1990, 75) and I have noted that the surface features of the boys' organization were the same. We both found that the boys had a "fluid hierarchy" and that, otherwise, there was no true ranking or permanent leader among the boys. Apparently, the presence of any type of hierarchy, whether "fluid" or permanent, was sufficient for Goodwin (1990) to label that social structure "a ranked society." However, in my data, the boys lacked a permanent leader, a social fact that placed their social structure closer to an egalitarian model. In egalitarian societies, situational leaders arise depending on the activity of the moment. In an egalitarian society, and for these boys, when there was no need for a leader, the group members operated with relative autonomy.

When the children themselves controlled and directed mixed-gender group activities, as they did to a large degree during the informal field trips, an interesting pattern emerged. The boys, who were intent upon investigating what interested them personally, inadvertently became Pied Pipers for the girls. The videotapes showed the girls following one or another of the boys on the trip. Each boy permitted the girls to tag along but made no accommodations for them. He explored what he wished, wandering and poking at his own pace, occasionally discussing an exhibit with them. If the girls kept up, it was fine. If the girls dawdled, that was fine, too. If more than one boy were in the group, at least one boy would wander off, return, make a pronouncement about some exhibit he had discovered, and then accompany the group to see it. These pronouncements were enticements and also served to establish the discoverer as temporary expert by virtue of his discovery.

In the context of a mixed-gender group interaction at the restored estate, Jasmine asked Moochie about rhododendrons. Her question allowed him to step into his role as science expert in order to explain. There was never any indication that he simply assumed either that role or the one of group leader. He did not direct the group's further activities. Instead, he ventured off to pursue his own interests, with one or both of the girls following, depending on where he went and what he announced he was going to investigate or had found.

At the natural history museum, Tatiana called Biggie the leader. There was never any indication he had assumed this role, had taken on a leader's responsibilities during this trip, or was even aware that she labeled him the group leader, since he was not present when she spoke.

There are different possibilities that might explain her designation. Chodorow (1978) mentioned one: in mixed-gender groups, in public spaces, boys will assume a leadership role, and the girls will acknowledge their subordinate positions by calling one boy the leader. I saw very little evidence that this was ever actually the case, since the girls never exhibited subordination or followed a single boy in mixed-gender group situations. This interpretation is further undermined when one considers that the boys have fluid leadership roles based on specializations and there is no fixed, permanent leader.

A second possibility is that, in a mixed-gender group with no fixed leader, the girls and other boys alike respond to statements made by a situational leader whose announcement of some discovery is designed to inform and draw the rest

Chapter 5: Social Structure

of the group. The difference between a *generalized* leader and a *situational* leader is that the generalized leader is expected to have overall knowledge about situations and things, whereas a situational leader or specialist is expected to have expertise only about certain situations, items, or things. A generalized leader has responsibility for the group all the time, whereas a situational or specialist leader has responsibility only when the group activity demands that specialty.

A third, highly plausible, explanation for Tatiana calling Biggie the leader raises another social dynamic issue altogether. If the girls are used to baby-sitting, as these girls were, they must keep track of all the children for whom they have responsibility. Perhaps Tatiana felt it was her responsibility, as the girls' traditional leader (baby-sitter in charge? mother-role?), to make an example of what not to do (i.e., wander off alone for a long time). She publicly chided Biggie *in absentia* for not staying with the group and wandering off on his own with no indication where he was going or when he would return. Perhaps she couched her public criticism of his behavior in ironic terms that implied the kind of role reversal that everyone in the group knew was impossible since these boys never assume a generalized leadership role ("Where Biggie? That's our leader. Where our leader go?"). Perhaps she, as the "real" leader of the mixed-gender group, chose irony and sarcasm to enforce social control and emphasize that the rest of the group had better stay together.

After I noted this occurrence on the videotape, I asked Tatiana what she had meant when she called Biggie the leader. She laughed and admitted she had just been kidding around, that boys were never the leaders. Princess, who was present at that time, agreed and added that if it were left up to the boys to do something, nothing would be done.

An examination of the children's use of directives raises some interesting questions about social class, pedagogy, and gender-specific social structures. The children's directives are actually codes that indicate "how a person sees the world, interprets the world, and bring that world back inside them [*sic*]," as Dickinson and Erben (1994, 260) maintained. *Codes* regulate and express social roles and conduct, as well as learning, as Bernstein (1971, 1973, 1975, and 1990) has shown. They can be *restricted* or *elaborated*, and many times they reflect social class.

In all-girl groups, these girls' leader used inclusive codes ("Com'on, y'all" or "Let's go!") to direct and pace the others. The girls' codes speak of group awareness and inclusiveness. They also definitely indicated the presence of a hierarchy ranking. The boys' codes were directed more toward an individual ("Com'on, man!" or "Lemme see!"). They suggested interactions between equals.

Neither the girls' nor the boys' directives were typically couched in what Bernstein (1990) would classify as elaborated codes. Again, there are three possible reasons for this non-elaboration: (1) the children were reproducing the kinds of directives with which they were familiar, (2) the contexts in which restricted codes were used did not require elaboration since the reasons for the directives were fully understood or at least acknowledged, or (3) that the children were sensitive to the fact that more elaboration of those directives could produce irritation rather than compliance.

Bernstein (1971, 1973, 1975, and 1990) raised an interesting point about control and codes that can be applied to discussions of these particular children's directives, although the contexts in which he discussed them were different from these contexts of child-to-child interactions. According to Bernstein (1990), individuals in lower socioeconomic groups tend to use restricted language codes. These codes are expressed as commands with little explanation and denote a hierarchical relationship between the speaker and recipient of the directive. It is distinctly possible that these children were using the kind of codes they heard at home when speaking with each other. It is clear, as I have documented in other chapters and above, that these children bring operating methods and organizational structures that they have learned outside the school to bear on their social relations inside the school and with each other.

Chapter 5: Social Structure

Bernstein's emphasis on identifying the specific contexts in which discourse occurs in order to analyze the social relations between the speaker and hearer is valuable in that it raises the issue of the contexts in which these children used restrictive code directives. When a girl gave a directive, it was given from her position as generalized leader. The context was one in which the group leader, whoever she might be, was supposed to make decisions. It is possible that the use of restricted codes to move a group activity along was all that was required. Leaders do not always explain the rationale behind their directives when they are sure their followers will follow. Followers do not often question their leader's decisions or ask why the decisions have been made, especially in situations where there is general agreement about the group's objective.

Let me clarify these statements. On informal field trips where the girls were at a museum, there were many things to see and do. The leader took the responsibility to pace and direct the group's activities so as much could been seen and done in the allotted time as possible. The girls understood the leader's role, the time constraints, and the group's objectives. They permitted the leader to direct them. No elaboration of her directives was required. Elaboration would have suggested that the leader thought the other girls were somehow unaware of time constraints and unclear regarding the reason they were at the museum and what they were supposed to see and do.

I have, however, also documented numerous cases in which the leader will explain a directive, using elaborated context-dependent and independent codes. For example, Jasmine's directive to me to move away from dragonflies was pedagogical and elaborated, as well as being both context-dependent and context-independent. She was trying to give me a reasonable rationale for both of us to move, while at the same time explaining the benefits of complying with her directive ("We gotta get away! They fight; they sting; they land on people. I ain't tellin' no stories!"). The elaboration was necessary because I expressed disbelief that dragonflies would hurt us and showed reluctance to heed her cautions. My reluctance required her to elaborate on the directive and to justify it by citing what she knew about dragonflies (true experiences?) to persuade me.

I am going to posit a somewhat different interpretation for these children's use of restricted codes other than social class. My data suggest that they used restricted codes because they were sensitive to the fact that more elaborated codes might be misconstrued as suggesting some deficit on the part of the directive's recipient. Actually, their restricted codes implied respect—that is, "I know you know my reasons for saying this, and I won't insult you or take up your time unnecessarily by going into things you already know." These children use elaborated codes when the hearer of the directive was reluctant to follow or asked for more information about the rationale behind the directive. Elaborated codes were never used as a matter of course.

Although the children were aware they were learners and frequently looked to adults to facilitate and direct their learning in school and in other social contexts, I often heard them complain when adults used elaborated codes in situations where the students felt they were not required. "She do go on an' on 'bout every little thing!" "She have to explain everything, like, she think we dumb or somethin'!"

These data raise interesting questions about the use of restricted and elaborated codes within the context of the classroom that bear further investigation. Does the teachers' use of elaborated codes in the classroom create tension and confusion, because the children, coming from a lower socioeconomic background, have only heard restricted codes in their home? Do the children misconstrue the elaborated codes an adult might use in pedagogical situations as insults, as showing "disrespect"? In what ways do the children's criticism of elaborated codes mean that they tune out any and all explanations, just on principle, thereby losing opportunities to learn new information?

The students lumped most of what they are taught in school and church into the category of "useful learnin'." They also indicated that church provided them opportunities for more diverse kinds of experience than school, thereby permitting them to choose the activities in which they wanted to become involved and to decide the degree of their involvement. Can some of the types of activities the children found so useful in church be brought into their school—for example, small group work and discussions followed by large group discussions, and longer amounts of time devoted to learning about and discussing a topic? Can the churches help the schools in their tasks to balance all the diverse influences to which the child is exposed? Could the churches help the children with their reading, not just through tutoring programs but also by encouraging them to read the Bible?

The children were divided on the subject of school-sponsored field trips. Most of them liked going on field trips and found them worthwhile, agreeing that learning takes place in school and outside of school. However, a number of the students felt it was their responsibility to help get the school off academic probation. Since the school's response to this situation has been to reduce the number of field trips the children take, two of the students, Coco and Corelle, were unsure they should be taking any field trips during the week at all but believed they should be using their school time to focus on increasing their academic skills instead. Perhaps their comments reflected a belief that the school was the only purveyor of useful and important skills and knowledge and that textbooks were the definitive authority. Dewey (1951/1991, 55) pointed out that such behaviors occurred and such attitudes were adopted when real learning was believed to be restricted to what happens inside a school.

The children were unanimous in their positive assessments of the informal field trips. However, the diverse reasons underlying their unanimity harken back to what Dewey (1949/1991, 351) has said about the ultimate valuation of any experience being required to come from the evaluator. Some of the students felt they learned "useful" information, specifically about their senses, heritage, and fire hazards. Some of the information may have been reclassified as useful after it appeared on the Iowa tests. Other students mentioned that the trips introduced them to things with which they had no previous experience, such as the knowledge that some frogs carry their babies on their backs or that bodies can naturally mummify under certain conditions. Some students believed that these trips provided them with opportunities to pursue their interests in different settings and test their already acquired knowledge against new observations. Others said they enjoyed the trips because they afforded them chances to revisit exhibits they had already seen, but that the trips' structure gave them additional time to explore and discover other things. Others simply called the trips "fun."

Interestingly, when they assessed these excursions, none of the children mentioned that these trips afforded them opportunities to use their imaginations, although it was quite obvious that they did. In order to recount their experiences at the Workout World and behind the scenes at the natural history museum, the children must have used their imaginations to repicture the events and their sequences and draw conclusions about those experiences. The children also engaged in imaginative play when they played house at the Workout World, pretended to be blind going through the Five Senses game, "drove" a car, journeyed to Mars, rode on a bus in Africa, stomped on the mummy's tomb in Egypt to resurrect it, and pulled water up from the Nile River. Perhaps their omission indicated that they have not realized that imaginative play has any "educative value" (Dewey 1902/1991, 263).

On the other hand, perhaps their omission was because they realize that imaginative play has a very large educative value. They did not typically distinguish between using their imaginations and the role playing they normally did in the course of living their lives. These adolescents (perhaps all adolescents?) tried on various roles every day. The girls tried on leadership, mother-type, and baby-sitter-in-charge roles; the boys tried out specialist roles (science guy, best reader, side-dish specialist, good rebounder). They all tried on different kinds of student and learner roles.

These are adolescents, and they are learners. They are aware that they are growing up and will be expected to operate in the larger society someday. They have no clear concept of everything that will be required to operate successfully in this future. They look to adults for guidance and as role models. They also try out different roles and the behaviors that they believe could be associated with their future activities. They practice what they have already learned, and they innovate. The children are always asking "What if —?" as they play through different scenarios, and they track others' reactions to their different behaviors. Perhaps it is only an adult who would distinguish between imaginative play and learning to live.

These data suggest that the children tried to use their already-in-place, gender-specific social structures in their churches and classrooms with varying degrees of success and conflict. The churches provided a number of different activities in which the students could become more or less involved according to their own wishes. Apparently, church-based activities and lessons were presented in a fashion that either did not conflict with the children's pre-existing social structures or that made accommodations for them. As Biggie mentioned, he was the Bible Study group leader and the side-dish specialist at his church. Jasmine joined a church to sing in the choir, as part of the group. She expressed no desire to direct the choir. She wanted to learn Bible lessons, not lead the Bible Study group. The children's churches are social institutions where a wide range of activities exist. The participants are free to pick and choose the ones that interest them, determine the degree to which they will become involved, and specify the role they wish to take in them.

However, at school, where there was a set curriculum and expectations for mastery, the students did not have many opportunities to structure the ways they preferred to participate in classroom lessons or much choice about becoming involved in different activities. The teacher generally determined the lessons' structure and pace and required full student participation. In the mixed-gender classroom, the differences in the girls' and boys' social structures can make teaching and learning difficult.

In classrooms where the teacher is the leader who sets the pace, sequence, and scope of learning, and all of the students are supposed to go along with his or her agenda, is it any surprise that the individualistic boys are often cited for disciplinary infractions? Would "Jig-Saw" strategies, such as are outlined in Kagan (1990, 13:3), be one method that might work especially well with boys since the strategy would permit each boy to have the opportunity to become a specialist? Would giving a boy the opportunity to choose his own classroom activity from a number of choices mean he would become more engaged in the lessons?

What these data suggest more than anything is that the children were not shopping for social structures or organization when they were playing and operating in nonadult-supervised situations. They brought pre-existing social structures and learned interaction patterns to those kinds of activities. The children's families and the churches have already fixed their sense of social options and self. These data do suggest, however, that the children were shopping at school for ways to fit their individual interests, identities, and social organizations into the classroom structure. Moreover, these students were looking to the school to provide additional routes to a social position among their peers, for skills they needed and found useful, and for help identifying areas in which they could excel.

CHAPTER 6

SCIENCE EXPLORATIONS

Three of the seventh-grade boys, Ken, Moochie, and Terrell, said their "hobby" was science. No girls claimed to be interested in science, per se, but two of them confided that they wanted to be doctors when they grew up. This was in keeping with the results of a school-sponsored survey of the 1996–97 seventh graders' attitudes toward school and their academic subjects. In that survey, 50 percent of the boys claimed their favorite subject was science, whereas no girls marked it as their favorite.

When I spoke with Kay about science, she said that she thought the seventh graders

> need more science [in school]. It's important to do science projects so it can help you with your Iowa. They ask science questions on the Iowa. They ask about the seasons, an' how plants grow, the name of plants. It helps you with the readin'. It help with comprehension. I expect to learn a whole lot of stuff [in school]—useful stuff, like the atmosphere, how trees grow. You have to know science to be a doctor, so you don't blow up the hospital!

I knew none of these girls ever went "up on the tracks" to observe or "live capture" garter snakes, rabbits, bugs, and other wildlife as the boys did. Unlike the girls, Ken and Terrell also rode buses to the local pet store, about one mile away, where they looked at animals and fish and sometimes bought them. The boys had very little money to spend, so they used the tracks as if they were not only a source of free animals but also a zoo; and they used the pet store as if it were a museum, aquarium, and zoo where they could see and observe a wide variety of small animals. I know some of the boys also regularly watched the Discovery Channel and other television programs on wildlife and fishing.

Terrell and I had long, involved conversations about science. He was fascinated with all kinds of animals, particularly dogs, snakes, and frogs. Once he called me to report he had purchased a

> vegetarian iguana.... He eat lettuce, a little piece of carrot, an' little bitty strips of cabbage... an' the vegetarian iguana live longer 'cause they be vegetarian. If you get a big iguana, the western iguana, they eat roaches an' bugs.

Then, almost as an afterthought, he asked, "You know anything about frog breathin'?" When I admitted ignorance and asked why he wanted to know, he sighed. "Oh, 'cause I bought a changin'-color tree frog an' I fed it a fly, an' it start chokin', so I give it CPR [cardio-pulmonary resuscitation], an' a piece of the skin come off, an' the frog just lyin' there not breathin' like usual."

I asked, "How is it different?"

"The chin place not goin' up an' down."

"Did you ask the pet store people what to feed the frog?"

"No, I just 'sume it eat flies."

The next day, Terrell reported the frog had died and the pet store people had offered to replace it, but that he thought he would get a snake instead because he knew what snakes ate.

With the above conversation in mind, I asked Terrell and Lemar to accompany me on an informal field trip to the aquarium to see the frog exhibit. Terrell and Lemar spent two hours looking at, marveling over, and speculating about the hundreds of different kinds of frogs on display. They learned that frogs are "predators" whose choice of prey is largely determined by size, that small frogs eat insects the size of ants and ladybugs, and that bigger frogs eat things the size of flies, beetles, crickets, and small fish. The boys jumped from glass tank to glass tank examining the frogs ("This one look dead!" and "Lookit that one up the tree!" were some of their observations), counting them ("There a one; there a one; there a one."), but not reading the accompanying identifying, explanatory cards. "I wonder why they got flat back legs, lookin' like rocks? Yah, they look like rocks. See, he breathin' in an' out. Why he be lookin' like a rock?" Terrell spent a long time wondering aloud about a particular frog, what kind it was, where it lived, if it grew bigger, why it looked "funny." He was prompted to read the sign next to the display case to get some of the particulars about the frog he was observing. "Oh, I see. This an African bullfrog. It got camouflage, like the army do, an' he have mottled—what that is? Mottled? Dark?" Lemar came over and, hearing Terrell struggle to define the word *mottled*, but without having read the sign, interjected: "*Modeled* is like sculpture, like a model, you show somebody how it look."

The boys went off in different directions again, looking at frogs in no particular order but still managing to cover the entire exhibit. By the time they reached the end of the exhibit, they were reading the signs and checking the information against their observations.

"Frogs' tongues wrap around they food. It say they don't have no teeth, they swallow."

"Looky this Kangaroo frog. It say she carry her babies on her back. I seen a frog doin' that back there."

"Leopard frog an' his kids, I mean her kids. It say they called *leopard* 'cause they got spots."

"Oooh, looky that frog! That tree frog! He stuck up there [on the glass]. It say they use those suction-things on they fingers, so he stuck up there with his fingers!"

When we headed toward the dolphin exhibit, Lemar stopped to read the identifying sign in front of a totem pole.

"This a Tlingit, that how you say it?—Tlingit totem pole, with a bear an' a eagle. They mythical. Mythical like, not quite true? Like, they have different gods, the bear god, the fish god, maybe the dog god? Yah, mythical. Tlingit."

During later conversations with the boys, some as far removed in time as six months, they brought up their aquarium experience and referred back to some of the things they had learned.

Terrell reported that, one time on television, he had seen "a black thorny thing that if it sting you, it be the worst sting you get. I forgets what it called, but the fishes, they eat it by pushin' it over on its underside where it don't have no spines. We saw 'em at the aquarium."

Terrell was also very interested in fishing. He generally went fishing with his father. During the past year, they had caught two painted turtles "in [name of suburb]—Churchill Road." He kept them in a cardboard box at home. He fed them crickets, meat, and raw hamburger; let them swim in the bathtub; watched them fight with each other; speculated that because they had not had babies, they were both the same sex; and held turtle races. He claimed "they *real* fast—they run real *fast*." Usually, he and his father caught blue gills or carp. They prepared for their fishing trips by making "blood bait," a smelly concoction of dough and fish guts, which he claimed was guaranteed to attract carp, catfish, and bull heads. One "cat" they caught was purported to have been twelve pounds and quite a fighter. They debated whether to take it home to eat. Instead, they decided to give it away to some other people who were fishing near them but who had caught nothing that day. Because he was so interested in fish, he and I searched through books on fish, their habits, and their skeletons and learned the names of their bones.

We spent time looking at animal tracks at the state beach near the Power Museum. He identified them as two kinds of dog and one set of raccoon tracks. We picked up water-rounded rocks to bring home. On March 25, 1997, he tested the school's water fountains for lead, nitrite, and pH.

Chapter 6: Science Explorations

He wrote the assistant principal the following note concerning his findings:

> I tested the water from [our school's] drinking fation [fountain] for lead. I found no lead. Then I tested for Nitrites. I found no nitrite. Then I checked the water for acidity. We have pure unpolluted water pH of 6.0. Am I glad now I know I can drink the water and its not polluted.

Terrell said he would like to be a scientist when he grows up, but added:

> I think I'm going to have to meet a personal scientist an' set up communication. Then, I'll have to do somethin' else to earn money to start to go to college. In ten years, I'll be in college an' get a degree. I have to have a whole bunch of master's [degrees] to be a scientist. I want to do animals. Well, I wouldn't like killin' them, but I could do it on a computer. In my future I want to study animals—communications an' they movements.

He later refined his aspirations. "I wanna be a herpe—herpetologist with the reptiles."

Moochie, too, was heavily involved in science. He had a microscope that he occasionally brought to school. Normally, he prepared his own slides. A set of prepared slides that he received for Christmas evoked the following comments: "Dissection slides! I been tryin' to get some for the longest time! Grasshoppers, flies, everything! A dragonfly! Man!"

Moochie has tried to replicate some of the experiments he has seen on television. However, he admitted that most of the time

> I be mixin' things, just everything I can find at home. Then I try it out, see what it do. One time, I made paint remover by error—took all the paint off behind the bathtub. I didn't never make no mustard gas, though. I know what that can do. My father, one time, he made mustard gas an' *whew*! We all be coughin' an' coughin'. No, I just mix things up an' then see what it do.

His mentor frequently took him to the university laboratory where he was working on a project having something to do with the soleus muscle in rats. He showed Moochie how to fill a syringe an' tap it an' inject the rats. Then we shave they legs, an' dissect the muscles. The fast muscles be in the back, an' I still got some 'a them with skin and muscles on at home. One time, one of the rats 'come to' when we was doin' that. After the rats go to sleep, we do that, an' then we drop 'em in nitrogen, an' afterward, we cremate 'em.

Moochie asked me if we could do dissections. He had a dissection kit as well as a microscope. Of course, I said, "Of course." I suggested he get a dead animal, maybe from a pet store, freeze it, and then we would dissect it. A few days later, Moochie triumphantly announced, "I got a rat! It's missing its soleus muscle. Is that okay?" We made a date to go to the university's anthropology department laboratory with him, Biggie, Terrell, and Art. While my husband, coerced into helping with this venture, was defrosting the rat under hot water with Moochie, the other boys investigated the alligator, gorilla, and chimpanzee skulls along with the human skeletons in the lab. Having a real alligator skull available, complete with mandible, meant that they were *required* to play having their hands and heads bitten off. Art talked about a video he had seen that described the differences between crocodile and alligator snout shapes and eye placements. I had already taught Terrell the names and locations of the bones in the human body, so he was quick to share with the others which bones were which on one of the articulated human skeletons standing in the laboratory.

My husband, a physical anthropologist, gave the boys the standard biology lesson he gives college students (dermis, epidermis, muscle, ligament, etc.). They wrote down the terms and definitions and recited them in order, committing them, at the minimum, to their short-term memory banks. Finally, they were ready to dissect. All the boys were instructed to don latex gloves for safety reasons. Each boy cut a different layer, and all of them examined the structures. Moochie commandeered the rat ovaries to make into a slide. He showed everybody the slides he had already made from rat muscles. Unfortunately, although he knew the tissues he had used, he had no idea which cells were showing on the slides. My husband pointed out the various structures to the boys, explaining the differences.

Chapter 6: Science Explorations

The boys were involved from 11 A.M. until 4 P.M., working on the rat. Hunger finally drove them to quit. Terrell wanted to keep what remained of the rat, so we packed it up. He left it in the car. A few days later, tracking down the origin of the very strange smell in my car, I found the rat remains. Terrell was terribly embarrassed when I told him. The next week, Moochie showed me an old lab manual he had purchased on rat dissection for $1.95 of his own money from a used bookstore where he had coerced his mentor to take him. "Can we do that again?"

In September 1997, Moochie called to report his bird had died, and did we "want to dissect it?" He said it was a "dwarf parakeet 'cause it just didn't never grow." He said he had "already got it on ice, 'long with my pet hamster that just up an' died, too."

"Sure," I said, "we'll dissect it, but are you sure you're not killing off your pets just so you can dissect them?" Even though I was teasing, he took me literally, assuring me "they was all *old*." I suggested he review the comparative anatomy book I had given him, paying special attention to bird bones to learn how they are different from mammal bones. He agreed without hesitation. "Okay, what time will you pick me up?"

We spent hours working over the bird bones in the basement. Moochie identified the bird as a female, discovered that its skeleton was perfectly formed, and marveled that the bones were extremely thin and that they really were hollow. We decided to boil the head so Moochie could mount it in the diorama case (a black velvet-lined box) he used to construct fantasy natural history scenes, such as an eagle attacking a cow or a snake striking a frog. Although the bird's head burned, Moochie took the rest of the skeleton home to mount. The hamster sat in my freezer, next to my dead frog, waiting for another dissection session for many months. Moochie was concerned that if we did not get to them "they be gettin' freezer burn," so we arranged another dissection session.

Moochie's teacher, late into the 1997 school year, gave him the responsibility of teaching three science lessons to his classmates. She permitted him to choose the topics. He picked hair, snails, and frogs. We searched the Internet for information about all those subjects. We videotaped his dissection of a frog so he could show the students every step and each organ without bringing the frog or a knife to school. Moochie then devised quizzes for the class and corrected them, as well. He related that he found his foray into teaching fun but also frustrating because some of his classmates either had not understood his lessons or had not taken them seriously.

Moochie has frequently said, "I want to be a scientist, a biologist." Much of his interest is supported at home because his parents have purchased him a microscope and allowed him to keep a variety of pets as well as science projects in his room. The only time I am aware that his mother complained was when, as Moochie related, "I had all them chemicals to test lichen [his latest science project] spread out all over the kitchen table, an' my mama made me take 'em to my room."

Moochie truly loved fishing. He talked about it whenever he was not discussing other scientific things, like rat muscles, dwarf parakeets, albino moths, and dissection. He watched a regularly scheduled fishing show on television. We spent a long time at a local sporting goods store picking out a fishing rod. It needed to be correctly balanced; it had to handle a left-hand reel; it had to be "priced right." He told me the best places to catch carp and catfish around the city and cautioned that one particular park lagoon was no good because "one time, peoples, they hook a dead body floatin' there. Truth." He was a font of information about fish and fishing, as well as about rats' soleus muscles.

I began my actual research into the students' attitudes about "science" by asking Terrell how he liked that class at school. He said:

> It could be more live. [We could do] actual stuff, team work, not work inside books all the time—like science experiments, like physical science, like heat. Only thing we did [in science class] was paper clips an' cups. We put paper clips on cups an' balanced them. An' we did hot water an' cold water, an' put it down an' add it up. That's all we did. We 'posed to learn hot an' cold water, I guess.

In early December 1996, I checked with him again. "What happened in science [class]?"

He replied, "[The teacher] say we got to do our science research but she just glanced at it [the project proposal] 'cause most of the kids didn't do it."

"What happened when the other kids didn't get theirs in?"

Terrell explained:

> [The teacher] got them F's. I got an A—100—I'm happy. We was goin' over the projects. Like Ed did 'What's a good bleach?', an' Moochie [did] 'What's the good pesticide for rats?' I didn't want to do no animals 'cause I got to fill out all sorts of forms in the office, an' I didn't want to go through all that.

In early December 1997, when I asked Moochie about science, he claimed:

> Well, we really don't have science lessons. We do assignments out of science books, an' little displays in the classroom. Like, for instance, we have to read about an egg, an' how to drop an egg out the window without the egg breakin'. It 'posed to teach you how to suspend things. Like, you could put a tissue in the box inside, or put strings cross up under the egg an' drop it, or, like I did, just boil the egg, or soak it in vinegar for a week. Gotta do that stuff at home, though. I wish we could do projects an' experiments [at school]. We spend an hour learnin' about projects out the book an' watchin' videos.

Biggie, who normally was nonjudgmental, felt this way:

> Well, science is not basically teached in our classes every day. Like, [our teacher], she'll give us these books. We readin' to ourself—myself. We got no teachin'. She'll read to us every now an' then. So, when we stop switchin' classes, we really had one class, for science, for everything. Before, we used to have a science class, an' she used to just talk 'bout the environment an' everything. This year, science is book learnin'. We watchin' a lotta videos on volcanoes—different kindsa videos. It's all right, but I like 'hands-on' science 'cause it lets me experience a lot. I get to touch it, see it. It's a great deal.
>
> Knowledge—that's what I get. See, some people might learn better from books, some from 'hands-on.' My better way to learn is from 'hands-on.' But see, math, readin', an' science is all the foundation. You gotta read your science for your project. You can't have one

without the other. It separate in our school in its own way. Science you can do everyday! You can do science everywhere. It's basically like, science is life—cookin', calendars, the seasons. Science is in your environment, pollution . . .

The boys' comments should be interpreted contextually and historically. Before the middle school became self-contained in January 1997, the students were scheduled for a regular science class period of forty-five minutes each week. I observed the children looking at drops of water under magnifying glasses, and learning about plants in the then eighth-grade classroom which was set up as a combined classroom and science laboratory. However, at the end of the first marking period, the teachers decided that "switching classes" was not working well, so the seventh-grade students' science lessons were handled from that point onward in their own classroom by their homeroom social studies teacher who, according to the children, showed them different videos.

Some of the students felt that this approach was definitely lacking, particularly since they were required to come up with a topic and experiment for the annual School Science Fair.

In late November 1996, before the middle school became self-contained, I asked Terrell if he went to science class that particular day.

"Yes," he answered. "She [the science teacher] told us to figure our science project. [I think I might pick] electricity—How do it work?"

I probed, "Do you know anything about electricity? Where do you plan to look it up?"

Without a moment's pause, he replied, "I plan to look it up in the dictionary."

"Well, you might also try the encyclopedia. Does anyone else have a project yet?"

"Moochie—he gonna do roaches."

"He already did roaches last year," I commented.

Referring to Moochie's winning sixth-grade Science Fair project, Terrell replied, "Well, he want to win again."

The school's yearly Science Fair was always a huge undertaking involving much preparation and lots of excitement. Judging in each classroom yields three class winners, whose projects are subsequently rated independently by judges in the school gym. The two winners from the gym judging then qualify for the Regional Science Fair (which the students interchangeably called the District Science Fair).

Winners at the Regional Fair go to the City Science Fair, and those winners travel to the State Fair. The state winners then are eligible to participate in an International Science Fair. No student in the school's history ever made it to the City Science Fair before 1997. The students may work on joint projects if they wish; but if a project is chosen for the Regional Fair, only one child's name can be on it. The justification is that the projects are only nominally *joint* ones, since, in truth, a single child has really done all the work.

When he was in sixth grade, Moochie's science project involved testing the efficacy of two different kinds of cockroach control products. He brought the live roaches to school where he demonstrated his conclusions to his classmates and the judges. Unfortunately, some of the other students were not as interested in his findings as he, and "when [he] had put the roaches in the backa the classroom, some kids come over, an' just start squashin' 'em." However, he won in the school and earned an honorable mention at the Regional Fair.

He figured he would win again in seventh grade by testing which kind of mousetrap (trigger/snap-trap or glue-board) worked better. "It used to be [we] never had rats 'cause this old guy live there, an' he a real rat killer. Just took him a broom, an' when he see a rat, take that broom an' push that rat to the wall, then take his shoe an' *bam*! beat that rat to death!" Unfortunately, the man had moved or died, and the building where Moochie lived during the months before the Science Fair had a rat problem again. Moochie really wanted to know how to trap them safely and effectively, and had already spoken to the housing project's rodent-control person.

Biggie's seventh-grade science project explored which of two colognes lasted longer. He said:

> What I was thinkin' about when I first started the project, well I was thinkin' 'bout winnin', goin' to the City an' downstate. I know kids that went to the City [Science Fair], you had a big opportunity to win money. An', well, I also was thinkin' 'bout women—women, really, an' which cologne was gonna last longer. I don't wanna waste my money. I was thinkin' 'bout that girl [at church], an' I wanted to see which cologne was gonna last longer.

In neither case did the science project arise out of anything the boys had learned about in school. If truth were told, neither project was terribly scientific, except on the surface. Each child had a hypothesis, a method to test that hypothesis, and a conclusion. Moochie's hypothesis was that snap-traps would work better than glue boards. He had no rationale for this hypothesis; his choice of snap-traps was not bolstered by research. His hypothesis could as easily have read: "Glue boards will work better than snap-traps." His methodology was to put a package of glue boards and a packet of snap-traps in his brother's garage, and see which traps caught more mice. He never considered that placement of the traps in the garage might affect how many mice were caught, that once a snap-trap had been sprung or had caught a rodent, it was no longer serviceable without resetting, that some mice might escape, that there might be a finite number of mice in the garage, etc. His conclusion was that glue boards catch more mice.

Biggie's hypothesis was that one cologne would last longer than another. To develop this hypothesis, he used his own experience that colognes vary in their intensity and longevity. His methodology was to put a dab of cologne on separate pieces of cloth, ask two people to smell each, rate the intensity, then put the cloths in the closet for a day, have the same people check them, rate the smell intensity, put them back in the closet for a week, check again, and have the same people rate the smell intensity again. His conclusion was: "[Name of cologne] lasts longer."

Chapter 6: Science Explorations

He did not consider how the chemical formulae, the amount and type of essential oils (natural or synthetic) used in the colognes, the smelling ability of the sniffers, the type of cloth used, the closet temperature, or other variables might affect the experiment.

At the school level, one of the judges wrote that Moochie's project would have been greatly improved if he had pictures of the mice he caught. Another judge suggested Biggie should have looked into the reactions of water and alcohol. After the boys won at the school level, I was asked to work with them to ready their projects for the Regional Fair. We had much work to do. To their credit, both boys became totally committed to doing whatever was required, although Biggie complained at first.

Moochie's project was redesigned from the ground up. He identified six locations where he saw evidence of mice. He placed snap-traps at sites one, three, four, and six and glue boards at sites two and five. He checked the traps and counted the catch. Then, he rotated the type of traps and counted the catch again. We went to a local wildlife museum to talk to the docents about mice. We learned about rodent habits. We checked the Internet for information on mice and traps, discovered the large amount of damage they did to crops and that farmers were concerned about how to control rodents without pesticides that might harm their animals or crops. Moochie read about rodent control efforts in the city where he lives. He dragged me around to photograph mice that were caught in his traps. He wrote a paper, made a show board, and went to the Regional Fair.

He was told he would not be allowed into the fair unless he removed the pictures of the mice from his show board. Then he was told he was disqualified because he had not secured the appropriate forms for working with vertebrates.

Moochie recounted the experience:

> They said I could not kill a rat or a mouse! They said—they read it out the book: 'Only do unto the animal what the student want done unto him,' so I couldn't show anything with a rat on it even though the guy from Science-On-The-Go told me to. I felt pretty bad. That hurt me.

> That what really hurt my project, so I couldn't go on from the District to the City. But, well, it improved my interest in science, because now I know what I can do an' what I cain't do.

I asked him how it was that he was allowed to go so far with a project that did not meet the rules. He said, "Nobody understand' the requirements. Nobody told me about animal testing until I got to the regional." During the entire next year, Moochie grumbled about what he perceived as the Regional judges' unfairness, vowing to "get to the City [Fair] yet."

Biggie's project was more complex to rework. His only real interest in colognes had been to discover which one lasted longer. As far as he was concerned, he had answered that question with his first experiment, and that was all. When he was told he would have to rework the project for the Regional Science Fair, he protested. However, because he was highly competitive and wanted to win money, he agreed to go along with the program.

> I really didn't want to know 'why' until I heard that I was going to the District. 'Cause if you made it that far past the school, you probably could win at the District. I knew I needed to dig deeper than into the longevity of the cologne. So, I needed to go into the 'why.' It was something that dawned on me, to look into. I decided to look at the Internet an' this crazy little lady was runnin' around screamin': 'Honey, this is your project an' not mine, an' you're goin' to the District, not me,' an' wouldn't let me forget it neither. So I do what a man gotta do, which was—do my project.

First, Biggie had to learn chemistry. He said he did not know any chemistry, and did not want to learn chemistry because he wanted to be a judge, not a scientist. He had said, however, that he liked to read "cookin' books," so it was through cooking that Biggie became hooked on chemistry. He knew heat changed foods. He knew that different spices interacted differently to produce different flavors, and he knew that boiling could transform liquids into gas. After I pointed out he already knew a lot of chemistry, he became more willing to work through additional experiments on colognes.

He researched colognes—their history; how they were made; the amounts of alcohol, water, and essential oils in them. He talked to perfume chemists in New York by telephone and to a cosmetic company's distributor in the suburbs about colognes after working up interview questions first. We investigated smelling, and whether smelling abilities varied according to sex and age. We devised two experiments: (1) testing the intensity of the two colognes over time using an adolescent, an adult male, and an adult female; and (2) testing the intensity and amount of essential oils in each cologne through extraction.

We did all of our experimentation in the kitchen, using mostly kitchen equipment: a scale, a microwave, pots, pans, and glass jars. It did not hurt his enthusiasm when, at the Scientific Supply Company buying litmus paper and a hydrometer, we were videoed for a local television news station's snippet about "neat places to go." He wrote his paper on colognes over a two-week period. He made his show board in a five-hour marathon session during which he sang Gospel songs and complained I was a slave driver. He practiced his presentation until he had it letter-perfect. He won at the Regional Fair and became the first student in his school's history to go to the City Science Fair.

Biggie's regional win meant he had to rework his show board, rewrite his paper, and add an experiment. He said:

> So with the Internet research, I learned about the different kindsa formulas, like essential oils an' water an' alcohol. The second experiment got me through the district, an' got me to the City [Fair]. It did excite me an' make me want to know more. It did, an' it didn't. 'Cause I did want to go to the City, but I didn't want to do all the hard work, like typing, talking, chart making, doin' interviews, making a journal, all other sorts of things that they wanted you to do. 'Cause I wanted to be lazy. I wanted somebody to do that for me. But, I had to do that myself because I wanted to win. It excited me 'cause I wouldn't have to do all my classroom work, but I knew I'd have to do all my homework still, even though I got out of classroom work.

For the third experiment, we decided to test the amount of water and alcohol in the colognes' formulae through distillation to see whether there were a difference and if that difference affected longevity of smell. Biggie found out the evaporation rate of alcohol and water, the temperatures at which they boil, and hypothesized that the alcohol would boil off quicker. We were back in the kitchen to "cook" the colognes. We set up two pans of water, put a weighed and measured amount of cologne in a sealed jar connected by a glass tube to another sealed jar, and boiled away. The seal was not tight; some alcohol escaped and the vapor ignited with a brilliant blue flash. We had to redo everything and learned firsthand about the volatility of alcohol.

Biggie recounted:

> I got excited about the cologne itself—the different material, like the fire we had, goin' out to do interviews, finding out what was in the cologne, figuring out the formulas. The interview, it was fun—the going to places, it was fun 'cause I got on TV—the eating part was fun—the Internet an' the library—It wasn't nothin' I couldn't handle. It seem easy once I got goin'.

We also decided to test the pH of the essential oils to see if there were differences in their acidity. We did not realize until we found a difference in the pH before and after boiling that heat might affect acidity and, hence, the smell and longevity of the cologne. The kitchen mishap figured largely in Biggie's presentation of his experiment at the City Science Fair. He received a savings bond and an award from a local shampoo manufacturer, plus an invitation to tour their plant and meet some of their scientists. He returned to his school in triumph, where he was dubbed the "Big Man on Campus" or "Biggie."

The head chemist at the shampoo company told me she had been impressed with his rendition of the fire and what he said he had learned from his experiments. When we toured the plant in June, we stopped in the gas chromatography lab. Biggie, using his best "market " English and the concepts and vocabulary he had learned while developing his science project, asked, "Do you have to be concerned with the volatility of a solution when you put it in for analysis?" When we

Chapter 6: Science Explorations

talked to the chemist who uses liquid chromatography to identify substances, he asked, "Does putting a solution in here affect the pH?"

Biggie discussed his experience at the fair.

> As you know, I went on from the District [Regional] Fair to the City Fair; but the District Fair, it seemed kinda, you know, easy, because the judges was like, kinda easy, an' people was bein' nice to me, an' I had more help at the school than I ever had before, an' that what made me get farther. 'Help' mean like, I had people to guide me. I still help myself, first. Then, I ask for other help.
>
> At the City Fair, I was kinda nervous. It was a great experience! I learn how to do different projects an' increase my project even better, an' learn which is the things that interest the people most that was the judges. The people who won were like, high school kids.
>
> I still got $100 savings bond due to my project, an' it was a great project! A great deal of it was experiments, an' a little part of it was an accident that was a fire that I learned about volatility from.
>
> It made me want to pursue science. Sure did, sure did, 'cause I love science, but science is not what I'm going to major in. But anything that give you a scholarship or a little grant or somethin', I'm all for it. It interested me enough so I will continue to look into chemistry an' all that.

Biggie had support from the teachers and administrators at his school once he had been selected to go to the City Fair. He said:

> "[My teacher], she bought me new clothes, took me out, an' talked to me. She talked to me 'bout all sorts of things. 'Give it your best. Be yourself an' don't get nervous,' an' that's about it. An' [the assistant principal], she got my samples together an' my board, an' made sure I had my materials, an' I thank her for that, an' I got enthusiasm from the teachers. I sum it up as—it was a great experience! I did my best, an' I got a savings bond, an' I *will* be seeing them again next year! They *will* see me next year!

Tatiana, Kay, and Ceana finally figured out their projects two weeks before the Classroom Science Fair in January 1997. Tatiana decided to measure which soap lasted the longest in her household of two adults and four children. She used the Internet to research soap ingredients but measured the bars' lengths and widths after every family member finished showering, instead of weighing and calculating the percentage of soap used. Ceana chose to look at molds to see if those on food were the same as on flower bulbs. She tracked down some moldy cheese and asked her mother, who worked in the school health clinic, to hold it while she was at gym class. A pre-kindergartner came in for treatment, saw the cheese, and ate it. Ceana did not complete her project.

Kay told me she had real trouble deciding on her project and was unhappy with the experiment on which she finally settled. "My science project is really stupid. It's 'What kind of toothpaste cleans the teeth best?'" She added she picked the topic at the last minute because she really "did not know how to set up our science project. I want someone to show us how to set up our science project. I'd like to have a book, but the boys took all the ones [in the classroom]."

Jasmine had wanted to do "somethin' with mealworms," but she never got the mealworms. She settled for having her classmates try to identify Kool-Aid® flavors while blindfolded, and then tabulating the results. She was not satisfied with the project but figured it had been easy to do. It also meant she had completed the assignment to develop and test a hypothesis and received a grade for the semester in science.

For her science project in November 1997, she returned to mealworms. This time, the science teacher at Jasmine's new school provided the bugs. Jasmine explored whether the amount of light made a difference in how fast mealworms turn into beetles. She researched mealworms on the Internet, wrote a proposal based on what she had read about past mealworm research, drew up a hypothesis, and kept a daily log tracking the life-stage progress of her mealworms. I received weekly reports on how many mealworms in the opaque container versus those in the see-through container had died, how many had turned into larvae, and how many had become beetles. Jasmine presented her project at her school fair but did

Chapter 6: Science Explorations
167

not win. Her non-win did not bother her very much. She had done some research with mealworms, found out something about them, and that was good enough.

I asked her to explain why she was so interested in mealworms. She shrugged and said that she just wanted to see how they turned into beetles from worms. She added that the previous year she had no idea where to get mealworms or how much they cost. When she learned one hundred worms were available from almost any pet store at $1.50, she was furious that she had not pursued her mealworm project earlier. She said, "Nobody tol' me." However, it should also be noted that she never asked.

I queried the boys about how they would design science lessons in their school if they had the opportunity. Moochie had some ideas for improvement.

> Well, I'd get better equipment, all the things that we need, an' I'd fix up a science lab, all with sinks, an' I'd have each kid do an experiment they want or pick out they science project, an' I'd help them get their stuff, an' spend a good amount of time helpin' them research what they like or see about previous science projects, brain-storm, an' come up with a project.

Biggie responded:

> If I'd be settin' it up, I'd have this table back there, an' goggles. They havin' they gloves, an' we'd dissect somethin', or we'd look at slides, or be fixin' things, or do chemistry. I'd have a separate time to do this for science projects.

The common thread that ran through many of the children's comments about science at their school was that their lessons were from textbooks. This is not unusual, even at the college and graduate level, as Kuhn (1977, 228) has pointed out.

> Let me briefly try to epitomize the nature of education in the natural sciences. . . . The single most striking feature of this education is that, to an extent totally unknown in other creative fields, it is conducted entirely through textbooks.

Dewey (1938/1963, 19) wrote that ideally, in democratic, progressive schools, learning shifts away from "texts and teachers, [to] learning through experience." Yet, can a school with limited resources, such as the one the children attended, really afford to buy the kinds of supplies necessary to teach science through different hands-on laboratory experiences? I wonder whether there is ever a point at which technology, such as the videos the children watched during their science classes, must or should substitute for live instruction? Is "something better than nothing," especially if the teacher feels insecure about her own knowledge of a subject?

Will those students, like Moochie and Terrell, who are truly fascinated with science, pursue their interests in spite of the way the subject matter was taught in their school? Will students who might have been interested in learning about science, like Kay, Jasmine, and Tatiana, be discouraged from exploring their interests because they receive a certain kind of instruction in their school or because no one has guided them or helped them find the right materials? Or will these students channel their interests into something else because hidden messages or social norms discourage them?

Moochie, Terrell, and Ken all claimed they want to be scientists when they grow up. Ken's interests seemed to be centered on "going up on the tracks" and visiting pet stores to look at animals. He never completed a single required science project and reportedly received poor grades in science on his report card.

Terrell's project, replicated from a book on science projects, was on plants and the atmosphere. He was one of the classroom winners in 1997, but did not win in the School Science Fair. He tried again the next year (1998), also using a plant and a book experiment, with the same results.

Moochie's negative experience with the Regional Science Fair while a seventh grader spurred him to try harder to develop a good project that would take him to different fairs, and to make sure his experiment conformed to the rules. He explained: "What compelled me to start really tryin' this year was really that I saw my associate, Biggie, went to the City [fair], an' I want to go." He began working on his science project in October 1997, well in advance of when the teacher announced that the Science Fair was coming up.

His eighth-grade project was to test whether lichen from highly polluted areas had different pH, nitrite, nitrate, lead, and ammonia levels than lichen from less polluted areas. He identified lichen species we collected through their chemical signatures. Because the school had no chemical supplies, we substituted acetone for paraphenylenediamine, Liquid-Plumr® for potassium hydroxide, and bleach for calcium hypochlorite. We used an aquarium water testing kit to check for nitrate, nitrite, and ammonia levels and an acid rain test kit to check for lead, oil, and pH. It was really nothing more than kitchen chemistry. He won in his classroom, and tied with Biggie for first place at the School Fair.

Biggie never has had a driving desire to be a scientist. However, his win at the School Science Fair and the realization that he needed to improve his project to win at the regional level, spurred him to delve into chemistry and look for reasons why some colognes lasted longer than others. The possibility of winning money and getting a job more easily because his science fair wins could be put on his resume were other motivating factors for Biggie.

> Next year, 'cause of what I see this year, I'm gonna do environment or computer skills. The reason I want to do that is to both make money an' learn, even though I don't wanna be a scientist. I told the people [at the City Science Fair] I didn't really want to be a scientist; I really wanted to go to law school, an' they said, 'Oh, that's great, but you know you could be a scientist.'
>
> I see an application for this, 'cause I see how to go back an' do it again an' make the biggest money in town. So, money's where it's at. Plus, I get a job quicker 'cause it [the City Science Fair] be on my file.

In keeping with this plan to impress the Science Fair judges with an environmental project, Biggie's eighth-grade project involved mapping lichen distribution in the city and suburbs, correlating the presence and amount of coverage with the degree of air pollution, sulfur dioxide, particulate matter, and building and road construction. He said that as a result of his projects, he saw connections between science and other useful skills that he had not seen before. He explained, "I can get more readin' ability by readin' science. An' you can carry on [research techniques] what you learn through high school an' make the straight A's."

Biggie's comments were in keeping with what Dewey (1979/1985, 163) said happened when children were encouraged to connect their learnings.

> While the little child takes only a near view of things, as he grows in experience he becomes capable of extending his range, and seeing an act, or a thing, or a fact not by itself, but part of a larger whole. If this whole belongs to him, if it is a mode of his own movement, then the thing or act which it includes gains interest too.

Biggie's interest in becoming a judge was recent. When he was in sixth grade, as part of the problem-based service learning program that operated only for that year at his school, Biggie met a female lawyer. He recounted the story.

> She was the kinda lawyer I want to model myself after. She had an office downtown. She say you have to have your own bachelor's degree, an' you couldn't do no crimes, you couldn't have no long record, an' [you needed to go to] law school.

> She told me I was gonna be a lawyer 'cause of the questions I ask her, like, could the students be held accountable for drugs, an' where [do] we put the students who use drugs, like do we kick 'em out the school, expel them, or do we put them in a special program? An' do they have a valid reason to search my locker? Is it valid for them to test a person for drugs without a reason?

> I want to be a successful young man. I want to achieve my goals to become a lawyer an' then to become a judge, 'cause I don't like the way people is treatin' our government system, an' I want to get rid of crime—like gangs, for instance, drugs, killin'. I want to stop all that.

None the less, until that future time, whenever the possibility of winning some money with a good science project presented itself, he would try for it.

Biggie's and Moochie's reasons for pursuing science were polar opposites. Moochie wants to become a scientist more than anything else in the world and relates everything he does and learns to science. He learned to make pottery at the local Boys and Girls Club and became interested in the different minerals that can

Chapter 6: Science Explorations

be used to produce the various color glazes. He was astonished to read that lichen were sometimes used as essential oils in perfumes, and to dye wool, and that different species of lichen make different color dyes. He thinks he might like to try dying things with lichen sometime. Biggie, on the other hand, wants to be a judge but sees science as a necessary part of his overall education, as well as an opportunity to win money. Would Biggie's involvement with science be a case of what Dewey (1979/1985, 164, 167–68) called "transferred interest"?

The boys' stories illustrate Dewey's (1949/1991, 351) point that the value placed on an object (or endeavor) can be very different depending on the person doing the evaluating. The stories also illustrate how "shopping" affects interests and choices. Moochie's family has always been supportive of his interest in science. They have legitimized it, as Holt (1972/1995, 80–82) explained is so necessary to encourage learning, by purchasing him a microscope, allowing him to mix chemicals in their bathtub, taking him fishing, permitting him to bring home the animals he catches, and allowing him to have a room full of pets and bugs. His kind of science shopping is producing an ensemble.

Biggie happened to meet a woman lawyer who flattered him by saying he could become a lawyer. Until he met her, he had no interest in becoming a lawyer and, in fact, still only knows the barest details about how to become a lawyer or how lawyers can specialize in different areas of the law. He wants to be a judge and change the world but has no idea what he would have to do to become elected. He has not followed up on his interest in law to the degree that Moochie has pursued his interest in science, although he claimed to have read a book about lawyers, and I know he tried to read the Law School Aptitude Test (LSAT) review booklet. Does his somewhat superficial interest in law and lawyers mean he really is not interested in becoming a lawyer? Does it mean that his interest is a passing one? Or does it mean that, for the moment, entertaining the idea about going to law school and dreaming of being a judge is enough, again as Holt

(1972/1995, 82) suggested? At the moment, what Biggie is doing most closely resembles window shopping.

Although the girls had varied amounts of enthusiasm for science and their science projects, and their reasons for abandoning their projects or picking projects at the last minute were different, all of their comments returned to the same point: none of them wanted to be a scientist when she grew up. As far as they were concerned, shopping at the "science store" was not something they particularly wished to do. They would, and did, use the slightest excuse not to participate. For most of the girls, if they shopped the science store at all, it would be under protest and with a very desultory approach.

I believe it would be stretching my data to say that the school had a hidden curriculum aimed at discouraging girls from pursuing or developing interests in science. Instead, what discouragement I noted might actually have come from home and from other girls, much as McRobbie (1978, cited in Apple 1995, 101) found. Any hidden message that discouraged science and science research in the school was given to boys and girls alike.

I am uncomfortable with the conclusions I can draw from my data. One set of conclusions is that the girls, as a group, were passive when it comes to science and, by extension, perhaps with other subjects. It is not that they were totally uninterested in science, believed that understanding scientific principles was unimportant, or saw no applications for science in their lives. Rather, it was that many of them were apparently waiting for someone to direct them or, failing direction, to assign them a project or give them a book so they could "do" science.

Their attitude might have been fostered, in part, by the manner in which many academic subjects were taught in their school, with strong boundaries between and with top-down, textbook instruction, the very opposite approach to learning that Dewey (1896/1972, 245–46, and 1901/1991, 218–23) advocated. Or perhaps since they were told their science grade depended on having a science project, it was easier to go through the motions of doing a science project in order

Chapter 6: Science Explorations

to get a grade than to push themselves to think of something they really might like to have investigated. It was undeniably easier to claim an inability to come up with a science project because the boys took the books, as Kay complained, than to find other books at the library or simply think about things that interested them that then could be turned into a project.

Dewey (1898/1972, 265) talked about this very phenomenon.

> How many teachers of science will tell you, for example, that when their students are instructed to find out something about an object, their first demand is for a book in which they can read about it; their first reaction, one of helplessness . . . it seems so much simpler to occupy the mind with what someone else has said about these things.

Kay said that she wished she could "bring my knowledge of cookin' [and] measurin' ingredients to school for math an' nutrition." Yet, she never gave any indication that she thought about bringing that knowledge to bear on a science project or ever tried to incorporate what she knew with what interested her in terms of science. In addition, her comments about doctors needing to know science so they would not blow up the hospital suggested a real lack of understanding about the connections between science and medicine.

I asked Kay about this and, when she answered, she said not a word about liking science as being part of her decision to be a doctor. "I used to think all doctors was the same, 'til I met a pediatrician at [the hospital clinic]. Now, I wanna be a general pediatrician. I like babies." Will this liking of babies be enough to carry her interest in pediatrics "beyond itself," as Dewey (1979/1985, 163) thought was crucial, to develop the next levels of interest in medicine as science and as a career?

Some of the girls and I went to the Academy of Science to get project ideas. Since it was Water Day, they were able to explore how water moves sand depending on landform and the water's speed and flow. Kay looked for microscopic organisms in pond water while the other girls hovered over her shoulder, pointing to the screen where the critters were displayed. The girls used computers to identify various waterfowl and fish. They watched while a docent filleted a bass. They examined and touched its scales, liver, and other organs.

Tatiana asked for, and received, a fish eye lens so she could do a project on that. She brought the lens to school to examine, but since the school's microscope was mysteriously missing that day, she took it home again. Soon she reported, "My mama made me throw it out 'cause it be stinkin' up her 'frigerator."

She asked if I could get her a fish skeleton, instead. I dutifully ordered catfish at a restaurant, took the skeleton home, and cleaned it. We examined its morphology, flexibility, and the translucency of the bones and looked up the reasons why fish bones were constructed the way they were. I suggested she might consider using different kinds of bones to test Archimedes's principle of buoyancy for her project, primarily because I thought it a good experiment that built on her expressed interest in fish bones, as well as one that could be done within the time span her teacher had allotted for the identification and development of a science project. (See Simmons 1996, 468–69, for a summary of Archimedes's *On Floating Bodies*). Instead, Tatiana chose to work with Twitty on a totally different science project. When I asked about the switch, Tatiana explained, "'Cause [name of a teacher] say my project would take too long."

A second conclusion I can draw with respect to the girls is that, although they have never actually said so, they saw science as a male thing or, at least, not a "typical" female thing. They have expressed a desire to incorporate their pre-existing knowledge with what they learn in school but indicated the setup of their school day and the lessons' structures did not permit this. Unlike the boys, the girls never mentioned asking their mentors for help with science. Whether this was because science was not the paramount interest of the moment for the girls, because their mentors never broached the subject, or for some other reason, I cannot say. Many times, in mixed company, when the topic was science, dissection, bugs, worms, or whatever, the girls—even Kay—showed they had already learned the "socially correct" (in their school only?) way for girls to respond:

"Ooh, icky!" Yet, when we were at the Academy of Science, touching fish and groping around in their guts, none of them said anything remotely like that.

Was this because we were all females? Or might it have been because the girls' acknowledged leader, Tatiana, became interested in fish, and her interest legitimized that of the others as has been suggested in the preceding chapter? Might this contradictory behavior be explained using Chodorow's (1978) model that the gender construction processes, in school and in the home, render girls socially and politically subordinate to boys in public spheres?

A third conclusion I can draw about the girls is that they feel no connection with science assignments, as they felt little connection with any of their assignments. The children's comments indicated that they believed that science was only stressed as being necessary to learn in order to pass the standardized tests in seventh grade. Consequently, it may well be that some of the girls have compartmentalized science, like they did with reading, into the category of activities that were necessary to do only for standardized tests. I wonder if the girls thought that science was something they need learn only in order to do well within a school context.

At the School Science Fair, several of the children from every grade in the school had show boards with misspellings, incorrect grammar, and even mixed-up conclusions. Were such errors indicative of a lack of attention to detail? In addition, might they not have also signified that perhaps the children and their teachers were simply going through the motions?

There is justification for separating the boys' stories from the girls' stories with regard to science. The teachers treated the boys and girls alike in terms of their science education. The children got the best that their teachers could give. The children's reactions, however, were very different; and, at least in the cases I documented, those differences fell along clear gender lines. But to say that gender-related, social factors were somehow solely responsible for the girls' lack of interest in science would be too simplistic and, more than likely, incorrect. Many of the boys had the same overt reactions to science as the girls. Science, for these children when they are in school, was perceived to be an individual pursuit. Learning about science, completing a science project, and winning a science fair depended on individual motivations, opportunities, and happenstance more than on school-based instruction, facilitation, and support. The girls might have had to work through the additional layer of societal or familial attitudes toward science in order to learn about the subject. The school's teaching of science as a separate, isolated subject might have reinforced, and have been the deciding factor in, the girls' decisions to become uninvolved.

Biggie's and Moochie's stories clearly showed the importance of positive reinforcement as they shopped in the "science store." The point is not that the encouragement led them to do the work but that they received encouragement that helped them to produce quality work that was competitive with similarly aged students as assessed by the objective standards of science fair judges. This distinction brings to light one of the points I will return to when discussing the children's scores on standardized tests: With a little help, encouragement, and direction, these children can do far better than the statistics for their school imply they should be able to do and have been doing.

The seventh graders with whom I spoke perceived science as another contested area (site). The students said they were unhappy about the way in which science was being taught or not taught in their classes. They adopted different strategies in response to what they perceived as an institutional failure to respond to their desires to learn science and to help them connect it to what they already knew and would like to learn. Some of the students shopped outside of school for the science they wanted, for what interested them and what they believed they would need in the future. Depending on their outside support, sources, and resourcefulness, some were more successful than others. Some students, unfortunately, no longer bothered to shop at all.

CHAPTER 7

STANDARDIZED TESTS

The students took five different standardized tests each year: The Illinois Goal Assessment Program test (IGAP), the Iowa Tests of Basic Skills (ITBS), the Stanford Diagnostic test, and both parts of the Gates-MacGinitie test battery. They scored equally as poorly on all the tests. Their low scores in reading and mathematics (i.e., fewer than 15 percent of the student body performed at or above national norms in both subject areas) were one of the reasons that the school had been placed on academic probation and the state's Watch List.

According to Kay, the students learned about the school's troubles when "[Name of administrator] called everybody together an' explain it. She say that the school could get closed, the principal could get fired, an' the kids might not pass into the next grades, so everybody had to get they Iowa tests up."

Some of the reasons that were offered as explanations for the students' poor showing on standardized tests included the following comments made by administrators, parents, and teachers, with occasional corroboration by the students:

- Perhaps the emphasis on scores was too stressful for the children, and they just "shut down."
- Maybe the children's former teachers were somehow at fault.

- Maybe the children were at fault because they did not take the tests seriously.
- There were no consequences for not passing the tests.
- The children were disengaged or resistant to learning.
- The students did not have the skills to pass.
- Possibly, some of the children were learning disabled but had not been identified as such.
- Maybe the children's social environments placed added stress and distractions on them.
- The teachers have tried, and the children have tried, but maybe the parents have not done anything additional to help the children.
- Maybe the parents were not informed about how to help or shown what to do to help.
- Maybe the teachers were not teaching.

The school's formal curriculum has always been aligned with the city and state goals and academic standards. The teachers said they have embedded the skills the children should master and the content on which they will be tested into the formal curriculum. The school restructured itself along a school-within-a-school model, and then also adopted the "accelerated school" philosophy (Levin 1994) to personalize and facilitate the children's learning process. Some of the teachers implemented Project Read®, to encourage the children to read and write more. (See Enfield and Greene 1996 for information about this reading program designed to make the abstract concrete through direct teaching of concepts and skills using multisensory techniques). The teachers used their locally developed version of an Afro-centric curriculum to foster pride, self-esteem, and knowledge of the students' roots. The principal hired a local university as an external partner to work with the teachers on strategies for improving instruction and the children's standardized test scores. The school's reputation, according to one of its administrators, was that of a "progressive" institution. The principal said, "Good things are happening here," and she was right. Everyone was trying his or her best for the children, although much of what they did appeared to be reactive, shaped and constrained by being on academic probation and the Watch List.

The administration and the teachers were stymied and frustrated by the students' low test scores. The children said they were tired of taking tests and weary of worrying about their scores. They were baffled about how to bring them up to the passing level. Many of the children worked with adults they called mentors on their academics, went to the free tutoring service at a local church on Saturdays, attended the after-school reading program four days each week, and went to the library to read. They practiced taking standardized tests during class and the after-school program, and then they practiced taking more standardized tests during school breaks. They still did poorly on standardized tests.

One mother, who said she worked with her son on his reading and comprehension every evening, told me:

> He's so concerned. He tells me his comprehension is low. I try to show him how to break down the sentences, learn the vocabulary, but he's so worried he won't pass. They're [the children] losing six days each year, at least, to the tests. They [the teachers] aren't teaching, just [focusing on] how to take the tests.
>
> It's like a building—you put the bricks up, the foundations, and you skip a few, you miss a row, and the building is wobbly and it crumbles. These children don't have the foundations, and you can't just open up their heads at this late date and pour it all in. It's like when you overfeed a baby, it throws up. They [the students] can't take it in all at once. They get headaches, and the stress is too much. The building is crumbling, and they [the teachers] should have taken care of it years ago!

Another complained that some of the school's emphasis on uniforms was misplaced since efforts should have been directed toward getting the school off probation.

> The school is under sweat with this probation, and I don't understand why they send seven or eight kids home because they're out of uniform. If the problem—the number one thing—is probation, why they so hung up on uniforms?

What the one parent mentioned about the emphasis on test taking and the time spent on them has been said before. The loss of six days of instruction to testing that she noted was exactly the amount of time Johnston (1992) documented for upper elementary students elsewhere in the nation. Her concerns over the tests—the prominent position that the tests have been allowed to take in shaping the pace and types of instruction; the content of the formal curriculum; student, school, and teacher assessment; and the school's emphasis on teaching test-taking skills—were no different than other teachers, principals, and parents have expressed elsewhere (Bizar 1997, 3).

A review of the seventh graders' individual standardized test scores going back to 1990 revealed that, in first grade, five students were reading at or above national norms as measured by the Iowa Tests of Basic Skills. By second grade, there were four. By third grade, the number had slipped to two. The number jumped to three in fourth and fifth grades, then fell back to two in the sixth and seventh grades. Two of the children in the seventh grade consistently scored at or above national norm levels on the standardized reading tests. For the rest of the students, they rarely and erratically achieved national norm levels. These seventh-grade students had raised their reading levels an average of nine months every academic year for the past three years, but, of course, this still left most of them reading below "grade level."

The breakdown of the seventh-grade children's 1997 performance on the IGAP test, which specifically assessed their performance in social science and science, showed that in no category except basic concepts in social science did the class average meet or exceed the state average. Their ITBS scores from 1997 showed an average reading grade of sixth grade eighth month, with a class range from third grade third month to eighth grade ninth month. The Gates-MacGinitie test, taken at the start of the 1997–98 school year, showed the class reading average to be fifth grade eighth month and the class comprehension average to be fifth grade third month. The reading scores ranged from third grade fourth month to ninth grade second month, and the comprehension scores ranged from third grade second month to tenth grade fifth month.

I was asked to look into why the children scored so low on these kinds of standardized tests. I jumped at the opportunity. I knew from my experiences with many of the seventh graders at museums, from interacting with them in teaching-learning settings, and from dealings with them in and out of school, that they operated on a much higher day-to-day level in terms of vocabulary, comprehension, and conceptualization than their standardized reading and comprehension test scores suggested. The disparity between what I perceived as the children's functional level and their "true" operating level according to national standards and norms made me curious about the reasons they scored so low. I hoped I could uncover patterns to the children's answers on standardized tests that might explain why there was such a huge discrepancy.

The principal provided me with statistics concerning every child in the school. The statistics recorded individual performances on the different standardized tests from the time each child had entered the school and been tested.

Although I focused on the seventh graders' scores, I charted every set of scores for every child in every class in the entire school. I broke down the test scores, individual by individual, by year and by class, and compared them to class, district, and state averages and to national norms by category of tested area.

I asked the entire group of seventh graders what they did when they took the standardized tests. Their replies fell into three main categories: (1) taking the tests seriously and trying to answer the questions as best they could; (2) randomly filling in the "bubbles" because of test anxiety; and (3) holding a general *laissez-faire* attitude toward tests because there were (*a*) no discernable consequences for poor or mediocre performances and (*b*) no rewards for good or improved scores either at school or at home. Some children indicated that their parents did not understand the reporting system. For example, one student told me his reading score, which according to the ITBS was fifth grade third month, was a "53, an' that pretty good." I asked him why he thought that was a good score. He replied his mother had told him it [the score] was "over 50 percent." The children's answers gave me an initial feel for the attitudes and understandings that they, and perhaps their parents, held toward and about standardized tests.

As part of my research, I interviewed a subgroup of ten seventh graders whose standardized test scores mimicked their class curve for the ITBS and Stanford tests. I asked these children, "Why do you think you should be coming to school?" None of them said they were required by law to be there. A single student alluded to the law when he claimed, "I'd rather be at home, lyin' 'round, watchin' TV, but my mama won't let me. She say I gotta come to school." All the others said they come to school to "learn" and "get an education." I was amazed at the unanimity of their responses, since I had heard so many complaints about the students' "disengagement" with school and school subjects.

There could be three reasons underlying this unanimity, two of which the children articulated themselves. The first possible reason, although never voiced by the children, might have been that they gave the answer they thought I wanted and expected to hear. (See Anyon 1980, for a discussion of how pedagogy in lower class and working-class schools trains children to give expected, stock answers and to follow the rules).

The second reason might well have been that they (and possibly their parents) distinguished between the type of learning that they believed was supposed to occur in a school setting and the kind of learning they did everywhere else. Kay said she expected to get "useful learnin'" in school. Biggie said that he learned "the how-to's an' the what-for's in school."

The third reason might well have been that the children had bought into the credentialing aspects of modern society. In plain language, the sequence of events they foresaw for themselves was an uninterrupted series of passings. After they passed elementary school, they would go to high school. After they graduated from high school, they would go to college. All the students advised that they wanted to go to college, graduate, and get a good job. When I asked the teacher who called the children "disengaged" why she thought the children even bothered to come to school, she said, "School's better than staying home."

Regardless of their performance levels, all the children professed to hold a positive attitude toward the vague, abstract category they called education. Kay said, "The reason I'm goin' to school is to get an education to do somethin', an' to be a better person, both." Kay's comments, corroborated by the other children, were in keeping with Mickelson's (1990) and Ogbu's (1978) findings, with Apple and Zenk's (1996, 86–87) data, and also with MacLeod's (1987) thesis that African-Americans have bought into the "achievement philosophy." Part of the students' professed faith in education might have sprung from hearing their parents talk about their own pasts and their aspirations for their children's futures. I found a widespread conviction among the parents of the children I studied that things were already better for their children than they had been for them, and a hope that things would be even better for them in the future. Some of the mothers' comments follow:

"I'm doing OK [economically], but my kids will do better because they will go to college."

"It's different now than when I was growing up. They [the children] have more opportunities now."

"I always tell him, 'You can be anything you want to be. You got to study hard and learn. It's gonna be some rough times, and it's gonna be some good times, but you got to keep on going.'"

Although the parents wanted their children to succeed academically and believed that the school was the place the children should learn their academics, not very many of those with whom I spoke seemed overtly upset about the school's probationary status or transferred their children to schools that were not on probation. I only heard one parent discuss anything about the school with reference to probation. She said, "The school is under sweat with this probation. To me, the parents are not really involved in it. The proper information is not getting out to the parents." One mother who transferred her daughter to a different school did so not because of the school's probationary status but because the child was having interpersonal relationship problems with one of the teachers. That student's new school was also on academic probation.

In the interviews with the ten children, I also asked them questions relating to their test-taking strategies. I wanted to (1) discover what approaches the children used, (2) see whether there were differences in their approaches, (3) identify the types of questions with which they were having trouble, and (4) find the rationale they used to answer the questions.

To do this, I administered old (1979) practice standardized tests by different publishers that I unearthed in the school counselor's cabinet to these students. Test 1 was for seventh graders, and test 2 was for levels nine through fourteen. Although in my opinion these particular test versions were, by and large, poorly written and ambiguous, they did contain what can be termed "questions that test fundamental, general knowledge," reading in specific curricular areas for content or to test inference abilities, and vocabulary words. I hypothesized that the children would all struggle to answer the poorly written questions, but would answer the fundamental knowledge questions easily and correctly. Their scores on the standardized reading tests led me to expect a wide range of answers in the vocabulary and inference sections of the tests I was about to administer. What I discovered was nowhere near what I had anticipated!

I administered the old tests under circumstances similar to that which the children would have experienced in an actual test situation. On these simulated tests, I allowed the children thirty minutes for each test. I figured that they could work on both tests during the one-hour period in which I had all ten of them out of their classroom.

I asked that they make a mark on the sheet at the point they had reached when I announced "Two minutes." They were instructed to do whatever they normally did when alerted that two minutes remained. I also permitted them to mark their answers on the sheets. The children had indicated that marking the wrong "bubble" was a common occurrence for them during tests where they were not permitted to mark the booklets and had to use a separate sheet for their answers.

While they were taking each test, I observed and took notes on their test reading—both the speed at which they read and the methods they used to read and answer the questions. Later, I asked each child, individually and in private, about his or her answers. My experience with the children had shown they did not respond as well to my questions when their answers were being taped, so I wrote their responses verbatim. The children's replies to what they did and how they reasoned through to the answers they chose were varied.

I asked these students to assess which test, 1 or 2, had been easier and why. Nine out of the ten children I asked said they found Test 1 easier. Their reasons centered on the fact that the paragraphs were "shorter an' less borin'." The questions were, therefore, perceived to be easier to answer.

Terrell claimed, "[Test 2] is easier. The readin' is interestin', an' they made me answer more questions more quicker. I read the story so good, so when the questions came, I answered them real quick."

Moochie disagreed. "[Test 1 is easier] because it got the answers right there, you just got to find 'em. Plus, it's more quicker. You don't got to go through a whole paragraph just to find the answer."

"[Test 1] is easier," Wynona maintained, "'cause on the Iowa you have lesser questions an' the story wasn't long, so you won't have to read all the words in the paragraph."

Kay echoed this sentiment. "[Test 1] is easiest 'cause they don't got paragraphs to read an' stuff. It get borin' [reading paragraphs]."

Biggie combined his reply to which test he believed was easier with an explanation of his test-taking strategy.

> [Test 1]'s easier, 'cause we didn't have to read a lot; 'cause your eyes tend to hurt when you takin' a test, an' you get nervous, an' you can't hold all the information you take. That's why a lot of us forget when you—we read.
>
> For myself, I read well, but I don't understand what I read a lot of the time. It's like when I read the passage an' they ask, 'What happen then?', I can't really go back into the passage, an' I don't really get a chance to review, an' that's why I don't really get most of my answers right.
>
> I read the questions, an' then I read the passage. I really don't read the whole passage; I skim, an' that's how come I go for to look at the questions, an' I can answer them.

Next, I asked them what they had done when they were taking these sample tests, and I also observed what they actually did while taking them. The children related they have been told by their teachers to read the questions and answers before reading the passage or poem. They have been advised to answer the questions on the test to the best of their abilities until they are told "Two minutes," then to randomly fill in as many of the remaining ovals as they can.

Jasmine claimed:

> I read the paragraph out loud in my brain—the short story, the little passage—an' then I answer the questions. I go back to the paragraph when I don't understand the questions, to try to find clues. Like, it say a question, so I scan it [the passage] an' get the answer.

Yet, during the test I administered, I noted Jasmine read each passage by placing her pen under a word and sometimes dotting or underlining it with her pen. Later, when we talked, she said she dotted and underlined when she came to a word she did not know or words she thought were important. She said she wished she had a piece of paper to jot those words down to look up later, but in real test situations, they are not allowed to have paper out. I never observed her moving her eyes back and forth between the passage and the questions during the practice tests.

Moochie said, "I reads the questions first an' then the paragraph, so's I know what I'm lookin' for, like [he reads the question]—number 1 [reads answer] is not right. Number 2? No. Number 3? Number 4? Well, I kinda forgot, an' looked up in the paragraph an' saw it."

During the test, he did not shift his eyes between questions and the passage at all. He proceeded to read the paragraph and answer the questions in order. Wynona, Waldo, and Lemar said essentially the same thing as Moochie and were all observed using the same reading-answering strategy as he.

Kay maintained, "First I read the answers an' then I read the story. I look for the words that in the answers, an' I find 'em in the paragraph, an' then I know which the right answer."

"What if the word isn't in the paragraph?" I asked.

She replied, "I guess."

I observed Kay reading the story first and then answering the questions. By her own admission, Kay answered many test questions with guesses.

Terrell claimed:

> First I look at what kind of questions they gonna ask me. I scan through the questions, an' then I scan through the readin'. If it borin', you scan through the readin' an' pick out the important points. I knows what's important by lookin' at the questions.
>
> If not borin', as I'm scannin' through it an' I see it interestin', then I read it carefully, like the [snake] story. I see [the word *snake*] an' I started readin'. At first I thought it wasn't true 'bout a snake crushin' a crocodile, an' after I saw how big it [this particular kind of snake] was at the museum—no, at [name of the university where he had seen a dried snake skin], I know it was true.
>
> I answer the questions by first, I read the passage, an' then I scan through the answers, an' then I begin to look for them in the paragraph, an' then answer it.

During the test, I noted that Terrell began reading the paragraph and then proceeded to answer the questions.

Art said, "First I read the paragraph, then I read the questions an' look at the answers, an' then back at the story, an' reread the sentences over. I knew what sentences to reread, like in Question 1, because they said something about a [word that was in the paragraph]."

During the test, Art was not observed going between the paragraph and questions, except in a single instance involving a poem and its related questions. When he came to the poem, he read the poem before looking at the questions; then he reread the poem, working his way through the questions in that fashion. He admitted, when we reached the discussion of the poem, its related questions, and his answers, that he had had problems with the poem and its related questions.

Ed, whose reading and comprehension scores were consistently the highest in the class, reported: "I read the questions an' answers first, an' then the paragraph, an' then the questions an' answers." This was the exact method I observed him using during the simulated tests.

I asked the children what they normally did on tests when alerted that time was running out.

Jasmine related, "At 'Two minutes,' I speed through. I can't go back an' check, an' then comes 'One minute' an' I can't go back. But some teachers say, 'Speed through an' you might get two out of five correct.'"

"When the 'Two minutes' warning come," Moochie said, "I try to go a little bit faster, start goin' faster, an' start marking anything on some of 'em, but some of 'em I read. Well, I kind of like, mark one, read one, mark one, read one."

I asked him who taught him this strategy, he said: "I did. Well, actually, my mama. She said if I hear 'Time's up,' go down [the page] an' mark something. I would of got farther [on the practice Iowa test] but I stopped payin' attention for a while. In general, I just mark anything when time is runnin' out an' I'm close to the end. Nine times out of ten you'll get somethin' wrong ." When I questioned

Chapter 7: Standardized Tests

that statement, Moochie corrected himself. "Nine times out of ten you'll get something *right*."

Wynona said, "When I hear 'Two minutes,' I scan the answers an' the questions, an' I put which one is the main idea, an' that's gonna be my answer. If I get a chance to go back, sometimes I go back an' change answers."

"I stop when I run out of time," noted Kay. "When I hear 'Two minutes,' I'll keep going 'til I run out of time. I read the questions an' then I be onto the paragraph an' I try to answer the questions."

Terrell replied to the question, "I hurry up. I used the technique [of marking any answer] 'cause [name of one of his former teachers] say 'Pick any answer, an' you'll eventually get one right.'"

Art explained, "At the two-minute warning, I try to read the rest quickly as I can, an' then, I read the questions, an' I try to remember all that went on an' answer the questions."

Biggie explained his approach once the test administrator gives the "Two minutes" notice:

> I answer my initials or A, B, C, C, B, A, dependin'. Because out all them bubbles, if you stick with one, ten of them should be right, 'stead of losin' all them bubbles. That why I stick to my name, usually, but sometimes you do one line A, next line B, next line C, and sometimes you do it backwards, an' you end up with a good grade. You might be shocked, but, after a while you see that what it was.

Waldo's approach: "Just quit."

Lemar said, "I just guess [from that point on through the end]."

"When 'Two minute' comes, I tries to speed up," said Ed. "On the Iowa test, you mark in any answer or you don't get no credit."

The children expressed awareness that shorter paragraphs meant they could get through a larger proportion of the test faster. They said they would prefer to actually answer questions because they believed they were correct rather than just "fill in the bubbles" because they have simply run out of time. Further, the children's discussions about how they reached their answers were illustrative in terms of the knowledge they brought to bear on test questions, their reasoning processes, and the strategies they used to "decode" the text.

For example, one question asked about the most frequent use for wool—shirts, ribbon, paper, or blankets.

Jasmine answered, "Blankets. I don't know; I shoulda chose *shirts* 'cause you see more wool shirts than blankets."

"Blankets," replied Moochie. "But how to answer the question? I guess' between shirts and blankets. Quilts is made outa wool sometimes; shirts is wool. I was thinkin' a quilts."

Art answered blankets as well.

> That one was kinda hard because I was gettin' confused between shirts an' blankets, 'cause lotsa people wear wool shirts, an' they keep you warm an' wool blankets, too, so I chose blankets 'cause some people use wool blankets in the summer when it really hot, an' they don't wear wool shirts when it's really hot.

"Shirts," Lemar responded. "You don't use wool for paper, [or] ribbons. You do use it for blankets, but you use it for shirts an' sweaters more, an' I thought *cotton* for blankets."

Ed chose shirts, "but now I think it blankets."

Biggie said, "It really blankets. I didn't get a good look at this one. My eyes be playin' tricks on me."

Waldo chose blankets, erased it, and then picked shirts. "'Cause when I pick blankets, I thought it take too many sheep wool to make blankets, so, since I usually see wool shirts, I pick that."

In some instances, the children interpreted the question literally, found none of the possible answers to be totally correct, and then reasoned to what would have been marked as an incorrect answer. In many instances, the children felt there were two correct answers. A few realized that only a single answer was allowed. For example, Wynona said, "It supposed 'a been two answers but you only

Chapter 7: Standardized Tests

get one, so I made a choice." Others insisted there were two correct answers, and marked them both. Jasmine, in particular, picked two answers more frequently than any other child. She claimed, "I pick two answers 'cause two of them's right." On a few test items, she picked three answers, the maximum allowed on the IGAP tests.

Multiple choices are permitted when taking the IGAP tests but not when answering the national versions of standardized tests. Those children who gave multiple answers might merely have assumed that the test instructions on all tests would be the same. Moochie told me he thinks mistakes like this happened because "nobody read the instructions." Maybe the students simply did not know where to look for the instructions or overlooked them in their desire to get through the tests. Maybe they never considered that instructions might change from test to test or vary within a single test. On the other hand, perhaps they believed "what's right is right" and no instructions could alter the facts.

In some cases, especially those where other words allowed the children to infer the meaning from context, their lack of a definition for a particular word did not affect their answering the test questions. For example, *soaring* with reference to *towers* was guessed as meaning "moving" or "great," but most of the children were able to circumvent not knowing the exact meaning of *soaring* because of the wording of the question. Most of them answered that question correctly. In other instances, not knowing the definition of a word meant they guessed. Some guesses were lucky; some were not.

The children found certain categories of vocabulary words, particularly homonyms/homophones, to be especially problematic. The children occasionally thought they knew the meaning of the vocabulary words and, hence, the answer to the question because they did not know that one of the "critical" words was a homophone/homonym.

One question asked about the type of crop that would require the use of a combine, a truck, a tractor, and a grain elevator. None of the students could read or define the vocabulary word *combine*. However, two of them "slid" over the word *grain* that would have given them an idea about the type of crop raised.

"On this one, they talkin' 'bout trucks, tractors, and an elevator, an' I put *cattle* 'cause they wasn't talkin' 'bout food an' they wasn't talkin' 'bout vegetables," Wynona said. "No, [I did not know what a *combine* was]—first I thought they was talkin' 'bout one of them houses out in the forest."

I asked, "A cabin?"

"Yes, that's what I thought they was talkin' 'bout. Then, I remember my grandma—she have a farm, an' she grow vegetables, an' she don't use none of them things, so I pick *cattle*."

Jasmine, who dotted/underscored *combine*, *truck*, *tractor*, and *grain elevator*, reasoned her way to an answer as follows:

> *Combine* means 'to join.' Because grain—grain an' wheat goes together. If you could combine a truck, tractor, an' a grain elevator into one machine, it would look weird, but you raisin' wheat.

Art said:

> *Combine* is like when you put something together, like a truck, a tractor, an' a grain elevator all put into one vehicle. After the grain elevator would cut down the wheat, the tractor would take the bottom part an' scoop it up, an' dump it in the back part of the truck, the open part, like a dump truck, an' the tractor part would be longer than the grain chute.

Waldo explained his reasoning.

> *Combine* is a thing you mix together. What it mean is, you don't have to use one thing for wheat. 'Cause if you raised cattle, it be like cows an' pigs, 'cause you wouldn't need a tractor, they could walk. Potatoes? No, you can handpick 'em. I saw it on my uncle's farm. An' lettuce, the same with lettuce. So I figure you need a tractor an' a truck with wheat.

In some cases, when the modifier or adjective was unknown, as in *textile mill* or *grain elevator*, they proceeded to answer the accompanying questions on the basis of the noun alone, as if the modifier did not exist. For example, *textile* was a term with which the children said they were unfamiliar, but since they knew what a mill did, they figured the answer would be something to do with wheat and grains.

Jasmine commented, "*Textile* I did not know, but because the little red hen went to the mill to get wheat, an' cereals an' flour come from wheat, so I pick 'flour and cereal from wheat'."

In passages that contained a number of vocabulary words that the children did not know, they made educated guesses about the sense of the passage and the answers. They misread or mispronounced many of the words that might have given them a better idea of the correct answer, such as "Scots" for *Scouts*, "soil" for *silo*, "skis" for *skies*, and "oaks" for *oars*. In other instances, there were misreadings, misunderstandings based on lack of experience with the referents, or mispronunciations of the words, perhaps based on poor phonics skills.

Other times, their unfamiliarity with specific terms that are used to "clue" the test-taker in to the subject matter presented a problem. For example, one question asked where one might find a silo, pasture, pasteurizer, and a barn with stalls.

Jasmine chose *racetrack* "'cause stalls, stalls is where you put horses." I asked if she knew the definitions of *silo, pasteurizer*, and *pasture*. She replied, "*Silo* is dirt, *pasture* is where you grind up stuff, an' I don't know *pasteurizer*."

Terrell explained his reasoning.

> 'Cause there is a soil—what this word is? Paste-or-izzy? Pas-tu?—an' a barn with many stalls. 'Cause I saw a soil paste-or-izzy. It roll an' put the lines in the dirt, an' the word *barn* tell me it a farm, an' many stalls, they got a lot of stalls. Like, it ain't a vegetable farm 'cause it woulda said 'with many vegetables and many fruits.'

Art gave this support for his answer.

> On a dairy farm you would have a lot of cows to give milk. An' I think it's not a vegetable farm, 'though out in the pasture you can grow wheat, potatoes, carrots, radishes, onions. They's a lot of vegetables you can grow on a pasture. I think I saw one once when I went to asthma camp—going there, I saw a pasture.

Biggie picked *dairy farm* but erased it contrary to what he professed he normally did in test situations. He admitted:

> This one, I plain didn't understand this. I read it aloud. I forgot what a pasteurizer is. I know what—I knew *pasture*. A dairy farm? I tried to stick with my first idea. [My teacher] say, 'If you don't know, your first answer gonna be the right one.'

Waldo, who did not know *pasteurizer,* answered "A vegetable farm—it grows wheat in stalls [stalks?]."

One question asked which fruits in the following sets were citrus fruits: grapes, melons, pears; apples, bananas, plums; lemons, limes, oranges; tomatoes and peaches. Most of the children did not know the definition of *citrus*. The strategies they used to answer this question were:

(Jasmine) "Cirky fruits—I knew oranges was cirky fruits, so I pick the one with *oranges* in it."

(Moochie) "Citrus fruits—I guessed on that 'cause time was runnin' out. I don't know what citrus fruits is."

(Wynona) "They was talkin' 'bout fruits, an' I didn't know what this mean," pointing to *citrus,* "so I just put my favorite fruits, an' my favorite fruits is apples, bananas an' plums."

(Terrell) "Circus fruits—Well, number 3—lemons, limes, an' oranges all have *SUNKIST* on 'em so I look for that an' that my answer."

(Biggie) "*Citrus* mean 'really round,' like a circle, so I look at 'apples, bananas, an' plums,' an' they ain't really round, so, when I got to 'tomatoes an' peaches,' an' they be really round, I pick them."

(Lemar) "*Curtis*? I didn't know what it is. I guessed you had to peel or cut it."

(Ed) "Leems, lemons, an' oranges is citrus fruits. I learn it by citrus fruits on TV."

Chapter 7: Standardized Tests

In one instance, the child's answer was wrong, but his reasoning was good; in another instance, the child's answer was correct, but his reasoning was suspect. This group of children chose every answer possible for this question.

Sometimes, the students' unfamiliarity with seeing a word spelled out in print, even though they may have heard the word or a shortened version of it, meant they answered test questions incorrectly. For example, Lemar underlined the word *sanitation* on his test pages and wrote next to it, "I never heard of it. Sorry." When we talked about this question, he said he had heard, however, of the Department of Streets and San and knew that it was responsible for garbage collection. He had simply never heard the department's full name used or seen it written anywhere.

At other times, the children's categorization of items led them to have difficulty answering a question. When coupled with unfamiliarity with spelling or with homonyms/homophones, these kinds of questions became problematic.

For example, in response to a question about which of the following—a lighthouse, a helicopter, a runway, or a hangar—might *not* be seen at an airport, some children said that you *would* expect to see a lighthouse at the airport. They placed the tall building at the airport with lights on it that guides airplanes in the same nominal category as the tall building out on the water with lights on it that guides boats. In other words, both were *lighthouses*. Most of the children chose *hangar* as the correct answer by reasoning that a helicopter was like an airplane, that planes needed runways and lighthouses because they had seen that on TV, and a *hangar* was the object you find in a closet and use to hang up clothes. That there might be a spelling difference between *hangar* and *hanger* did not occur to them, or, if they were aware that there was a difference, they paid no attention to it.

In other instances, the children did not read carefully or they missed modifying words, such as *not*, that changed the meaning of the questions. Had they read the sentences more attentively, they might have been able to answer a larger number of those questions. Misreading sometimes meant that the children spent an inordinate amount of time trying to fit the passage material and the proposed answers into something that made sense to them and to discover a rational scheme for answering the questions. In other instances, misreadings were not so critical to answering test questions.

Occasionally, the children read only the first syllable of a word and assumed they knew the rest of the word but ended up substituting a totally different word for the one that was written. For example, once Jasmine was reading aloud to me about a luggage conveyor belt at an airport. She saw *con* at the beginning of *conveyor* and misread the word as *convenience*. I asked her to paraphrase the sentence she had just read, keying in on her use of *convenience* instead of *conveyor*. During our discussion, she said she had never seen or heard the word before and had never been to an airport, but she had seen a similar kind of belt at the grocery store. She said she had misread the word in her haste to finish the sentence and because she thought she knew what the word was once she saw the first syllable. She noted, in retrospect, that she thought *convenience* was equally as accurate as *conveyor* in terms of what the belt did.

Occasionally, however, when the students read too fast, they missed a clause that would have provided them with information that was crucial to answering the test question correctly. One question asked about the best way to obtain something without using money. Many of the children overlooked or forgot the modifying clause.

Wynona, for instance, explained, "Rent it for a month, 'cause if you payin' on it, it eventually be yours."

Waldo said:

> Rent's not like you own it, but if you gonna rent it forever, might as well buy it. Borrow it? No, 'cause somebody probably waitin' for it. Trade? No, you could probably sell it for more money. So, you take it when no one lookin'. Like, you want a building, you gotta do it when nobody's lookin'.

Jasmine related, "It ask like, 'How could you be the owner of a buildin'?' That means to me, 'Look at it when nobody else is lookin' so you can buy it [without competition].'"

In another instance, the use of an adverbial modifier confounded some of the children who interpreted the question literally. For example, one question concerned places that usually *do not* have accommodations for travelers to sleep overnight. The possible answer choices ranged from campgrounds, restaurants, and motels to hotels.

Lemar said he had problems with this question because he knew that some hotels had restaurants in them. Terrell picked "campgrounds." His answer hinged on the word "usually." He reasoned that you could *never* sleep in restaurants, but you *could* sleep in hotels and motels. Since the only remaining choice was *campgrounds*, he chose that one.

In some cases, the children's experiences led them to answers that the test-makers probably never anticipated. The students had difficulty with a question that asked what is *not* true about city parks, where the choices were (1) workers are usually paid to keep parks clean, (2) it is all right to drop gum wrappers on the ground in a park, (3) playgrounds in parks should be safe places to play, and (4) tax money is sometimes used to buy land for a park. Some children explained it was *not* true that "workers are usually paid to clean up a park." They said they never saw workers in the parks cleaning up. In fact, they said they rarely saw anybody in the parks because those were places where "gang-bangers hang." Furthermore, they could not fathom that anybody would actually be paid to clean up the parks, although they felt this would be a good idea.

One question asked what a boy who needed to present a talk about communication would most likely be reading about (churches and clubs; people's jobs; farms, factories, and stores; newspapers, radio and television). Six of the children answered with *churches and clubs*. They reasoned that churches and clubs were places where lots of communication occurs, so they chose that answer, never looked further in that answer set, and went on to the next question.

The variety of answers these questions garnered show that, once again, some of the children read no further than the first answer in the set and then went to the next question. Some found none of the answers plausible based on their personal experiences and simply guessed.

A question about what was *not* true about a public library was also very problematic for these students. The possible answers were (1) a library's main business is to sell books; (2) a library is supported by tax dollars; (3) a library card allows a person to take books home; (4) a library makes it possible for people to share books.

The children all said they knew you could take books home to read if you had a library card. They all had library cards. Some said, however, that the [local professional sports team], not tax dollars, supported libraries, because their local library had been "adopted" by the local professional sports team and they saw signs announcing that fact in front of the library as well as on the computers in the library. Some said that libraries sold books because they have attended book sales at the library; and some maintained that libraries do not make it possible for people to share books, since when you checked out a book, you were not sharing it.

In response to a question asking that they identify the best example of cooperation from four possible choices—looking for a lost toy, helping friends collect trash, reading a book for fun, and following a fire truck to a fire—some children answered *reading a book for fun*. They said they answered in that fashion because, as part of their reading program in fifth grade, they read to younger students in cooperative groups, and they thought this activity was "fun."

In response to a question about the job a *chairperson* performs, the children tapped into a variety of information sources.

Chapter 7: Standardized Tests *199*

For Jasmine, the source was something she had read. "[To keep a record of a group's work], that usually what a chairperson do. It says somethin' similar in the Constitution book."

Moochie and Wynona drew on examples in their community to select their answers. Said Moochie, "Like the chairperson on the [local school council], be 'voted on for that job.'"

"Oh, I put 'to keep a record of a group's work'" said Wynona, "an' I think that they [a chairperson] be like a city council—a few people who keep records."

Kay claimed, "I didn't understand that one. I ain't understandin' what a chairperson do. I thought it was like a chair an' a person, or a person who made chairs."

Art explained that he made his selection "'cause it mean 'lead a meetin',' as [in] calls meetings or [is] in charge of a council."

Ed told how he selected the *to lead a meeting* answer. "I found out 'bout that 'cause of Ceana's mother bein' the chairperson of the [local school council], an' 'cause we went to that student forum an' saw the chairperson."

One child, however, answered this seemingly culture-free question about a chairperson's job by saying that a chairperson "collects money." In his experience, a chairperson sits in a chair at church or at a club, collecting money at the door before a sponsored event. He related that his mother had often directed him to "be the chairperson" at his church.

The children also had a difficult time with a question that asked them to define a city council. More than a few of them picked "a few persons chosen to look after the city schools" because, in their experience, the city council and the mayor in the city where they live did exactly that.

Another question concerned garbage and the safest way to dispose of it in a city. The choices were (1) to leave it in the sun to dry, (2) to burn or bury it, (3) to feed it to pigs, or (4) to dump it in the river. Art reread the question as: "What the fastest way . . ."

He explained his answer. "I pick 'leave it in the sun' 'cause if you burn or bury it, that would be pollution to the ground, an' 'dump it in the river' would be the same, an' 'burn or bury it' that would be somethin' like pollution, too, an' pigs do carry germs, so I think 'spread it out in the sun to dry.'"

Waldo picked the second choice because "if you spread, it'll be like pollution. Pigs—pigs won't eat all of it, probably get sick. If you burn it, ashes be left, an' you can use 'em to help grow trees. Don't dump it, 'cause the fish or somethin' could die, or you eat 'em an' get sick."

Ed chose the same answer. "I figure number 1 make it stink; number 3 be a lot like pollution, an' number 4, well, people an' animals got to drink from the river, so number 2 the answer."

Lemar justified choosing number 3. "See, I didn't know this one. They don't do nothin' with the trash 'round our house. Guess the ozone a problem if they burn it; but spreadin' it out, I think that pollution, too."

Surprisingly, no child directly questioned what pigs would be doing in a city. However, Jasmine confided that the listed choices for answers were "so dumb" that she assumed the test-makers were "funning" her, so she "funned" them back and chose "feed it to pigs." All of the children added that bagged garbage should be placed in covered bins because that was really the safest way to dispose of it. They all said they felt that none of the possible answers was really correct.

Terrell, in response to a question about where subways would be found, reasoned they were located in "a large town." He said he lives in a city where the trains run right by his house, so cities have trains. His relatives live in [name of town], Michigan, which is smaller than his city. There are subways there. Since where he lives is a city, [name of town in Michigan] must be a large town; and, therefore, since his city has trains, and [the Michigan town] where his cousins live has subways, subways are in large towns. He added he never rode the trains in his city or went downtown because his mother says it was too dangerous, what with gang-bangers and all. Therefore, he had no knowledge of the subway system that exists in his own city.

The children frequently used information they had learned from television, movies, and videos to answer test questions and to shape their responses to things with which they came in contact. For example, Art interpreted the passage in the practice test about an artist in terms of a documentary video he had seen. Ed answered the question about citrus fruits based on television commercials about orange juice. Lemar answered three practice test questions about the East Coast shoreline, the use of a compass, and the way to power a pirate ship, based on televised fictional movies ("When I was real little, I look at *Star Trek*, an' then boat movies come on, an' I see them usin' sails.").

When Terrell, Lemar, and I were at the aquarium, Lemar commented that "dolphins help you if you get in trouble in the water." When I asked how he knew this, he said, "I saw it on a movie, *Free Willy*." Another time, when I asked Kiki why she did not want to see the exhibit on spiders at the natural history museum, she declared, "I don't like spiders," and cited the movie *Arachnophobia* as justification.

These seventh graders were extremely verbal. However, their predominantly oral *home language* patterns, primarily in the areas of sentence structure (word order) and grammar rules, were frequently at odds with written *market* language. Their attempts to "decode" what they read in standardized tests ("standardized test-ese") were further complicated because those paragraphs and questions are not written as they would be in market English (Bizar 1997, 2).

I asked the children to read a test question aloud to me and then to tell me what the question was asking. I never said, "Tell me in your own words." I have noted in other situations, when the children spoke, they ignored, elided, or dropped certain parts of speech, such as suffixes. They did not typically treat the suffix categories (*-ing*, *-s* for plural, *'s* for possessive, *it's* for *it is*, *you're* for *you are*) differently. Their readings of the test questions were no different from their normal speech. When they told me what they thought the questions meant in their own words, they shuffled the word order, sometimes completely confounding the meaning of the questions. Adjectives were frequently dropped and adverbs were relocated within the sentence(s). Anyon (1997, 25–26), basing her statements on linguistic research (that of Labov, in particular), claimed that material written in "standard English"

> interferes in important ways with ['nonstandard' English speakers'] reading achievement.... This interference is caused in part by the subtlety in the differences between standard and nonstandard English. Baratz and others demonstrated long ago that it is extremely difficult to learn to read a language you do not speak . . .

Yet, the students with whom I worked were able to speak market English when they wanted and when they felt the situation warranted. For example, once, when I was videotaping the girls, Coco said, "I don't got no . . ." and Tatiana interrupted her with "Proper English! 'I don't *have* . . .'"; and Biggie, as is shown in the chapter on science explorations, used market English when speaking with, and asking questions of, chemists.

Apparently unlike the children Anyon (1997, 25) studied at Marcy School, these students have been taught that market English is to be used at all times in the classroom. Except during their interactions with other children during lunch or in conversations with each other, such as in gym class and after-school sports, they tried to adhere to the school rules regarding market English. Most times when they were interacting with me, even in a school setting, the students spoke in their home language. Other times, when we were at school, once the classroom teacher was not around, the children began speaking in market English, but quickly switched to their home language. At those times, market English dropped out, sometimes mid-sentence, as the students became more excited about or more involved in what we were discussing. The children also used home language when they were explaining what they really meant or did not have the vocabulary words to define their thoughts completely in market English. I called this *code switching* and interpreted it as evidence that the children have been dialect shopping. Anderson (1990, 173) documented a similar instance that he also called *switching codes*, except that in the example he reported, an African-American, middle-class male "switched codes" from market English to street language in order to avoid a mugging.

I have observed that these children most often spoke totally in their home language when they were at ease in a social situation, excited, or angry. Perhaps they used, or tried to use, market English in situations where they had little control, such as in the classroom. Then, as they gained control or realized they could take control of a situation, such as when they were interacting with each other, they switched to their home language. Essentially, I interpreted the switch from market English to home language as signaling the degree of control that the students believed they possessed "over the selection, organisation, pacing and timing of the knowledge transmitted and received" (Bernstein 1996, 187). Although Bernstein (1996, 185–87) was referring to pedagogic communication in the above quotation, I believe his *framing* thesis can be applied to discourse among the students themselves.

Anyon (1997, 27) mentioned that she overheard African-American teachers and principals speak in what she termed "nonstandard" English when teaching and interacting with each other. I did not document any instances where the teachers used anything but market English when addressing or teaching the students in this school. I cannot say whether this is because the teachers were trying to teach the children another method for acquiring "cultural capital" or whether it was because the teachers valued and taught their "middle class . . . cultural capital over that of the students" (Yeo 1997, 100), believing market English superior to the children's home language. During parent conferences, I never heard the teachers use anything but market English. Yeo (1997, 105) has called market English the "voice of authority," the "dominant, official, administrative rhetoric (white, middle class)" and observed that teachers used it when they spoke from their positions of authority. However, it should also be noted that the board of education has mandated "Standard English" as the instructional language in the city schools. Whatever the reason(s), the teachers' use of market English with the students, and with the students' parents, was deliberate.

On the other hand, I noted that a number of the African-American teachers, when speaking with each other during staff meetings, might shift into home language. This shift occurred when they wanted to stress a certain point and make sure it was understood or when they made a joke. Among many of the teachers in this school, the social context and the management of interaction and communication shaped the language "style" they used, just as it did for the students (Bernstein 1996, 154).

Not all of the children used their home language as much, or as consistently, as some of the other children; and not every child's home language, vocabulary, grammar, or syntax was identical. The vocabulary, grammar, and syntax that every child learns initially come from the home. Consequently, each child had a somewhat different, individualized version of his or her home language. Moreover, I suspect that those children who heard home language exclusively spoken in their homes were more facile in that dialect than those children whose parents switched codes for whatever reasons.

The children were well aware there was a difference between their home language and market English and that regional differences, other than accents, exist among home languages.

Lemar pointed out that "Down South, people use different words than we do sometimes. Like, they say *folk*, an' up here, we say *folks*."

Moochie remarked that one girl who attended their school but who lived in the general area he called "up north" spoke "northside." He defined the *northside* dialect as being differently accented with a slightly different vocabulary, than *westside*. "Like, she say *fittin'a*, an' we say *fin'a*, like 'fin'a go someplace'." He added that he thought it was funny how, when this girl was at school, she tried to speak westside, shifted into a westside accent and used westside words, but did not always succeed.

Moochie also pointed out vocabulary differences between market English and the students' home language, using my pronunciation and my vocabulary as illustrations. For example, once while directing me to take a shortcut to his apartment building, he said, "Go down there, an' take a left." I asked, "Through the alley?" He laughed and corrected me. "It call a *fah-lane* [fire lane]. Use your Ebonics! It fah-lane, not *alley*."

Part of the children's poor test performance on standardized tests might have been due to their habit of translating and rephrasing what they read. They were perfectly capable of reading the words in a sentence in order, and most often they did read the words in order when they performed their first read. However, sometimes, to understand the true meaning of the sentence and answer the questions, they reread the words, often shuffling them until they fit the home language pattern.

Biggie claimed:

> To get a clear picture, you got to see it more than one time to get it clear. My mama always told me to understand readin', you gotta read over an' over again, until you get the clearin' of it, an' since I been doin' that, it gave me a better clearin'.

Unfortunately, if the words made little sense on the first reading, or if certain words were unfamiliar, misread, or routinely ignored, or the negatives were slid over because they did not appear where the children have been led to expect them, what remained, when shuffled, perhaps made less sense than the original sentence. In fact, the children constantly complained that many of the test questions and answers made no sense to them. I thought they were referring to the *content* alone; but after they reiterated what they thought the test-authors were asking, I saw that, oftentimes, their reworking of the words and word order had (further) confused them about the sentences and about the possible answers to the questions. Their rephrasing also frequently precluded using word placement to help them infer meaning from context or vocabulary words.

A clear example of this retranslation, dropped or ignored suffixes, dropped or reordered adjectives/adverbs, and reshuffling is illustrated by the test question asking what smoke signals, flags, blinking lights, and telephones have in common.

The answer choices were (1) that they require daylight for their use, (2) they all must be used in code, (3) they can all be used for sending messages, and (4) they are used in Scout training. Admittedly, some children did not know the meaning of *Scout training*. When orally reading the question, Terrell substituted *Scots* for *Scouts*, then identified *Scots* as "policemens" on a SWAT team. Jasmine cued in on the word *training* and thought that Scouts were people who trained you for a job. What job required learning how to send smoke signals was a question she could not answer, but she admitted she thought the question was another "dumb" one. When I asked Waldo to specify the meaning of *Scout*, his definition closely approximated what Scouts might do in terms of training: "[A] *Scout* is a person who helps with things, like really puts out a campfire with dirt or sand, an' tells you how to make a fire with sticks, although I ain't never seen a Scout."

A number of the children orally rephrased the question as "Smoke signals, flags, blinkin' lights, an' telephones—What they have in common?" They reiterated the possible answers as "They all be used in daylight; they all be used in code; they all send messages; and they used for trainin'." Terrell, Jasmine, and Waldo left *Scout* or *Scots* in front of *trainin'* when they reread the sentence, but the rest of the children did not mention that word. Biggie also complained:

> I mean, people use so many things in old times, an' old-time things, they—we really didn't know about. That's why I think these be real screwball questions they be givin' us, 'cause we ain't been born back then, so how we know?

His answer implied that, at least for him, the principle way to learn about or know something was through direct experience.

The idiosyncratic rephrasing of questions after reading them through one time undoubtedly cost the children both time and comprehension. The experientially based vocabulary problem of not knowing the reference for *Scout* and *Scout training* thus became a very minor issue when exploring the reasons behind the students' struggle to answer this purportedly general-knowledge test question. The children's mistakes in translation and rephrasing more than likely led them into many similar kinds of mistakes in interpretation and into marking incorrect answers on the tests. This rereading, rephrasing, restructuring, and reworking could explain why so many of the children protested, time and time again, "This question don't make *no sense!*"

The children also used another strategy to answer test questions that on the surface appeared logical and efficient but that, more often than not, actually worked to their detriment. If, after all their manipulations, the test passage or questions still made no sense, some students looked to see if the same word occurred in both places. Their reasoning was that if the same word appeared, it signaled the correct answer.

Kay used this strategy frequently, but admitted she often did not even bother to read the passages and questions first. She said looking for the same word in both places saved her time. She called what she did "skimming." She said that the students have been encouraged to "skim" or "scan" the test items for the main ideas and important points rather than waste time by reading every word. Moreover, along with all the other children, she claimed to have been told to guess as a last resort.

Biggie discussed skimming and guessing.

> For myself, tests is a little hard at the readin' part because I usually didn't finish it, but what I figure out is you have to skim through some of the test because there is only a certain amount of time to finish the test, an' what one of my teachers tell me is, 'If the time is gettin' short, start fillin' in the bubbles.'

Have the students misunderstood, or taken too literally, their teachers' instructions to rephrase test passages and questions? Have they interpreted those instructions to mean they should *reread* everything instead of simply *restating* the passage in their own words to decode it?

On most standardized tests, unmarked answers are scored as wrong. Nine of the children admitted to making random choices as a last resort, at the last minute. Most of the children admitted that usually, when time was running out, they tried to randomly mark bubbles in order to "finish" the test. They conceded, however, they were usually unable to mark all of them. None of the children actually returned to mark answers to the questions left blank earlier in the simulated test, although one student said she normally tried to do this in real test situations.

Biggie said, "I don't think the kids do that on purpose [skip a problem or leave a problem with which they are having trouble, and go on to the next one]. It's just they don't come back like they 'posed to."

Many of the students inferred that they suffered from the "high test anxiety/low test performance" cycle that is difficult to reverse (Ornstein 1993, 15). Moochie told me, "I gets nervous before I take the test. I don't do anything special to get over it. It just go away."

Biggie claimed, however, that test anxiety had a huge impact on him and his performance:

> You get nervous, an' you can't hold all the information you take. That's why a lot of us forget when you—we read. As a child, I knew I was 'right' before the test, but when the test day came, everything went blank. I think the problems with us kids today [is], we know the test, but when the test come, our minds go blank an' we get shooken up about it. We don't think as well 'cause we think we gonna score low.

It is impossible to tell how much test anxiety actually affected their performances in real testing situations. I thought that the children should have no stress at all during the practice tests, since they were not being scored, and I made it clear that I was not interested in whether their answers were right or wrong. Apparently, this was not the case. Lemar, Biggie, and Moochie all skipped questions without noticing. Wynona marked incorrect answers that she noted only after we went back to discuss her choices. No child offered an explanation for overlooking questions. Only Biggie and Lemar suggested a reason for marking answers other than the ones that were intended. Biggie claimed his "eyes be playin' tricks" on him and that his mind frequently went blank during tests. In addition, when we were reviewing his answers, Lemar frequently admitted, "I didn't read this one correctly." Perhaps these children suffer from a high test anxiety/low performance syndrome no matter under what circumstances they take tests. I suspect that the word *test* triggered their responses.

I attempted to determine if any of the strategies the children said they used when alerted to two remaining minutes actually produced higher numbers of correct answers and, therefore, higher scores. There were over one hundred questions on the practice tests that I administered to the children. When I said "Two minutes," the children marked the place where they were working. Then they did what they usually did on standardized tests. Two kept working on the questions in order, only reading a little faster, marking the answers as best they could. One described his technique as "read one, mark one. . ." They did not finish answering the test questions. One child said he "just quit," but when I looked at his test sheets, they both showed that he had circled more answers after he marked his place when I said "Two minutes." I can only assume he misinterpreted my question, and thought I was asking what he did when he ran out of time. The rest of the students stopped reading and tried to randomly mark more answers. Even using this strategy, only two finished marking all the questions.

Obviously, if no credit is given for blank answers or if blanks lower the overall scores, with statistical probability, the children *do* stand a better chance of scoring higher on standardized tests if they answer whatever questions they can as best they can and then, when faced with a time crunch, fill in as many of the remaining bubbles as possible. However, there is always the real possibility that students will simply randomly fill in bubbles for the entire test.

Biggie thought that the test-makers deliberately tried to slow the test-takers down.

> Another problem is—why the kids don't ace their test is 'cause they stay on one problem. They don't know how to move on an' come back. That's wastin' up. That's how they gonna get low. That how they [the test-makers] try to slow you down, to see if the hard problems slow you down in the beginnin'.

What became clear during my investigation was that the slow, deliberate, careful worker is penalized by the way standardized tests are scored. Regular schoolwork, homework, reading, and research require careful attention to details, and this attention is usually rewarded with A's. However, standardized test scoring encourages a "completion without regard to correctness" strategy, with a higher score as a reward.

The children, as they have been told, drew upon their own knowledge and experiences to answer the questions. However, I am almost certain that some of their experience-based knowledge and their reactions to the questions were quite different from those the test writers believe to be common to children across the United States.

In one instance where the practice test questions asked for inferences that could be drawn about an artist in a specific paragraph, Art drew so much upon his own experience gleaned from seeing a documentary video about an artist and interpreting what he had seen in terms of how he might feel if he were an artist, he lost sight of the fact that the questions concerned information presented *in that specific passage*. Art answered all the questions in that sample test section. Had they actually been scored, they would have all been marked incorrect.

One question asked the student to infer the source of the artist's greatest satisfaction: (1) helping others express themselves through art, (2) making mosaic bowls, (3) winning praise, or (4) working alone. Art said, "It say the artist like to make molded mosaic bowls. I saw that in a movie. You take a lot of wet clay an' you mold it up an' shape it, an' put it in the oven an' let it get hard."

His inferences, however, about what is required to produce art were very insightful. He thought, "like, if you doin' sculpture, you shouldn't be scared. If you moldin' clay, you shouldn't be scared to get it on your vest, or like, if you make somethin', you shouldn't be shy to show it to somebody, so lack of fear is what needed."

Unfortunately, the test questions were unresponsive to what Art knew about art and the processes involved in producing a work of art, because "the Iowa, and other norm-referenced tests, are standardized to ask the same questions across different populations so that scores can be compared. Items are chosen to discriminate between students and rank them against one another, rather than to determine what children actually do know" (Bizar 1997, 2). But, Biggie believed that the standardized tests "show what the teacher's doin', an' what the kids learn so far."

The children's answers to standardized test questions revealed that there was no single reason for their trouble with taking standardized tests and suggested there was no simple solution to raising their tests scores. Numerous problems are associated with the tests themselves (the use of "standardized test-ese," ambiguous questions and answers, cultural- and class-biased questions, etc.), with the uses to which test scores are being placed, and with the school's response to the "tyranny of the tests," as well as with the students' test-taking strategies.

Many times, at museums or during discussions, the children used information they learned on television or from movies or videos to interpret exhibits or explain why they knew about something ("I saw that on *Free Willy*." "Well, in *Anaconda*, that big snake jus' come up out the water an' eat everybody on the boat..."). This same strategy carried over to testing situations where, when the topic was one with which they thought they were familiar, they answered the questions in terms of what they thought they had already learned or knew about the subject matter. They never suggested they distinguished between fictionalized accounts and documentaries. Perhaps they were never told there was a difference.

Some of the children indicated that they answered test questions based on other types of information sources. Some cited books they had read ("I read that in a book 'bout Indians"). Still others said they had learned the information they used to answer some test questions in school ("When I was up in kindergarten [or whatever grade]"), from personal experiences ("Then, I remember my grandma—she have a farm an' she grow vegetables, an' she don't use none of them things"), on a field trip ("'Cause we went to that student forum"), or from a school visitor ("I learned that once when Ronald McDonald came to our school"). Still others, like Moochie, Biggie, Art and Ed, claimed they "visualized" what they were reading and used that visualization to help them figure out what test passages meant and how to answer test questions. Ed advised, "Readin' ain't just callin' words. You gotta get a picture in your mind of whatcher readin'."

Dewey (1901/1991, 250–52) discussed the worth of visualizing when it comes to academic subjects such as geography, history, and literature. He believed that the ability to visualize enriched the student's experience with the subject matter and was indicative of mental independence. The boys said they had never been instructed to use visualization techniques to decode text but simply developed it as a method to enable them to make sense out of the "collection of words" (Dewey 1901/1991, 252) they saw.

CHAPTER 8

FAIR TESTING?

At the start of the 1996 school year, the city mayor and the head of the public school system instituted a new "get tough" policy designed to eliminate "social promotions" and raise the public school children's test scores. All public schools in which fewer than 15 percent of the student body tested at or above national norms in mathematics and reading on standardized tests were placed on " academic probation" (Franczek-Sullivan, 1996). Those same schools were required to demonstrate that 20 percent of their students were reading at or above the norm following the next year's set of standardized tests in order to be taken off probation. This action occurred despite some educators' assertions that "tests that measure as little and as poorly as multiple-choice tests cannot provide genuine accountability" (FairTest 1997, 2).

Gregory Anrig, president of the Educational Testing Service, now deceased, "believe[d] that testing has been overused and misused. Anrig complain[ed] that tests are being used to make decisions they were never designed to make" (Bizar 1997, 3). Standardized test results have sometimes been used to determine the fate of elementary school children, to track them and, under the guise of "trying to maximize a child's chances for success in high school," limited the actual high schools they might attend. Test results have also been used as indicators of poor teaching and so have impacted the fate of teachers, principals, and whole schools (Olson 1998, 1).

The children's school was placed on academic probation and informed that henceforth it would be held accountable for the students' poor performances on standardized tests. Next, the school administration was informed that the school had also been placed on the state's Watch List, an action taken because the students' scores on the Illinois Goal Assessment Program (IGAP) tests were poor. Failure to raise scores meant that the school faced the following possibilities: the principal might be replaced, or the school might be closed permanently or temporarily. If closed and then reopened, it most likely would be *reconstituted*—that is, teachers would be required to interview for their old positions with no guarantee of rehire. The Office of Accountability, Department of School Intervention provided the school with what came to be called a probation-management team. This team helped identify problem areas in the school that ranged from the physical plant and maintenance to textbooks and the lack thereof. The school also linked with a local university, which served as an external partner to assist with instruction design and organization and with pedagogical techniques. Parents and students were informed about the actions that the city and state boards of education had taken. Despite the school's attempts to relay accurate information about the situation, at least one parent felt that the school was keeping the true seriousness of its probationary status from the parents.

According to FairTest (1997), the measures the school undertook to remove itself from academic probation and the state's Watch List were similar to those that other schools under pressure to show improvement have taken. Yet, these kinds of actions do not necessarily address the problems that are inherent in some tests; nor do they necessarily make up for poor teaching or deficiencies in the students' educational backgrounds. However, although a number of organizations such as FairTest advocate working to end the abuses, misuses, and flaws of standardized testing and ensure that evaluation of students is fair, open, and educationally sound, they primarily "place special emphasis on eliminating the racial, class, gender and cultural barriers to equal opportunity posed by standardized tests, and preventing their damage to the quality of education" (FairTest 1998, 1).

> In many districts, raising test scores has become the single most important indicator of school improvement. As a result, teachers and administrators feel enormous pressure to ensure that test scores go up (FairTest 1997, 1).

At this particular school, the teachers felt the pressure acutely, as their revised School Improvement Plan for Advancing Academic Achievement (1997–98) indicated. On page 1 of this document, the Executive Summary noted the following as primary goals: "Priority Goal #1: Increase IOWA Reading scores by 7 percent; Priority Goal # 2: Increase IOWA Math scores by 8 percent."

In an attempt to achieve this goal, which, incidentally, would raise the number of children meeting or exceeding national norms to the level required to remove the school from probationary status, the students were required, as part of the external university-partner program, to write their own multiple-choice questions. The rationale seemed to be that if the children wrote their own questions, following the format of one obviously wrong answer, two distracters, and one obviously right answer, they would better understand how to choose the correct answers on their tests. "Methods of teaching conform to the multiple-choice format of the tests.... Since this kind of teaching to the test leads primarily to improved test-taking skills, increases in test scores do not necessarily mean improvement in real academic performance" (FairTest 1997, 2). In fact, one parent commented on the change in instructional emphasis and pedagogical techniques since the school had been placed on probation. She bemoaned the pace and the kind of education that her son was receiving. She was upset about the stress he suffered due to the school's emphasis on standardized test scores.

Moreover, students in the after-school reading program took practice standardized tests and learned to break down test passages to get the main idea. Biggie said he thought this kind of exercise might be helpful in the long run.

> You gotta understand, it's like on the test. Find a main idea—So-an'-So made two kindsa cake, but Kimberly ate one, now So-an'-So is mad—so what's the cause? Kimberly ate the cake, so who cares who is So-an'-So? The name don't really matter.

Because of the probationary status of the children's school, a situation that was directly tied to the student body's overall substandard performance on standardized tests, much effort was devoted toward increasing the children's test scores. Terrell felt that "bein' off probation mean the kids could learn more." His statement was quite similar to one FairTest (1997, 1) has made: "Schools narrow and change the curriculum to match the test. Teachers teach only what is covered on the test. . . . Test content is a very poor basis for determining curriculum content, and teaching methods based on the test are themselves harmful."

Biggie's complaint, echoed by other students, was that "bein' on probation is added to our academics. They more tough on us now, an' it cuttin' our activities mostly—like, we used to have basketball games every other day; we used to go on field trips more; teachers used to be more looser."

Biggie's comment matched ideas that Meisels (1989, 17) has expressed: "The results [of using tests for purposes for which they were not designed] are a narrowing of the curriculum, a concentration on those skills most amenable to testing, a constraint on the creativity and flexibility of teachers, and a demeaning of teachers' professional judgment."

The children also believed that their teacher assigned their report card grades in reading solely on the basis of their most recent Gates-MacGinitie test scores. Biggie, for example, earned a report card grade of C in reading. He said he thought he received this grade because those test scores "sucked." When asked how he did on the Gates-MacGinitie test, he reeled off his scores. His reading level was fifth grade third month, and his comprehension was third grade second month, with a composite score of fourth grade second month.

The seventh-grade students who failed to achieve a fifth grade eighth month level in reading and mathematics on the ITBS tests were held back. True or not, they attributed their being flunked directly to their standardized test scores. Fair-Test (1997, 1, emphasis in the original) has claimed:

> No test is good enough to serve as the sole or primary basis for important educational decisions. . . . *Retention in grade*, or flunking or leaving a student back, is almost always academically and emotionally harmful, not helpful . . . Students from low-income and minority-group backgrounds are more likely to be retained in grade, placed in a lower track, or put in special or remedial education programs when it is not necessary. [Students] are likely to be given a watered-down or 'dummied-down' curriculum, based heavily on rote drill and test practice. This only ensures they will fall further and further behind their peers.

Terrell talked about the strategies he used on the Iowa test that he came to believe were responsible for his being retained in seventh grade.

> I skipped to the back of the book 'cause [name of a teacher] say the end is what bring you to another level. First, I did all the questions I knew, an' then I went back an' made sure I got the answers right. I ran out of time. I was workin' too slow an' I was erasin' the marks on the paper too much, an' when I went back, I had messed up. I had messed the questions up goin' from back to front.

Jasmine related that she frequently "messed up" when taking standardized tests. The ITBS test she took in March 1997 was a particularly bad test for her. She called me in May 1997 when the results of that test were in.

> I failed. I don't get to go to eighth grade. My scores—I went down in readin' but up seven months in math. I figure it 'cause I got on the wrong line with the bubbles. I figure I was off 'bout five lines. The proctor pointed it out, an' I figure since we was doin' spellin' an' I was up in vocabulary, I was on the wrong line. But when I found out [about not passing], I didn't even cry.

She added, "I was a little mad [at being flunked] because I know I tried my best."

Kay, whose comments were similar to those of other students, said:

> There's no time for the teachers to explain what we have to do an' go over the work. We don't know what to do, an' that's why we get bad grades. [If there were more time], then we'd understand, 'stead of havin' lots of tests to get our comprehension up.

"Pressure to teach to the test distorts and narrows education. Instead of being accountable to parents, community, teachers and students, schools become 'accountable' to a completely unregulated testing industry" (FairTest 1997, 2). Notices were posted in classrooms about the number of students needed from a particular class to meet national norms in mathematics and reading in order to get the school off probation. Still, when the results of the 1997 Stanford test were returned for these seventh graders, the class average in reading was lower than it had been at the end of sixth grade. Only a single student's score had dramatically increased. The children intimated that they viewed what they had to do in order to score at or above national norms on their standardized tests as distinct and separate from their "regular schoolwork." Taking the mandated tests was simply another (unquestioned? unchallenged?) "thing" they were required to do because they were in school. The tests and "passing" them became a focal concern for more than one student.

Tatiana, referring to the kind of academic help she might ask of her mentor, said:

> I'd ask my mentor, 'Could you give me some tutoring for say seven hours?' So, when I get to the Iowa tests, I would be ready. When I get to the Iowa tests, I'd go straight to the ones I know, do the estimation, then do the ones I don't know, so, without a mentor? [shrugged.]

Kay wished there were more of a connection between the standardized test instruction and her academic subjects:

> We need more science. It's important to do science projects so it can help you with your Iowa. They ask science questions on the Iowa. They ask about the seasons an' how plants grow, the name of plants. It helps you with the readin'. It help with comprehension. We need recreation

Chapter 8: Fair Testing?

> time—play games, an' stuff like that, so we can rest our brains. If we did that, we'd get our Iowa test scores up an' get us to high schools an' colleges.

In response to how he would organize instruction if he were in charge, Biggie advised:

> In my school, we will also teach our students the easy way of acing the test, because there is a lot of readin' goin' on, on the test, but you can't really finish it on time, so we gonna teach 'em how to skim through it.

I did not have standardized tests in mind when I asked Princess to write a daily journal, a sort of informal "learning log," discussing what she thought about what she had learned every day in school. The journal begins March 18, 1997 and ends May 8, 1997. She was not in school from March 27 until April 10, 1997, so there are no entries for those dates. The entries have been typed exactly as written.

March 18, 1997—"What I learned? We're working for the IOWA test, Today make sure we do the best. Because when I go to college, and they ask me a problem, I'll be surely glad to solve them."

April 17, 1997—"I think we need to learn percents. They will appear on the Iowa test."

April 27, 1997—"Poem—I'm trying to learn about percents, But first I got to prevent. I got to learn all of the rules, Because I'm trying to get an A in school. I know 50 percent of 200 is 100. I hope that question be on the test, because I'm trying to learn the rest, but I hope I survive on the Iowa test."

May 1, 1997—"I think it's important to learn to reduce fractions because on the Iowa test they will appear. Poem! I'm glad I learned something today, Because it'll help me all the way, and now I'm going to try my best, Because coming soon we have the Iowa test. I know I can study in the tree, because I'm trying to get a 7.3!"

May 2, 1997 (the day the school held a pep rally before the ITBS test during which the cheerleaders cheered and the students chanted "I will do my best on the Iowa test!" and sang the popular song, *I Believe I Can Fly!*)—"Today I learned what it [*sic*] a rilly. Well I don't know if that's spelled correctly, but we had one in the gym this afternoon. It's when people perform, and you just make a lot of noise. I didn't learn anything else."

May 5, 1997—"Today we had the Iowa test, 1997, and we had to do puncutions, capitilizations, and something about usage, I hope I past my Iowa test. It's important to do the Iowa test to see what you know or already learned. Is it based on this to pass?"

May 6, 1997—"Today we have taken the vocabulary and the reading comprehension. In reading we had to do a lot of reading passage, and it was only for 40 mins. Although I didn't get done I had one story left, so I panic and circled anything. If you didn't finish would they let you go back another time? I think it's a NO! I'm just trying to do my best, and survive on the Iowa test."

May 7, 1997—"Today we had the math part on the Iowa Test, some problems was easy and some I didn't get. It was three sections. Tomorrow we are having a car wash to raise money. Now I have to go! Bye!"

In the after-school reading program, the children dutifully took practice tests, marked their answers right or wrong, and then put the booklets away. I reviewed a random sample of these practice test booklets. Even when correcting those practice tests, some of the children got on the wrong line and, consequently, marked answers wrong that should have been right and vice versa! It is in instances such as these that Haberman's (1991) idea about the pedagogy of poverty and Anyon's (1980) thesis about working-class schools can be applied.

Rote learning, drill and test practices, giving tests, reviewing tests, are (re)producing situations in which these minority children are denied the possibilities to learn the social knowledge and skills in school that would help them become the critical thinkers who will be able to "alertly preserve democracy" (Farr and Greene 1993, 27). Perhaps the heavy emphasis on taking timed practice standardized tests permitted the children no "ownership" of their own learning, its pace, content, or direction. Perhaps the emphasis on standardized tests contributed to what has been called the students' "disengagement."

Yet, I found no concrete evidence that the children's poor test performance should be attributed to the "worker's resistance" that both Haberman (1991, 292) and Anyon (1980; 1997, 33) described, unless one counted the *laissez-faire* attitudes some of the children professed about the tests *before* they learned there *were* consequences for poor performance (i.e., they could be retained in grade or required to attend summer school and retake the tests). Every child in the subgroup of ten with whom I spoke wanted to at least attain his or her grade level. Every child was worried he or she would not be able to achieve the passing score, resulting in retention in grade or summer school attendance.

It appears that *resistance*, if it ever existed as a general phenomenon, had been replaced by a very pervasive and personal *fear* of the consequences for substandard test performance. Did this fear lead to bad learning and bad thinking habits, as both Biggie and Holt (1968, 49) suggested? Were the students' emphases on raising their scores enough to pass the "'cynical bargain' of doing just enough to get by that Linda McNeill has shown characterizes so much of their school experience" (Apple 1996, 103)?

This interchange between Biggie, Moochie, and Art made clear the students' belief that much of the reason they attend school is to learn what they need to know to take standardized tests.

Biggie initiated, "After the Iowa test, people get pretty silly."

"I know," agreed Moochie, "it like they just don't care anymore. They say they just don't have nothin' left to learn."

"After the Iowa test, they countin' the days 'til we get outa school," Biggie commented.

"It's dumb," said Art. "You gotta take more tests outa school, in school. You're basically—Your whole lifetime you gotta take tests."

"They think you don't have to do nothin' just 'cause you took the Iowa test," said Biggie.

Unlike Anyon's (1997) assertion, my data did not support the contention that market English was difficult for the children to read because they did not speak it. They can, and do, speak and read market English. However, it is true that "standardized test-ese" was difficult for them to read because they did not speak it. There is a difference between market English and "standardized test-ese." The latter "bear[s] no resemblance to natural text and lack[s] the connective elaboration that makes text readable and meaningful" (Bizar 1997, 2).

My data show that the children were perfectly capable of reading words in a sentence as they were written, in both market English and "standardized test-ese." Yet, when and if they did not comprehend what was written, they would read it again. At this second reading, they often shuffled the words into their home language pattern.

This is a subtle, but important, distinction that explains *one* of the children's problems with standardized tests. It also explains *one* of the reasons why they were so slow in answering the questions and rarely finished the tests.

Some of the problems the students encountered also arose because their experiences differed dramatically from those the test-makers have considered to be universal for students at their grade level. One could broaden these children's experiential base by taking them, for example, on subway rides, to see a mechanized farm, on a tour of a textile mill; by showing them documentary, scientific videos; or by providing them with books about the kinds of things likely to appear on a standardized test. However, all the possibilities could never be covered. Further, would not such efforts be teaching to the test, standardizing what children learn, making certain that they all know exactly what every other child in America knows (Apple 1996, 20)? Should one then teach children to ignore their own experientially based knowledge when answering test questions? Or should one try to teach them when it is appropriate to draw on their own knowledge to answer test questions, when to answer questions based on the passage information, and when to answer a question with what has been called *common cultural* or *global* knowledge? And even if that were a viable option, how ever would one do it?

The variability in these children's, and most likely all children's, explanations of how they reasoned to their answers for test questions, and the seemingly disparate kinds of information and vocabulary they commanded, can be explained if one considers that they "shopped" at different times and at different "stores." For example, one child might have a tremendous amount of information about DNA because he or she had watched and read about the O.J. Simpson trial, whereas another child might have little or none of that vocabulary or understanding because the trial in which DNA was discussed in depth was not high on his or her list of priorities. Since the children were shopping at different times without any sense of what kinds of information might be important or without any understanding that there might be differences in their sources' reliability, is it any wonder that their knowledge bases and vocabulary were so diverse?

The children repeatedly asked me to tell them whether their answers to the practice test questions were right or wrong according to the answer keys. It had not been my intention to score their answers in any fashion, but because they insisted, I told them. When I told them a specific answer was wrong, they asked "Why?" When I told them an answer was correct, they nodded and asked about their next answer. Their focus on correctness can be interpreted either as concern for scoring better on the tests, having already succumbed to the "tyranny of the tests," or as shopping for additional information to increase their knowledge.

What was accomplished when I told the child who did not know the definition of *citrus*, but who nonetheless picked the correct answer of "lemons, limes, and oranges" because he recalled they were all marked *SUNKIST*, that his answer was correct? Did explaining the correct answer to the questions about a chairperson, a city council, subways, lighthouses, garbage disposal, cooperative activities, communication, parks, and libraries teach the children anything except that the knowledge they had gleaned from their personal experiences was somehow wrong to use when answering test questions?

I do not intend to debate "deficit/difference" here. (See Bernstein 1996, 151, 153; Labov 1982; and Kellaghan et al. 1993, 88–92, for the distinctions, and Murray and Fairchild 1989, for examples of *difference* and *deficit*). I only wish to mention that had I been scoring the student's answers to the questions I would have been tempted to mark many of them correct because, based on their own personal knowledge and experiences, the children reasoned through to answers that, within those parameters, were often valid.

At school, the children's teacher frequently read to them. When she did this, she directed the class to follow along silently. Haberman (1991, 291) mentioned this as a negative practice common in urban schools. Considering that the teacher might be giving the children real, factual information, is this practice always wrong? Does the "goodness" or "badness" of this practice depend on whether the teacher is reading fact or fiction?

Biggie, referring to those times when their teacher read to the class, commented that "we read the chapter alone by ourselves, an' she'll [the teacher] read it aloud, all by herself. She'll read the whole chapter. I like it. It's a good way to read, 'cause it break down the books."

On the one hand, is this "reading to" truly the teacher's attempt to control the distribution of knowledge? (See Bernstein 1996, 25–28, and Yeo 1997, 99–106, for discussions of control of the distribution of knowledge and of cultural capital). Since the Office of Accountability, Department of School Intervention team noted that "reading textbooks [were] lacking in some upper-grade classrooms," and I have noticed that the children often worked with photocopied chapters of paperbacks during their reading lessons, perhaps the teacher really did need to read to the seventh graders. Jasmine confirmed this observation. "We don't have no readin' books."

Yet, I also noted that even if there were enough copies of some article or worksheet to go around, teachers might read the instructions, the directions, full text, and sometimes even every question to the students. Is it ever justifiable as a regular practice in school after first or second grade? How much of their reading to the students is simply habit born of necessity? How many of the students actually read along with the teacher? Does reading *to* adolescents help them read, better their pronunciation, add to their vocabulary, and increase their word recognition? How much does reading *to* the students on a regular basis raise their reading speed?

Their homeroom teacher encouraged the seventh-grade children to read at least twenty minutes every night. Most of the girls were fond of the *Babysitter's Club* and *Goosebumps* series that have been written for nine- through eleven-year-olds. A few of the better girl readers said they liked the *Sweet Valley High* series, while the boys mostly read books on sports figures, mysteries like *the Encyclopedia Brown* series, and wildlife.

The average *Babysitter's Club, Goosebumps,* and *Encyclopedia Brown* book has fewer than two hundred pages. Jasmine informed me that it took her between three and four days to finish one of those books. Kay confided that she liked to read stories "because stories, like 'Once upon a time,' gives you ideas. They tell you how you can think about stuff."

One boy advised, "At home my mama still get on me to read—read sports, newspapers, magazines." Waldo read a fifty-page book on archaeology, written with a fourth-grade vocabulary and sentence structure. He said it took him two hours to finish. Biggie took a book about Michael Jordan out from the library. He claimed he read the required twenty minutes every night, with a dictionary in hand. It took him seven nights to finish its one hundred-fifty pages.

Most of the children were slow readers, both silently, as the above data indicate, and when they read aloud. Sprick and Howard (1997, 24–25) wrote:

> Reading is a multidimensional skill. . . . Oral reading fluency is a measure of both the rate and the accuracy of a student's reading. . . . Although fluency alone is not sufficient for reading with understanding, it is clear that it is a necessary prerequisite for understanding, interpreting, and responding to print. Fluency allows, but does not guarantee, that readers can construct meaning. If students must search for appropriate words . . .comprehension suffers. . . . Fluency allows, but does not guarantee, that readers will be motivated to read . . . that readers can read strategically (i.e., adjust the way they read, depending on their purpose and the type of material being read).

There are norms that provide rough guidelines for determining adequate oral reading fluency for grades two through five (Hasbrouck and Tindal 1992, cited in Sprick and Howard 1997, 27). There are no norms for seventh grade but, according to Sprick and Howard (1997, 27), a seventh grader should be able to read aloud at a rate of approximately 150 words per minute without errors. At one point, following my mentioning of this fact, Waldo attempted to demonstrate how fast 150 words per minute actually was. He logged in at 143 words with no mistakes. However, he was unable to summarize the main idea in the paragraphs that he had just reeled off.

During every week of the 1997–98 school year, I worked with a self-selected group of children on their reading skills. My objective was to have fun reading; to encourage the students to read more; and also to help them increase their reading speed, comprehension, and vocabulary. We used *jump-in* techniques to read aloud from a biography of Amos Fortune, an eighteenth-century African freed slave.

Jump-in reading is a term I use to describe the following: anyone who wished could read aloud to the others in the group who followed along silently. At the end of the page, the next person who wished to read aloud jumped in and took over reading to the group. Sometimes jump-in reading inadvertently led to a chorus of readers who were all reading the same words aloud. Eventually, all but one of the choir dropped out. When "choral reading" happened, it usually provoked laughter and giggles.

Chapter 8: Fair Testing?

We also read with a dictionary close at hand. If we encountered a word whose meaning I was fairly certain the children would not know, I asked if anyone knew it even if the person reading had pronounced the word correctly. If no one did, we raced to see who could find that word the fastest in the dictionary. After it was located, the locator read the meaning(s) aloud, and each child wrote that word and its meaning(s) written down for future reference. We reiterated the correct pronunciation, spelled those words, and thought up antonyms for every one. We used them in sentences. Occasionally, we acted the words out.

I also asked each child who stumbled over a word when reading aloud if he or she knew what that word meant. Sometimes the stumble was because the child did not know the meaning or the pronunciation, or sometimes it occurred because the child did not know the pronunciation but knew the meaning or could infer it from the context. In either case, we looked up the word in the dictionary, noting the correct pronunciation and its meaning(s).

When we finished the book, which incidentally took almost the entire school year, the children devised ways to demonstrate their understanding. Some of the girls collaborated on writing a play. A portion of that play is reproduced below, exactly as it was written.

> Scene 2. A crowd of people had already gathered near the auction block, men for the most part. But a few women hovered on the outskirts. There were chains on their wrist and ankles.
>
> Auctioner: "Here's a fine specimen of the Gold Coast."
>
> The auctioner began slapping At-Mun's should[er] and running his hands down the strong arms.
>
> "You train them the way you want them to go."
>
> A voice shouted out from the crowd: "Defects? Why, none at all. Can't you see for yourself? Hey, it says here that no one is allowed to talk."
>
> Auctioner: "Is that so? Come on now let's see you say something."
>
> Man: "What is the little boy name?"

Auctioner: Laugh. "None of them have names."

At-Mun never heard English. He didn't know what they were talking about.

Quaker: "Friend, will thee take £30 and do no bidding on this man."

The auctioner thought for a moment realizing he was being offered almost twice.

Auctioner: "He's yours!" Paused. "He's an intelligent lad. Give him plenty of work and you'll soon have him in the shape you want him. Call him Amos."

Caleb Copeland was not sure what he would say of his wife when he arrived home with no money.

Celia: "How did thee come by the boy?"

Quaker: "I bought him at the wharf. A ship had just come in and they were selling the merchandise."

Two boys drew pictures of what they felt were the most significant events in Amos's life. Others wrote a rap song about Amos and his life which they then "produced" for the group.

> Hit you with my man Amos.
> So what ya sayin' yo
>
> It's silly he wasn't free
> So stop your playin' jo
>
> While he up in the slavery
> Long he knew his dutio
>
> He was a prince before he
> Got snatched into slaveryo
>
> He had a dream to free
> A young cutio—

Another worked on a short poem that went through a large number of revisions before it was declared "done":

Chapter 8: Fair Testing?

> Amos Fortune had dreams to be free.
> In the jungles of Africa, he was thinking,
> Just let me be.
> Then came the Portuguese,
> And they captured him with ease.
> He paid for his freedom, then he didn't have to flee.

After all the projects were completed and the presentations finished, Biggie confided he "ain't never read no book like this before."

Based primarily on the discussions following our reading of every chapter, and partly on these projects, I decided that the children had indeed grasped the book's fundamental ideas and had learned some new vocabulary words. I also felt that their projects had demonstrated comprehension of the story's main ideas far better than their answers to any test questions I might have devised. Could such alternative assessment vehicles be used in every learning situation? Who would determine whether such assessments were valid?

During these reading sessions I discovered that the children did not approach the fluency rate that one might expect for seventh and eighth graders based on Sprick and Howard's (1997, 27) projections from the norms for grades two through five. How much of their slow speed was because they did not normally read aloud, I cannot say. Jasmine said that when they were in fifth grade, they read aloud to younger students, but that they no longer did so. In July 1997, Biggie's mother told me that she had started working with him at home on reading aloud. When he stumbled on a word, she insisted he sound it out, spell it, and remember it. I have infrequently heard the children reading aloud to their entire class; and, even on those occasions, they usually read just a sentence or two that had been written on the chalkboard. Reading aloud in a classroom setting, when it occurred, happened in small group situations. There was a designated reader in each group of four students. The reader read aloud, while the three other group members silently read along with him or her. Sometimes, when there were not enough copies to go around, the designated reader read to his or her group while they listened.

Based on my observations, I am not certain that oral reading fluency measures either comprehension or lack thereof. Like Sprick and Howard (1997, 24–25), I noted that oral reading fluency did not guarantee that the students comprehended what they were reading. Nevertheless, I also noticed that oral reading nonfluency did not mean the children did *not* comprehend what they were reading.

Let me explain this seeming contradiction. Some of the students might not have known some of the vocabulary words and stumbled over pronouncing them. Others whose phonics backgrounds were strong could pronounce the words but might have had no understanding of their meanings; still others systematically mispronounced words but, when questioned, knew their meanings. Are not these data somewhat at odds with the above statements about reading competency? Is it that the students have placed phonics in one shopping bag, vocabulary in another, and reading in still another? Is it because some children have shopped for phonics, but perhaps missed the vocabulary store, that they have such difficulty reading?

Additionally, the children said they sped through some test questions because they knew the answers off the "top of the head." Other passages and questions required that the children read them over and over "to get a clearin'," as Biggie explained. The passages they read over, shuffled, and placed in their more familiar home language pattern might or might not have contained what the testmakers would define as difficult or important information.

Sprick and Howard (1997, 25) have asserted, "Fluent readers quickly skim through text when the material is familiar and read deeply when important or difficult information is presented." They continued by saying that oral reading fluency strongly suggests that a student can read strategically. My data show that there was little connection between these students' oral reading fluency and their abilities to read strategically. Not all of the children were fluent oral readers. Even Ed, who consistently scored above grade level on his standardized tests, had occasional trouble. Keesie, the most fluent oral reader in the class, had very little comprehension of what she read because she read too fast and her vocabulary was not large.

The students' lack of oral reading fluency never noticeably affected their motivations to read, contrary to what Sprick and Howard (1997, 25) asserted usually happened with poor oral readers. Approximately 50 percent of the seventh-grade students volunteered to join a weekly reading group. The children also reported they read at the library after school, with their mentors, and at home.

Biggie believed:

> Readin', that is one of your main keys, sort of like math. Like if you don't know how to read, you don't know how to do nothin'. The reason why you have to learn to read is because people out there in society—you got your own business, right? An' you have to sign a contract, you need to learn what that contract says, else they goin' to take all you' money, you' place, and you be left jobless an' you' business just go to waste.
>
> That's why readin' is the most important thing to learn because you got to read the numbers, the fine print, an' also you got to read the check, 'cause most people cheat you nowadays . . .
>
> One thing I found out, you blind if you don't know how to read. You got to read little books, move on to the medium, an' then the big, an' start learnin' more.

Yet, when the children discussed reading, they always mentioned it as an activity they did most often at home or outside of school. Kay said, "I wish I could read more at school."

The students' comments suggested that they were receiving a subliminal message in their classroom. I am certain, because I know the children's teachers well on a personal and professional basis, that the message was unintentional; and I am also certain it would have been denied, if I had pointed it out. The message was that reading in school was something reserved primarily for standardized tests. Reading was not really required to function in class. Lessons were most often oral and aural. Although things were written on the board, what had been written was then frequently read aloud, ostensibly for the benefit of the poorer readers in the class, to make certain that everyone understood. The children were not reminded to consult written texts for information on a regular basis. The children watched videos whose topics were part of their core curriculum, specifically social studies (*Washington, D.C., Our Nation's Capital*; *Once Upon A Time When We Were Colored*; *Mandela, The Man*, and *Martin Luther King, I Have A Dream*), and science (volcanoes, earthquakes, microscopic life forms, and bears). Who can blame them for preferring to see videos on these subjects rather than struggle through reading about them? When videos are frequently used for instruction and as substitutes for real-life experiences, who can blame the children for thinking all videos or movies, such as *Free Willy*, *Anaconda*, or *Arachnophobia*, are equally valid information sources to use when answering standardized test questions? Was it totally the students' faults they were not achieving at or above national norms on their standardized tests?

CHAPTER 9

TEACH ME

On the first day of school, when the children were new seventh graders, they wrote out their wishes for the future and for the kind of society in which they would like to be adults. As far as I know, although their wishes were posted in their classroom, they were never sent to anyone. They are listed below exactly as the students wrote them.

Shanita: "Fresh clean air. Wishes Come True."

Princess: "In my country I wish we could all get along."

Tatiana: "Let all people join together."

Jasmine: "I wish people would stop all rasism because people are dieing and people are not careing."

Kiki: "My wish is to stop the people in the country from doing drugs."

Lemar: "My wish is to stop all this hatetred & violence."

Waldo: "I wish for the churches stop getting burned down. I wish for stick-ups stop and the robbings."

Twitty: "I wish to stop all the killing."

Moochie: "I wish all gangs would stop."

Lia: "To stop the raping."

Biggie: "I wish for P.E.A.C.E."

Tracy: "I wish all poeple should have a house & food & should not be poor."

Keesie: "I wish that kids would stop ditching school and come to school and get his/her education."

Crissa: "My wish for the country is for the teachers and students to walk in better schools."

The children's wishes should be interpreted within the contexts of their lifeworld and some of the "reforms" that had been simultaneously initiated on a number of fronts and that were personally affecting them. Some of these reforms are what Apple (1993) has classified as part of a neoconservative resurgence. Moreover, these reform efforts, whether imposed by the system or organically flowing from the community members, are touching all the social areas that comprise "living" for these children and their parents.

Things are changing and many of the changes are reactive. The children's neighborhood, deteriorating over the past one hundred years, further gutted by the creation of the segregated sixty-acre housing project, but truly decimated thirty years ago in the riotous wake of Martin Luther King's assassination, has been designated an *empowerment zone*. This designation means that funds have been made available to woo businesses and spur commercial and economic development. A new sports arena has been constructed to replace a much older building. Some businesses are moving back into the community. A large food chain has built a store close by. Where few, if any, restaurants were left standing following the 1968 riots, new, trendy eating establishments have been opened. A large bank has established a branch office. Empty commercial property is once again selling at premium prices.

Churches are taking a more active, public role in trying to change social conditions. At least one religious institution has begun a student-tutoring program in response to a felt need to help the children read better. One minister coordinated a street-corner prayer vigil. He involved all the local churches, those with large congregations and those whose numbers fit into small storefront spaces alike. This vigil demonstrated the church members' solidarity with efforts to eliminate violence in the neighborhood. The demonstrators held hands on the corners in front of their churches, sang, and prayed for change. A local hospital is sponsoring an effort to provide science equipment and curricular support for thirty-seven local elementary schools' mathematics and science programs. Four churches have allied themselves with that hospital to encourage and reward local elementary students who excel in those subjects.

The large public university located a few blocks away from the housing project has become involved in numerous outreach ventures designed to improve both life and health for the neighborhood children, their parents, and other community members. These programs are run and staffed by university personnel and students, but they also hire local residents to fill auxiliary positions.

These changes are accompanied by *regentrification.* Expensive loft condominiums are being built in abandoned factories; Victorian row houses are being restored to their former glory. The children have expressed fear, perhaps because of things their parents have said or perhaps because of what they have seen happening around them, that they will be forced to move out of their community by rising prices and the attitudes that the new community residents might hold toward living so close to public housing and "project kids."

Some people are being moved to different buildings within the children's housing project; some are being provided an opportunity to move into newly constructed town houses; and others are being relocated to different neighborhoods altogether on Section 8 rent vouchers. The city and federal government have stepped in and, using federal, state, and local funds, have begun major renovations of the project buildings themselves. The larger buildings are coming down; the smaller ones are being reconditioned. Fixing up the buildings may well be a typical "emphasis on physical solutions to urban woes" that Smith (1996, 95) deplored, but something along these lines really needed to be done. As Kotlowitz (1991) and Jones and Newman (1997) have so vividly revealed, public housing was and, to a certain degree, still is rife with mismanagement, rats, roaches, gangs, and despair.

From what the children reported, some of the project's tenants are moving into leadership roles in their local community action groups, taking some control and responsibility for what goes on in their neighborhood. Buildings now have paid *building captains* tasked with keeping an in-house, supervisory eye on the buildings. Two of the students said their mothers are captains. There is a men's association whose members, according to these students, keep a watch out for gang and drug activities in and around the projects. Members of this group also help out at school graduations and community events. They play with the children and sometimes organize impromptu football games. Two of the boys said their fathers belong to the association. In the students' teenage vernacular, this group is "cold" (i.e., one step above cool), a really good group of men.

I did not determine whether these cadres developed as grass-roots phenomena or in response to invitations from those in power to participate in the direction that the reforms are taking. The children said that people just got tired of the gangs and the conditions under which they were living and are finally doing something to change it.

The welfare system that supported so many of the children's families for so long is being revamped. The children are aware of the changes. As Jasmine said, "It is important to learn [in order] to get jobs because . . . welfare bein' cut off." Welfare is no longer the "womb to tomb" entitlement it once was. Apple (1993, 21) has classified this change, and others that accompany it, as the "attempted dismantling of the welfare state" under the guise of anti-statism.

Whatever the reasons behind the changes, they have resulted in new educational opportunities and employment for some of the children's parents. For instance, two of the children's parents work in the projects, supervising breakfast and lunch at the day care center; another has a supervisory job at a hotel in the suburbs; another manages a food court downtown; one father is a public school janitor; another works the concessions at the new sports arena; one mother works in a nursing home; still another is a secretary. In addition, two mothers with whom I spoke related that they were currently attending school after which they hoped to find jobs.

In some cases, their parents' schooling or employment has caused shifts in the children's activities and responsibilities after school and on weekends. Their in-home duties must be done in addition to their schoolwork. I never understood why one particular girl did not accompany us to the library on Thursdays after school, or why she was rarely able to get her assignments completed on time. Then, I discovered she had full responsibility three evenings each week for her nieces and nephews until their parents returned from work or her mother returned from night school. Another girl baby-sat two small children every day after school until after seven o'clock in the evening for a woman who worked. That girl's homework was put off until late each night. Sometimes she completed her work. At other times, she did not.

The city took control of its public schools in June 1995. At one time, a former state governor likened these schools to a "black hole" (Ayers and Ford 1996, 89). Teachers and principals are now, more than ever, being held accountable for their students' performances. Schools are placed on academic probation when 15 percent of the student body does not meet or exceed national norms in reading and mathematics. The threat of reconstitution hangs over these schools, their principals, and the teachers.

According to the seventh graders I studied, they believe the children have been given the sole responsibility to raise those scores. Of course, the teachers and administrators feel it is their responsibility to teach the students well enough so that they will "meet or exceed national norms," but somehow the children believe it is up to them alone. The sense of personal responsibility for what happens to their school, principal, and teachers, whether the result of their own feelings or because they have been made to feel responsible, affects the children and their learning greatly, but not always in positive, productive ways, as has been shown.

The risk of closure and reconstitution shapes and, in some ways, constrains instruction and the children's learning in school, as has been discussed at length in the foregoing chapters on standardized tests, science in the school, and field trips. The children's assessments of what being on academic probation has meant to them personally suggest they feel constrained.

The chief operating officer and the mayor have announced that, as a result of their new public school policies and the concentrated efforts of the administrators and teachers, the system's high school students have posted the highest standardized test scores in a decade (Martinez 1997, page 4, section 2). The mayor used the test results to urge the General Assembly for more funding for school reform in the city. He did not mention that the scores already had a very high price attached to them. As much as some of the students claimed they believe the standardized tests "show what the teachers doin', an' what the kids learn so far," all of them worried about their performance on them and the ramifications of not passing.

At the same time, being on probation means that the schools receive additional funds for teacher training and long-overdue physical improvements. The Office of Accountability, Department of School Intervention team noted that the school needed a new boiler, new windows, and better maintenance, among other things. Better physical conditions, and radiators that do not heat with staccato clanks, will make the school a nicer place to spend time and in which to learn.

These students believed that coming to school and becoming credentialed will help them secure the jobs they want when they are grown and, perhaps, the power to create the society they envision. Ogbu (1978), MacLeod (1987), and Apple and Zenk (1996, 86–87) have documented similar beliefs among other groups of young African-Americans. These same researchers have also noted that the reality of the types of jobs African-Americans can usually find are nowhere near what they hope. However, these adolescents do not know this yet. So when Kay said, "The reason I'm goin' to school is to get an education to do somethin', an' to be a better person, both," her comments are reflecting a sincere belief that the school can play the integrating and educative role in children's social life that Dewey (1916/1985, 25–26) envisioned. These students want to become doctors, lawyers, scientists, actors, writers, teachers, and architects. They want to take their places as productive members of society, to own their own homes, and raise their families.

One school administrator has called these children "bounded." I understand why she did. Their families are far from wealthy, and they belong to a minority group that is traditionally repressed and discriminated against. Their poverty and that of their school district has a strong impact on their lives, on what they can do, and on the resources they can muster so they can do what they want to do. Some of them are given a great deal of responsibility at home for themselves, their siblings, and other family members at a far earlier age than nonminority, middle-class children.

These children have seen and experienced more of death and violence than perhaps other adolescents who do not live in ghettos have or could conceive. During the space of a few months, two of their friends were shot in gang-related incidents; another was stabbed to death; one girl was gang-raped.

They have learned, through experience, that the projects are places where police, fire personnel, ambulance drivers, welfare workers, and even telephone installers do not like to come. Perhaps their knowledge of these kinds of social facts is why the students often sounded wise beyond their years.

The children are being swept along by some of the real and fundamental changes happening around them and to them and their families. They cannot alter where they live or the conditions under which they live. They cannot change the stereotypes people might have of them because of their residence, their age, or their skin color. They cannot control what the government does about the welfare system. Nor can they influence much of what the state and city have set as the goals and objectives for them to master in order to graduate from elementary school. They have been made aware of the requirements and say that they are trying to meet them. Biggie claimed, "We're actually good kids." By and large, he is right.

In some instances, their efforts to do the right things, as they understand them, are stymied, most likely unintentionally, by many of the adults with whom they are in contact. When this happens, these children are not loath to look elsewhere for the help they think they need, as they did when some of them individually found mentors.

The phenomenon of interest that brought me to the door of this particular school was a broadly phrased curiosity about what young adolescent children want to know, and why and how they think they could learn what they want to know. My question was based in Schubert's (1993, 42; and 1986, 411) recurrent exhortation to think about "what is worth knowing and experiencing."

I was lucky to have been provided what amounted to free rein with a class of seventh-grade, middle-school children. At the conclusion of our first talk, in April 1996, the principal said, "Welcome to the family." At the time, I did not realize what those words implied. Her designation of me as "family member" meant that I was essentially given "free rein" to collect whatever data I thought I might need for my study. Any records I requested were collected, photocopied, and given to me. I was invited to attend every committee and faculty meeting that took place in the school during the two academic years I was there. I was asked to join any number of committees. I was sent on school-sponsored field trips, to out-of-state and in-state conferences and workshops at the school's expense, invited to attend lectures and teachers' in-service meetings, and provided with a mailbox in the office. I was even given a position title—resident anthropologist—although I think this title simply made it easier for the school personnel to talk about me to those who inquired about the woman running around with a video camera and hordes of children in tow. The principal, assistant principal, teachers, and auxiliary personnel could not have been more kind or open. I will never be able to thank them adequately. The principal's designation of me as a family member was quite different from the children's designation of me as fictive kin. In the first case, the designation conveyed rights and privileges. In the second, it also included responsibilities.

The data that treat my phenomenon of interest have been presented, for the most part, in these children's own words. They represent a collaborative effort between a particular group of students and me that lasted over two years. During that time, we explored what it is they want to know, and why, as well as how they approach learning. The quotations reflect and explain the children's worldviews, which are not necessarily those of the adults in their communities or of their teachers. I have tried to analyze, synthesize, and interpret them within the children's own conceptual frames.

My conclusions are simple. These children are learners like children everywhere, as Dewey so frequently pointed out. They have no clear idea about the exact steps required to reach their goals or what precise information they will need to take their places in society as adults. This is a factor more of their ages than anything else. They have a general idea that to achieve, they need to pass, and to pass, they need to "know [their] academics." They look to the school to supply them with "the how-to's an' what-for's" of those academic skills. They look to their families to provide models for their social interactions, and they look to their churches for some of the moral lessons they want and believe they need. They look to nonrelated adults for financial help, advice, and academic assistance.

What I learned during my work with the children is that they are not *culture bearers* because they are learning about their culture and how it operates. They know that they do not know, but they do not yet realize the full extent of what they do not know. They do not operate with a sense of culture as an integrated whole or with a sense that their actions should be directed toward creating that ideal. They function on a daily basis in a restricted environment, more because of their young age than because of their parents' socioeconomic status, and more because of that status than because of discrimination. However, socioeconomic status and discrimination are certainly contributory factors in their "boundedness." Perhaps it is because of these kinds of restrictions that they often sound so naive.

These students have grown up in a primarily African-American community and have attended a school with a locally defined version of an Afro-centric curriculum. The school's version of an Afro-centric curriculum stresses pride in themselves, their abilities, and their heritage, and emphasizes learning to value cultural differences. That political message comes across clearly. The students with whom I worked most closely have a clear sense of self and a can-do attitude. As my data clearly show, it is when their desires run up against barriers that the system has placed in their way that they become frustrated. My data strongly suggest that this can-do attitude may be responsible, in part, for the students' devising ways to circumvent the restrictions they feel are a direct result of academic probation's shaping and constraining of their school experiences. Very likely, it is their school's Afro-centric curriculum and the children's responses to it that enable them to push what Dewey (1934/1987, 197) called their "bounding horizon[s]" so frequently and so successfully.

Because they have been isolated by living in a public housing project and attending a school where the student body is all African-American, they have been subjected to discrimination on the basis of where they live, their age, skin color, and stereotypical assumptions about their activities, as the data have shown. But, these same social facts, along with the efforts of many of the adults in their community, their teachers, and school personnel, have also shielded them from much of the discrimination they might have experienced had they lived in a different community and attended a school where students were of different ethnicities. (See Hollingshead 1949/1963 for a classic study of older adolescents that at-

Chapter 9: Teach Me 243

tributed much of what they did and how they thought to class-based social forces influencing their lives and activities. See also Hersch 1998 for a more recent study of adolescents that attributed their "separate teen community" where there were rules without structure, values without clear morality, and codes without consistency to a society that has relinquished its responsibility to connect with, advise, and supervise teenagers).

Because these children are young and without much money, they did not venture out of their neighborhood alone often. The children said that when they traveled locally, it was generally with their parents or relatives. Their excursions were most often limited to stores, relatives' houses, and, less frequently, to shopping malls. Perhaps these social facts have isolated them from additional discrimination they might have encountered had they roamed more freely, and more regularly, alone.

These children pick and choose, accept and reject what they want to learn and investigate from the choices that are available to them and from the opportunities they can create, without necessarily having an overarching scheme or end-picture to guide those decisions. Moreover, the very fact that they do pick, choose, accept, reject, and innovate shows a typical adolescent awareness of their "dawning capacities" (Dewey 1897/1972, 92) to do so. The model that most closely describes what these adolescents do as they live their daily lives is *cultural shopping*. I have repeatedly stressed this model because it fits the data of what the students do and explains what drives their behaviors.

Yet, because these children are shopping, they also have the power to be agents of change in their own and the next generation, too. *Change*, especially as it relates to culture, has always been problematic to explain. What causes it? How fast does it occur? Under what circumstances does it occur? Is it permanent?

Change is usually thought of as happening slowly. It requires, and results in, shifts in political power bases. Generally, adults are considered the instigators and implementers of change and the ones most resistant to change. Changes that happen in times of stress, whether social, political, or economic, are usually part of what Wallace (1956), among others, has called secular "revitalist" movements.

A revitalist movement is clearly now under way in this community, fueled, in part, by regentrification, welfare reforms, community empowerment initiatives, and grass-roots efforts bolstered by macrosocial institutions (e.g., the police, the housing authority, and schools) to eliminate the gangs and improve the quality of life for neighborhood residents. Changes are coming fast and laying the foundations for future changes and political alliances. Revitalist movements provide a way in which radical changes that impact the current and future shape of culture can occur within a single generation.

In the past, children have simply not been considered as having much—or, more truthfully, any—role in shaping their culture or in the conduct of social institutions. They have not typically been included in the category of "agents of change" because they have not been seen as having power. These data clearly show otherwise.

I see the children as having significant roles in effecting culture change in the following areas:

- By independently deciding not to join gangs, they are decreasing the power and influence of those gangs now and in the future.
- By identifying where they believe the system has failed them and going outside their school to get the skills and information they believe they need to succeed in school, they are challenging the idea that school is the only place where learning can occur and that textbooks contain all the information it is necessary to know. If and when they become teachers and parents, they may bring some of those realizations to bear on their own pedagogies, thereby changing the way the next generation of learners thinks about and structures learning, and how those children will be taught.

Chapter 9: Teach Me 245

- By incorporating mentoring into their social, academic, and spiritual lives, they have already brought about changes that might have long-lasting and important ramifications. Adults and children are interacting on a sustained basis that benefits and enriches the lives of all parties, as the data have shown. Some of the teachers have re-instituted a Friday advisory program that is aimed at helping the students. It remains to be seen whether the mentoring concept and the advisory program become institutionalized at the school, thereby changing the "school culture" for the next set of students.

When I began my research with these particular students, I thought that I would write an ethnographic account of what they did and said when I was following them around. I intended to couple my observations with their explanations about what they were doing, why, and their rationales, analyzing the data according to an already existing theoretical framework. I never anticipated that the children would modify what they did to the degree that much of the data I collected involves their interactions with me, and me trying to teach them some of what they wanted to know.

I wanted to learn about the children's community; they decided that if I were to follow them around, they had to teach me survival skills. I wanted to investigate their families, focusing on the out-of-school socialization that occurs in that institution, and they "adopted" me so I came to know firsthand what *family* means to them. I wanted to explore what they did during their playtime and free time, so they taught me how to jump and twirl rope, what to look for "up on the tracks," and how to play house. I was interested in documenting their learning, using science as a focal point, and they reshaped their science lessons so that I became a person who taught them some of the "how-to's and what-for's." The principal was interested in learning why the children were scoring so poorly on their standardized tests; but when I asked them to explain what they did when they took the tests, they insisted I show them where they had gone wrong and teach them better test-taking strategies. I wanted to record what museum exhibits intrigued the children and why; instead, they showed me that almost everything they came across could be interesting and taught me to think in terms of using their pre-existing, gender-based social organization as a possible pedagogical method.

These data forced me to reconsider how I had thought about culture and to ask what they were telling me about how children go about learning their culture. The end result was that the data required the development of a different theoretical model (*cultural shopping*) in order to make sense.

There is a repetitive theme that runs through the children's ethnography and which strongly emerges in every chapter. The students want to learn, and are willing to do whatever it takes to learn about the things that interest them. They will even suffer through things that do not immediately interest them in the event that those things might be "useful learnin'" someday. They want to sample wide varieties of experiences and willingly participate in activities that broaden their horizons. Where opportunities do not exist, for whatever structural reasons, they will do what they can, and what they can conceive, to create them. These students intend to be "successful young [people]" and toward that goal, they ask almost everyone they meet: "Teach me." My wish is that their wishes come true.

CHAPTER 10

AFTERWORD

The 1997–98 school year was essentially finished two weeks before June began, although graduation was not until the middle of that month. By that time, the children had already taken their standardized tests and were preparing to go on their class trip. They had worked for the last four months to amass the monies they needed for their African-American Heritage Tour of Charleston, St. Helena Island, Savannah, and Atlanta. The trip cost $550, and, on top of this, there were graduation fees and luncheon costs to be paid. Some of the seventh and eighth graders were unable to save the required sums, despite the help of church sponsors, teachers, and other adults, and monies generated by doing odd jobs and participating in fund-raisers such as car washes, pickle days, and candy sales. However, no child who had at least made a down payment on the trip was left behind. When they returned home and stepped off the tour bus, they learned the results of their Iowa tests.

The children took the IGAP tests in mid-April. The eighth graders took the complete battery of the ITBS during the second week of May. Tatiana confided that "[Our teacher] say she think ten of us'll pass." Out of twenty-four children who entered seventh grade in 1996, five were retained in that grade (one of them had transferred to a different school) following their May 1997 ITBS tests. Of the remaining nineteen children who entered eighth grade, three are classified as learning disabled (LD). Sixteen eighth-grade children from the original group I began to study in 1996 took grade-level ITBS examinations in May 1998. Twelve of them scored at the seventh-grade level or better in reading; fourteen scored seventh grade second month or better in mathematics, but only twelve scored above the required levels in both the mathematics and reading sections. Seven students scored at the eighth-grade level or above in reading; seven scored at grade level in mathematics, although they were not all the same students. Only six children scored at grade level (8.0) in both reading and mathematics. The reading scores for the class ranged from fourth grade sixth month through tenth grade sixth month. Princess, Art, Biggie, Ed, Ken, Fred, Waldo, Tatiana, Keesie, Twan, Corelle, and Lemar all "survive[d] on the Iowa test" with scores good enough to move them out of eighth grade. However, Keesie, Ken, Corelle, Twan, and Fred did not score at grade level in reading, while Ken, Princess, Corelle, and Keesie did not score at grade level in mathematics.

Interestingly, when I polled the eighth graders following the ITBS battery, all said they felt they had done well on the tests. Tatiana identified the final reading section as "long an' hard." She said she did not finish it. Lavinia, almost with embarrassment, related that she had "just marked them bubbles." Despite the fact that she, as a learning-disabled student, was entitled to additional time to work through the tests, she claimed she forgot, and randomly filled in bubbles. Her latest reading score is sixth grade eighth month, and her mathematics score is seventh grade seventh month. Kay, DeDe, Kiki, and Terrell were all retained in seventh grade at the end of the 1997 school year. Only DeDe qualifies to pass seventh grade this year if promotion decisions are made solely on the basis of her ITBS scores.

The school remains on academic probation with only 14 percent of its students testing at or above national norms in reading (up from 11.7 percent in 1997), as measured by the ITBS. Slightly more than 23 percent of the student body scored at the national norm level in mathematics (up from 17.1 percent in

Chapter 10: Afterword

1997). However, to be taken off the probation list, the school needed 20 percent scoring at those levels in both tested subject areas.

Graduation Day will be bittersweet this year, as it was last year. The teachers make a big fuss over graduation because, as one of them confided, "This might be the last one some of them [the children] ever have." The Graduation Committee, composed of the assistant principal, seventh- and eighth-grade teachers along with other staff members, spends much time and effort to assure every child receives a special recognition award, whether it is for "Perfect Attendance," "Citizenship," "Most Improved," "Honor Roll," or "Class Officer."

Much thought is also given to designing the printed programs for the event. The class valedictorian and salutatorian are chosen with special care since each will present a speech during the graduation ceremony. The children rehearse for days.

The ceremony will take place in sanctuary of the corner church that shares its parking lot with the school. The graduates will wear white caps and gowns, and four seventh graders carrying African staffs will act as the honor guard. The eighth graders will file down the aisle to the sound of live music, courtesy of the music teacher and some of the other men who work at the school. The valedictorian and salutatorian will each present the speech he or she wrote. The principal and assistant principal will talk, as will a guest speaker.

In 1997, their alderman presented the keynote address. His speech was designed to encourage the children to continue to achieve. He recounted his own life history as an example of how it is possible to overcome poverty by having a good attitude, working hard, and remaining determined. The graduates will sing. They will receive flowers and congratulations from everyone. When they emerge from the church, if last year was any indication, there will be hugs, tears, cheers, balloons, and maybe even a limousine or two to take the students to family celebrations. The graduates will not be allowed to re-enter the school when the other students return to classes. These children are supposed to be "movin' on."

As happened last year, some of the eighth graders will not march in the graduation procession. Instead, because graduation is on a regular school day, they will sit at the back of the church, watching their classmates receive their diplomas. They will be the ones who did not achieve the board-required levels on their ITBS tests in mathematics and reading; who were not approved for waivers; or whose teachers, in consultation with the principal, decided they were not going to pass. These students will attend summer school and try to meet the grade-level requirements again. If they do not succeed, they will be back in eighth grade next year. If they turn fifteen years old by December 1, 1998, they will go to a transitional school until they pass. Some will undoubtedly "make the grade." One or more of them might drop out of school all together.

Tatiana plans to spend the summer months tutoring younger students at her elementary school, along with Twan, Coco, Ceana, Sierra, and a couple of the other eighth graders. They all will be fourteen years old before the end of May 1998 and can then legally work twenty hours each week. These students are looking forward to working with, teaching, and interacting with younger children and being paid for it. Ceana says she will buy clothes with her money. Tatiana says she will save her salary for "trips an' stuff."

Jasmine has kept in contact with me although she attended a different school during the 1997–98 academic year. She enjoys her new school more than her old one but confesses to having some social and academic problems there, too. She reports that her teacher has had a number of conversations with her about her "attitude." Apparently, he believes many of her problems stem from "people doin' stuff to get me hyper an' I respond to it, so now, I just keep my mouth closed." She has vowed to work on this along with her academic subjects.

In April 1998, Jasmine's teacher assigned the Spring Break homework of taking practice ITBS tests under simulated test conditions (forty minutes for each section). Jasmine corrected the tests herself using teacher-provided answer keys. She said no one double-checked her answers or her scoring, either at home or at school. She said she did not finish reading the test paragraphs or questions during the allotted time. Because she was running out of time, she bounced around from paragraph to paragraph, and filled in "answer-bubbles" at random. She felt that she "did all right" on these practice tests because she scored "'round sixty percent correct." She assured me she "didn't cheat" either on the tests or the scoring.

Before the actual tests, she confided that she held very little hope of achieving the sixth-grade level in reading and mathematics on the ITBS that she needs to pass out of seventh grade. However, Jasmine also mentioned that her "mama talked to my teacher an' he say he was gonna promote me, even if I don't have the scores." Can the classroom teacher make that kind of decision when the board of education has set minimum score requirements for promotion to the next grade? If Jasmine does not achieve those scores, will she be required to repeat seventh grade a third time despite her teacher's recommendation that she pass?

Jasmine has grown and matured during the past school year. Although not yet fourteen years of age, she now stands six feet tall! When I allude to her height, she moans that her mother calls her "a giant, an' I don't wanna be no giant." She really hopes to work this summer because she has outgrown almost everything she owns and says: "I'll be savin' to buy me school clothes." She has applied for a job at the Park District facility near her house, "an' I'm waitin' on them to call me back. I'll get minimal [sic] wages, but it gonna add up quick."

Biggie, Moochie, and I composed their resumes so they could apply for part-time summer employment tutoring at a local grade school (Biggie) and working at a city-run art gallery (Moochie). Each boy used a preloaded template on my computer to type his own resume.

Biggie's mentor from church secured him his job for the second year in a row. He is going to take public transportation to work by himself this year. His practice run using buses and transfers was to come out to my house to type his resume. He plans to apply for a second job at the company where his mother works following the end of the summer school tutoring project. He anticipates he will need to update his resume before applying for this second job.

Moochie holds little hope for getting the job at the city art gallery where he would really like to work. He reported that when he went to apply for the position, there were two thousand applicants for such city-sponsored summer jobs. He thinks that since he attached a printed resume to his application, he might stand a better chance than those who did not have resumes. If he does not get called for the city job, he added that he might try to get a paid position at the Boys and Girls Club or, if that attempt fails, work around the house with his father.

Although the children want to save their money, none of them has a savings account. They tell me the Bank-in-School program is defunct, and that they consider the local bank's practices to be "unfair." Earlier in the year, when the children began talking about how to earn the money for their class trip, I suggested they establish personal savings accounts at the neighborhood branch bank to earn a little interest.

Moochie liked the idea of making money on his money. He went over to the bank to talk with someone about opening a savings account. He claimed the bank officer with whom he spoke said the bank charged a monthly service fee on accounts under a certain amount. He said that he was told that there would be no fee if his class participated in the Bank-in-School program, but unless every student contributed $5.00 weekly, there would be a monthly service fee deducted from every savings account. It did not take Moochie long to figure out that he would be losing money on this venture.

The other children accepted his word as gospel, even though I found it difficult to believe, and everyone dismissed the idea of opening accounts. Twan's bank account is, therefore, most often located in his pocket. And Moochie's is hidden in his room, safe from his little cousins, nieces, and nephews.

Chapter 10: Afterword

This past school year has been one of great physical changes for Biggie and Moochie. Both boys grew taller and their voices deepened. They developed an interest in girls and in improving their physiques.

Biggie also became more serious about his schoolwork and extremely focused on improving his reading. He attended Saturday tutoring classes at his church in addition to working on his reading and vocabulary skills with his mother and me. His ITBS reading score rose fifteen months above the score he earned at the end of seventh grade. Moochie's score improved twelve months over where it had been at the end of seventh grade. Although he is still involved in various science projects and investigations, he has recently branched out into lifting weights.

Biggie's family moved out of the projects. Their new apartment is on the first floor of a three-flat building owned by an African-American. It is located in an area where a Latino gang's borders abut those of an African-American gang's. The building's front door was recently tagged with the Latino gang's graffiti. The mark was subsequently reworked into a design that promised death to that gang. Biggie said he had heard that property owners on the block were considering putting fences around their properties, "so if anyone go on 'em, they [the property owners] can legally shoot 'em." He also confided that some of the neighborhood children wondered if I were his "patrol officer" [sic]. He added that perhaps if they thought he were bad enough to have one [a parole officer], no one would bother him.

In February 1998, Moochie's family bought their own house in a different neighborhood. The move surprised Moochie. His father had told me about six months before the actual closing that he was looking for a house. At the time of our conversation, he was not committed to any specific area of the city.

The brick bungalow-style house they finally bought is seven miles away from where Moochie grew up. It is, however, two blocks from one of Moochie's brothers, around the corner from a group of cousins, and down the street from his auntie. Moochie's sister and her children live in the basement "in-law" apartment. Moochie is monitoring a pear tree in the backyard for fruit and he has staked out an entire (unheated) attic as a private domain where he can perform science experiments and lift weights. He has already discovered an area called "the hills" near his house that is analogous to "the tracks." He says geese nest there and he wants to find out "what else it got."

Bibliography

Abrahams, R. D. 1963. Some jump rope rhymes from South Philadelphia. *Keystone Folklore Quarterly* 8:3–5.

Abrahams, R. D., ed. 1969. *Jumping rope rhymes: A dictionary.* Austin: University of Texas Press.

Allen, W. R. 1985. Race, income and family dynamics: A study of adolescent male socialization processes and outcomes. In *Beginnings: The social and affective development of black children,* eds. W. B. Spencer, G. K. Brookins, and W. R. Allen, 271–90. Hillsdale: Lawrence Erlbaum Associates.

Anderson, E. 1990. *Streetwise: Race, class, and change in an urban community.* Chicago: The University of Chicago Press.

Anyon, J. 1980. Social class and the hidden curriculum of work. *Journal of Education* 162:67–92.

———. 1997. *Ghetto schooling: A political economy of urban educational reform.* New York: Teachers College Columbia University.

Appiah, K. A. 1994. Identity, authenticity, survival: Multicultural societies and social reproduction. In *Multiculturalism,* ed. A. Gutman, 149–63. Princeton: Princeton University Press.

Apple, M. W. 1993. *Official knowledge: Democratic education in a conservative age.* New York: Routledge.

———. 1995. *Education and power.* 2d ed. New York: Routledge.

———. 1996. *Cultural politics and education.* New York: Teachers College Press.

Apple, M. W., and C. Zenk. 1996. American realities: Poverty, economy, and education. In Cultural *politics and education,* ed. M. W. Apple, 68–90. New York: Teachers College Press.

Asante, M. K. 1988. *Afrocentricity.* Trenton: Africa World Press.

Aschenbrenner, J. 1975. *Lifelines: Black families in Chicago.* New York: Holt, Rinehart and Winston, Inc.

Ayers, W., and P. Ford. 1996. Chaos and opportunity. In *City kids, city teachers,* eds. W. Ayers and P. Ford, 81–90. New York: The New Press.

Bernstein, B. 1971. *Class, codes and control*, vol. 1. London: Routledge and Kegan Paul.

———. 1973. *Class, codes and control*, vol. 2. London: Routledge and Kegan Paul.

———. 1975. *Class, codes and control*, vol. 3. London: Routledge and Kegan Paul.

———. 1990. *Class, codes and control*, vol. 4. London: Routledge and Kegan Paul.

———. 1996. *Pedagogy, symbolic control and identity: Theory, research, critique*. Bristol: Taylor and Francis.

Bizar, M. 1997. Standardized testing is undermining the goals of reform. On-line document available on the Internet at http://www.ncrel.org/mands/docs4-2.html.

Bourgois, P. 1995. *In search of respect: Selling crack in El Barrio*. New York: Cambridge University Press.

Bruner, J. S. 1975. Play is serious business. *Psychology Today* 9:81–83.

Campbell, D. T. 1996. Can we overcome worldview incommensurability/relativity in trying to understand the other? In *Ethnography and human development: Context and meaning in social inquiry*, eds. R. Djazair, A. Colby, and R. A. Shweder, 153–72. Chicago: The University of Chicago Press.

Carpenter, C., B. Glassner, B. D. Johnson, and J. Loughlin, eds. 1988. *Kids, drugs, and crime*. Lexington: Lexington Books.

Chodorow, N. 1978. *The reproduction of mothering: Psychoanalysis and the sociology of gender*. Berkeley: University of California Press.

Delpit, L. D. 1993. *The silenced dialogue: Power and pedagogy in educating other people's children*. In *Beyond silenced voices: Class, race, and gender in United States schools*, eds. L. Weis and M. Fine, 119–375. Albany: State University of New York Press.

Dewey, J. 1896/1972. A pedagogical experiment. In *John Dewey, early essays*, ed. J. A. Boydston, 244–46. Carbondale and Edwardsville: Southern Illinois University Press.

———. 1896/1972. The influence of the high school upon educational models. In *John Dewey, early essays*, ed. J. A. Boydston, 270–80. Carbondale and Edwardsville: Southern Illinois University Press.

Bibliography

———. 1896/1981. Experience is pedagogical. In *The philosophy of John Dewey*, ed. J. J. McDermott, 421–523. Chicago: University of Chicago Press.

———. 1897/1972. My pedagogic creed. In *John Dewey, early essays*, ed. J. A. Boydston, 84–95. Carbondale and Edwardsville: Southern Illinois University Press.

———. 1898/1972. The primary-education fetich. In *John Dewey, early essays*, ed. J. A. Boydston, 254–69. Carbondale and Edwardsville: Southern Illinois University Press.

———. 1900/1990. *The child and the curriculum*. Chicago: University of Chicago Press.

———. 1901/1991. How the mind learns. Brigham Young educational lectures. In *John Dewey, miscellaneous writings*, ed. J. A. Boydston, 213–25. Carbondale and Edwardsville: Southern Illinois University Press.

———. 1901/1991. The social aspects of education. Brigham Young educational lectures. In *John Dewey, miscellaneous writings*, ed. J. A. Boydston, 226–41. Carbondale and Edwardsville: Southern Illinois University Press.

———. 1901/1991. Imagination. Brigham Young educational lectures. In *John Dewey, miscellaneous writings*, ed. J. A. Boydston, 242–54. Carbondale and Edwardsville: Southern Illinois University Press.

———. 1902/1991. Periods of growth. Brigham Young educational lectures. In *John Dewey, miscellaneous writings*, ed. J. A. Boydston, 255–68. Carbondale and Edwardsville: Southern Illinois University Press.

———. 1910/1985. *How we think*. In *How we think and selected essays*, ed. J. A. Boydston, 182–356. Carbondale and Edwardsville: Southern Illinois University Press.

———. 1916/1985. *Democracy and education*. Carbondale and Edwardsville: Southern Illinois University Press.

———. 1934/1987. *Art as experience*. In *John Dewey, the later works*, ed. J. A. Boydston, 9–352. Carbondale and Edwardsville: Southern University Press.

———. 1938/1963. *Experience and education*. New York: Macmillan Publishing Company.

———. 1949/1991. *The field of "value."* In *John Dewey, essays, typescripts, and knowing and the known*, ed. J. A. Boydston, 343–57. Carbondale and Edwardsville: Southern Illinois University Press.

———. 1951/1991. *Introduction to William Heard Kilpatrick: Trail blazer in education*. In *John Dewey, miscellaneous writings*, ed. J. A. Boydston, 52–56. Carbondale and Edwardsville: Southern Illinois University Press.

———. 1979/1985. Interest and effort in education. In *John Dewey, essays on philosophy and psychology, 1912–1914*, ed. J. A. Boydston, 153–97. Carbondale and Edwardsville: Southern Illinois University Press.

Dickinson, H., and M. Erben. 1994. Bernstein and Ricoeur: Contours for the social understanding of narratives and selves. In *Discourse and reproduction: Essays in honor of Basil Bernstein*, eds. P. Atkinson, B. Davies, and S. Delamont, 253–68. Cresskill: Hampton Press, Inc.

Enfied, M. L., and V. Greene. 1996. What Is Project Read®. On-line document available on the Internet at http://www.project.read.com/whatis.html.

FairTest. 1997. How standardized testing damages education. *Parent Directory*. Cambridge, Mass.: FairTest. On-line document dated Aug. 28 available on the Internet at http://www.fairtest.org/facts/howharm.html.

———. 1998. FairTest introduction. *National center for fair and open testing*. Cambridge, Mass: FairTest. On-line document available on the Internet at http://www.fairtest.org/.

Farr, R., and B. Greene. 1993. Improving reading assessments: Understanding the social and political agenda for testing. *Educational Horizons* 72:20–27.

Folb, E. A. 1980. *Runnin' down some lines*. Cambridge: Harvard University Press.

Fordham, S. 1985. Black students' school success: Coping with the burden of 'acting white'. ERIC Document Reproduction Service No. ED281948.

———. 1986. Black students' school success: An ethnographic study in a large urban public school system. Preliminary report submitted to the Spencer Foundation. ERIC Document Reproduction Service No. ED281949.

———. 1988. Racelessness as a factor in black students' school success: Pragmatic strategy or Pyrrhic victory? *Harvard Educational Review* 59:54–84.

Franczek-Sullivan, __. 1996. Placing non-performing schools on probation. (Sept. 15). Np: Np.

Gilligan, C. 1979. Woman's place in man's life cycle. *Harvard Educational Review* 49:431–46.

Goodwin, M. H. 1990. *He-said-she-said: Talk as social organization among black children*. Bloomington: Indiana University Press.

Haberman, M. 1991. The pedagogy of poverty versus good teaching. *Phi Delta Kappan* (December 1991): 290–94.

Hare, R. B. and L. A. Castenell, Jr. 1985. No place to run, no place to hide: Comparative status and future prospects of black boys. In *Beginnings: The social and affective development of black children*, eds. M. B. Spencer, G. K. Brookins, and W. R. Allen, 201–14. Hillsdale: Lawrence Erlbaum Associates.

Harris, M. 1964. *Patterns of race relations in the Americas*. New York: WW Norton.

Hersch, P. 1998. *A tribe apart: A journey into the heart of American adolescence*. New York: The Ballentine Publishing Group.

Herskovits, M. J. 1941. *The myth of the Negro past*. Boston: Beacon Press.

———. 1966. *The New World Negro*. Bloomington: Indiana University Press.

Hollingshead, A. B. 1949/1963. *Elmtown's youth*. New York: Science Editions.

Holt, J. 1968. *How children fail*. New York: Pitman Publishing Corporation.

———. 1972/1995. *Freedom and beyond*. Portsmouth: Boynton/Cook Publishers.

Johnston, P. H. 1992. *Constructive evaluation of literacy activity*. New York: Longman.

Jones, L., and L. Newman. 1997. *Our America*. New York: Scribner.

Kagan, S. 1990. *Cooperative learning resources for teachers*. San Juan Capistrano: Resources for Teachers.

Kellaghan, T., K. Sloane, B. Alvarez, and B. S. Bloom. 1993. *The home environment and school learning*. San Francisco: Jossey-Bass Publishers.

Kohlberg, L., and C. Gilligan. 1971. The adolescent as a philosopher: The discovery of the self in a postconventional world. *Daedalus* 100:1051–86.

Kondo, D. 1992. *Crafting selves: Power, gender, and discourses of identity in a Japanese workplace*. Chicago: University of Chicago Press.

Kotlowitz, A. 1991. *There are no children here*. New York: Anchor Books.

Koziol, N. A. 1997. Mentors give students a big push in the right direction. *Chicago Tribune* (July 20) sec. 18:17–27.

Ksander, M., and B. Berg. 1988. The deterrent effect of adult versus juvenile jurisdiction. In *Kids, drugs and crime*, eds. C. Carpenter, B. Glassner, B. D. Johnson, and J. Loughlin, 209–18. Lexington: Lexington Books.

Kuhn, T. S. 1977. *The essential tension: Selected studies in scientific tradition and change*. Chicago: The University of Chicago Press.

Labov, W. 1982. Competing value systems in the inner-city schools. In *Children in and out of school: Ethnography and education*, eds. P. Gilmore and A. A. Glatthorn, 148–71. Washington, D.C.: Center for Applied Linguistics.

Lee, R. 1974. Male-female residence arrangements and political power in human hunter-gatherers. *Archaeology of Sexual Behavior* 3:167–73.

Lees, S. 1993. *Sugar and spice: Sexuality and adolescent girls*. London: Penguin Books.

Lemann, N. 1992. *The promised land: The great black migration and how it changed America*. New York: Vintage Books.

Lever, J. 1976. Sex differences in the games children play. *Social Problems* 23:478–87.

Levin, H. M. 1994. Accelerated schools after eight years. Stanford University, *Accelerated Schools Project* (December 1994), Palo Alto, CA.

Lincoln, C. E., and L. H. Mamiya. 1990. *The black church in the African American experience*. Durham: Duke University Press.

Lowe, F. H. 1997. Uniforms are a fitting subject for 70 percent of schools. *Chicago Educator* 2 (January 8): 5.

Macintyre, M. 1993. Fictive kinship or mistaken identity? Fieldwork on Tubetube Island, Papua New Guinea. In *Gendered fields: Women, men and ethnography*, eds. D. Bell, P. Caplan, and W. J. Karim, 44–62. London: Routledge.

McLaughlin, M. W., and S. B. Heath. 1993. Casting the self: Frames for identity and dilemmas for policy. In *Identity and inner-city youth: Beyond ethnicity and gender*, eds. M. W. McLaughlin and S. B. Heath, 213. New York and London: Teachers College Press.

MacLeod, J. 1987. *Ain't no makin' it*. Boulder: Westview Press.

Martin, J. M., and E. P. Martin. 1985. *The helping tradition in the black family and community*. Silver Spring: National Association of Social Workers.

Martinez, M. 1997. Test scores in math, reading bring praise for Chicago's high schools. *Chicago Tribune* (May 1) sec. 2: 4.

Mead, G. H. 1934. *Mind, self and society*. Chicago: University of Chicago Press.

Mead, M. 1928. *Coming of age in Samoa: A psychological study of primitive youth for western civilization*. New York: W. Morrow & Co.

Meisels, S. J. 1989. High-stakes testing in kindergarten. *Educational Leadership* 46:16–22.

Mickelson, R. A. 1990. The attitude-achievement paradox among black adolescents. *Sociology of Education* 63:44–61.

Monti, D. J. 1994. *Wannabe: Gangs in schools and suburbs*. Oxford: Blackwell.

Murray, C. B., and H. H. Fairchild. 1989. Models of black adolescent academic underachievement. In *Black adolescents*, ed. R. L. Jones, 229–45. Berkeley: Cobb & Henry.

Myers, W. D. 1993. *Malcolm X: By any means necessary*. New York: Scholastic Press.

Nichols, L. M. 1991. Reducing economic inequality can stop racism. In *Racism in America: Opposing viewpoints*, ed. W. Dudley, 240–46. San Diego: Greenhaven Press, Inc.

Noddings, N. 1992. *The challenge to care in schools: An alternative approach to education*. New York: Teachers College Press.

Ogbu, J. 1978. *Minority education and caste: The American system in cross-cultural perspective*. New York: Academic Press.

———. 1985. Ecology of competence among inner-city blacks. In *Beginnings: The social and affective development of black children*, eds. M. B. Spencer, G. K. Brookins, and W. R. Allen, 50–73. Hillsdale: Lawrence Erlbaum Associates.

Olson, L. 1998. Study warns against reliance on testing data. *Education Week on the Web*. On-line document dated March 25 available on the Internet at http://www.edweek.org/ew/vol-17/28chic.h17.

Opie, I. 1994. *The people in the playground*. Oxford: Oxford University Press.

Ornstein, A. C. 1993. Strategies for testing. *Educational Horizons* 72:11–16.

Piaget, J. 1932/1965. *The moral judgment of the child*. New York: Free Press.

Pitman, M. A., R. A. Eisikovits, and M. L. Dobbert. 1989. *Culture acquisition: A holistic approach to human learning*. New York: Praeger.

Rawick, G. P. 1972. *The American slave: A composite autobiography: From sundown to sunup: The making of the black community*. Westport: Greenwood Publishing Co.

Rhone, E. 1992. Improving negative behavior in adolescent pupils through collaborative initiatives. ERIC Document Reproduction Service No. ED346418.

Schonert-Reich, K. A., and D. Offer. 1992. Seeking help and social support in adolescence: The role of non-related adults. ERIC Document Reproduction Service No. ED354295.

Schubert, W. H. 1986. *Curriculum: Perspective, paradigm, and possibility*. New York: Macmillan Publishing Company.

———. 1993. Teacher and student lore: Their ways of looking at it. *Contemporary Education* 65:42–46.

Schubert, W. H., and A. L. Lopez-Schubert. 1981. Toward curricula that are of, by, and therefore for students. *The Journal of Curriculum Theorizing* 3:239–51.

Schubert, W. H., and A. L. Lopez. 1994. Students' curriculum experiences. In *The international encyclopedia of education* (2d ed., vol. 10), eds. T. Husen and T. N. Postlethwaite, 5813–18. Oxford: Pergamon.

Schultz, E. A., and R. H. Lavenda. 1995. *Anthropology: A Perspective on the human condition*. Mountain View: Mayfield Publishing Company.

Schwartzman, H. B. 1976. The anthropological study of children's play. *Annual Review of Anthropology* 5:289–328.

Shepard, S. 1997. Grandma. *The Journal of Ordinary Thought* 23:12.

Simmons, J. 1996. *The scientific 100: A ranking of the most influential scientists, past and present*. Secaucus: Carol Publishing Group.

Sipe, C. L. 1996. Mentoring: A synthesis of P/PV's research: 1988–1995. ERIC Document Reproduction Service No. ED404410.

Smith, R. 1970. The nuclear family in Afro-American kinship. *Journal of Comparative Family Studies* 1:55–70.

Smith, S. 1996. Saving our cities from the experts. In *City kids, city teachers*, eds. W. Ayers and P. Ford, 91–109. New York: The New Press.

Sprick, R. S., and L. M. Howard. 1997. *The teacher's encyclopedia of behavior management*. Longmont: Sopris West.

Stack, C. 1974. *All our kin*. New York: BasicBooks.

Staples, R. 1973. *The black women in America: Sex, marriage, and the family*. Chicago: Nelson-Hall Publishers.

———. 1985. Changes in black family structure: The conflict between family ideology and structural conditions. *Journal of Marriage and the Family* 47:1005–13.

Staples, R., and L. B. Johnson. 1993. *Black families at the crossroads: Challenges and prospects*. San Francisco: Jossey-Bass Publishers.

Taylor, R. L. 1989. *Black youth, role models and the social construction of identity*. In *Black adolescents*, ed. R. L. Jones, 155–74. Berkeley: Cobb & Henry.

Teens and self-image: Survey results. 1998. *Chicago Sun-Times* (May 1–3) USA Weekend section: 18.

Thorne, B. 1993. *Gender play: Girls and boys at school*. New Brunswick: Rutgers University Press.

Thrasher, F. M. 1927. *The gang: A study of 1,313 gangs in Chicago*. Chicago: University of Chicago Press.

Turner, V. 1967. *Forest of Symbols*. Ithaca: Cornell University Press.

Vanover, B., and W. E. Utesch. 1993. Mentoring as an intervention for adolescents in the school setting with potential or actual gang involvement. ERIC Document Reproduction Service No. ED383938.

Wallace, A. 1956. Revitalization movements. *American Anthropologist* 58:264–81.

Watkins, W. H. 1993. Black curriculum orientations: A preliminary inquiry. *Harvard Educational Review* 63:321–38.

———. 1994. Multicultural education: Toward a historical and political inquiry. *Educational Theory* 44:99–117.

White, M. 1993. *The material child: Coming of age in Japan and America*. New York: Free Press.

Yeo, F. 1997. The inner-city school and critical pedagogy: Locations of possibility and difference. In *Issues and trends in critical pedagogy*, ed. B. Kanapol, 93–110. Cresskill: Hampton Press, Inc.

Index

Abrahams, R. D., 89

Academic performance statistics, 1, 248

Academic probation
 perceived effects of, 81-82, 145, 179, 238
 reasons behind, 1, 2

Accelerated schools, 178

Afro-centrism
 local definition, 38-39

Allen, W. R., 42

Alternative assessment, 227-229

Alvarez, B., 224

Anderson, E., 19, 203

Anrig. *See* Bizar

Anyon, J., 182, 202, 203, 220, 221, 222

Appiah, K. A., 80

Apple, M. W., 33, 172, 183, 221, 222, 234, 236, 238

Archimedes. *See* Simmons

Asante, M. K., 38

Aschenbrenner, J., 40, 41, 42, 43, 53, 54

Ayers, W., 237

Bateson. *See* Schwartzman

Berg, B., 20

Bernstein, B., 142, 143, 203, 204, 224

Bizar, M., 180, 201, 211, 213, 222

Bloom, B. S., 224

Bourgois, P., 18, 31

Bruner, J. S., 113

Campbell, D. T., 38

Carpenter, C., 6

Castenell, L. A., 80

Change
 generalized, 234-238
 children as agents, 243, 244
 regentrification, 11-14
 revitalism movement, 33-34

Chicago Sun-Times, 38

Chodorow, N., 140, 175

Codes
 elaborated, 141-144
 inclusive, 110, 137, 142, 143
 restricted, 142-144, 145
 switching, 203
 use for control, 141, 142

Cultural shopping
 definition, 7, 8
 examples
  church, 121
  gangs, 12-13
  fictive kin, 54, 79

learning, 243, 246
mentors, 79
play, 113-114
science, 170-171, 172, 174, 176
field trips,148

Culture
aspects of, 5, 6, 32

Curriculum, 9, 10
curriculum studies, 9-10
educational lore,vi, 9-10
student lore, 9-10

Delpit, L. D., 68

Dewey, J., v, 2, 3, 6, 30, 39, 56, 93, 113, 115, 119, 145, 146, 167, 170, 171, 172, 173, 212, 239, 241, 242, 243

Dickinson, H., 141

Dobbert, M. L., 7

Ehrmann. *See* Schwartzman

Eisikovits, R. A., 7

Enfield, M. L., 178

Erben, M., 142

Ethnicity
student body, 1
students' definition, 36-38
related to fictive kin, 45
related to mentors, 74

Fairchild, H. H., 224

FairTest, 213, 214, 215, 216, 218

Family. *See* Fictive kinship

Farr, R., 220

Fictive kinship
new categories, 41, 43, 45-47, 55-56
play relatives, 39, 41, 42
tradition, 40-41, 46-47

Field trips
leadership roles, 127-128, 130, 132, 137, 138
social organization, 138, 139, 140
structuring language 137-138, 139, 141-145

Folb, E. A., 19, 25, 29

Ford, P. 237

Fordham, S., 40, 41, 51, 53, 54

Franczek-Sullivan, —, 213

Games and activities
child-initiated, 86-88
basketball, 96-99
gender of participants, 96-97
noncompetition aspect, 98-99
hand-claps, 86, 90-91
gender of participants, 86, 90-91
house, 106-109
gender of participants, 106, 107
jump rope, 86-87, 92
gender of participants, 86, 93, 96-97
rhymes, 87-89
school, 109
gender of participants, 109
tag, 86
gender of participants, 86

Index

the tracks, 99-101
   gender of participants, 100
toy feasts, 103
   gender of participants, 104
macrosocial models, 110
  purposes of play, 93, 94, 95, 102, 112-116
  gender-based models, 110, 113

Gangs
  activities, 12-13
    drive-bys, 22-23
    random shootings, 23-24
    walk-ups, 23
    wars, 14-15
  avoidance mechanisms, 19-20
  city efforts to deter, 14
  cost of involvement, 30
  generational component, 25, 31-32
  initiation rites, 20-21, 27
  rationale for joining, 18, 27
  rationale for not joining, 18, 20-21, 30
  school efforts to deter, 15, 26-27, 30-31
  signs, 15, 16
  sweeps, 25-26, 33

Gilligan, C., 84, 93, 113

Glassner, B., 6

Goffman. *See* Goodwin

Goodwin, M. H., 44, 93, 94, 95, 96, 102, 109, 110, 111, 112, 113, 137, 138, 139

Greene, B., 220

Greene, V., 178

Haberman, M., 76, 220, 221, 224

Hare, R. B., 80

Harris, M., 37

Hasbrouck, *See* Sprick and Howard

Heath, S. B., 38, 114

Hersch, P., 243

Herskovits, M. J., 40

Hollingshead, A. B., 242

Holt, J., 171, 221

Howard, L. M., 225-226, 229, 230, 231

Johnson, B. D., 6

Johnson, L. B., 40

Johnston, P. H., 180

Jones, L., 235

Kagan, S., 148

Kellaghan, T., 224

Klapp. *See* Taylor

Kohlberg, L., 84

Kondo, D., 54

Kotlowitz, A., 13, 100, 235

Koziol, N. A., 59

Ksander, M., 20

Kuhn, T. S., 167

Labov, W., 83, 224

Lavenda, R. H., 54

Lee, R., 110

Lees, S., 74, 75

Lemann, N., 11, 16, 20, 24

Lever, J., 44, 93, 96, 111, 113

Levin, H. M., 178

Lincoln, C. E., 121, 122

Lopez, A. L., 9

Lopez-Schubert. *See* Lopez

Loughlin, J., 6

Lowe, F. H., 15

Macintyre, M., 54

McLaughlin, M.W., 38, 114

MacLeod, J., 183, 238

McNeill. *See* Apple

McRobbie. *See* Apple

Malcolm X. *See* Myers

Mamiya, L. H., 121, 122

Martin, E. P., 40

Martin, J. M., 40

Martinez, M., 238

Mathematics
  standardized test scores, 1-2

Mead, G. H., 113

Mead, M., 6S.J., 216

Meisels,

Mentors
  origins of mentoring at school, 57-58, 61, 62
  roles for mentors 59, 61-62, 64, 66, 67-69
    changes through time, 66, 68, 72
    gender preferences for mentors, 69, 74-76
  types and characteristics, 59, 65-66
    formal, 59
    informal, 59

Mickelson, R. A., 183

Monti, 2, 6, 18, 29, 30, 31, 32

Murray, 224

Myers, W. D., 33

Newman, L., 235

Neighborhood demographics, 1

Nichols, L. M., 30

Noddings, N., 56

Offer, D., 2, 57, 59

Ogbu, J., 42, 48, 51, 183, 238

Olson, L., 214

Opie, I., 88, 109

Ornstein, A. C., 208

Piaget, J., 113

Pitman, M. A., 7

Powdermaker. *See* Martin and Martin

Project Read®. *See* Enfield and Greene, V.

Rawick, G.P., 40

Index

Reading
  cooperative groups, 82, 229
  jump-in techniques, 226-229
  teacher-led, 224-225

Revitalism movement. *See* Change

Rhone, E., 59, 79

Science
  attitudes toward subject, 167-169
    boys, 100-102, 149-150, 153, 168
    girls, 100, 165-167, 172-175
    fairs and projects, 159, 165-167, 175
    teaching methods, 156-157, 158, 168

Schonert-Reich, K. A., 2, 57, 59

Schubert, W. H., 9, 10, 111, 240

Schultz, E. A., 54

Schwartzman, H. B., 114

Shepard, S., 56

Simmons, J., 174

Sipe, C. L., 59, 66, 74

Sloane, K., 224

Smith, R., 41

Smith, S., 235

Sprick, R. S., 225-226, 229, 230, 231

Stack, C., 40, 41, 43, 49, 50, 53, 54

Standardized tests
  performance scores 1997, 1-2, 180-181
  performance scores 1998, 248-249
  possible reasons for nonperformance, 181-182, 205-209, 211
  home language vs. market English vs. "standardized test-ese", 201-202, 204
  school efforts to raise scores, 178
  uses for tests, 211, 213

Staples, R., 40

Taylor, R. L., 76, 78, 79, 80, 81

Thorne, B., 44, 109

Thrasher, F. M., 6, 29

Tindal. *See* Sprick and Howard

Turner, V., 6

Useful learning
  church teachings, 121, 124, 144-145
  definitions, 6, 125, 144, 149, 170, 182, 246
  gender differences, 115, 117-119

Utesch, W. E., 59

Vanover, B., 59

Wallace, A., 34, 244

Watkins, W. H., 38

White, M., 6

Wishes, 233-234

Yeo, F., 203, 224

Zenk, C., 183, 238